Civil Society, the Third Sector and Social Enterprise

If the twentieth century was only focused on the complementarity and the opposition of market and state, the twenty-first century has now to deal with the prominence of the third sector, the emergence of social enterprises and other solidarity hybrid forms. The concept of civil society organisations (CSO) spans this diversity and addresses this new complexity.

The first part of the book highlights the organizational dimensions of CSOs and analyses the growing role of management models and their limits. Too often, the study of CSO governance has been centered on the role of the board and has not sufficiently taken into account the different types of accountability environments. Thus, the conversation about CSO governance rises to the level of networks rather than simple organizations per se, and the role of these networks in setting the agenda in a democratic society.

In this perspective, the second part emphasizes the institutional dimensions of CSO governance by opening new avenues on democracy. First, the work of Ostrom about governing the commons provides us new insights to think community self-governance. Second, the work of Habermas and Fraser opens the question of deliberative governance and the role of public sphere to enlarge our vision of CSO governance. Third, the concepts of substantive rationality and economy proposed respectively by Ramos and Polanyi reframe the context in which the question can be addressed. Lastly, this book argues for a stronger intercultural approach useful for the renewal of paradigms in CSOs research.

This book aims to present a unique collective work in bringing together 33 authors coming from 11 countries to share perpectives on civil society governance and will be of interest to an international audience of researchers and policy-makers.

Jean-Louis Laville is a professor at the Conservatoire National des Arts et Métiers (CNAM, Paris), European coordinator for the Karl Polanyi Institute of Political Economy, and a researcher in Lise (CNRS-Cnam) and Ifris.

Dennis R. Young is a professor of Public Management and Policy at Georgia State University, USA.

Philippe Eynaud is an associate professor at Panthéon Sorbonne University and a researcher in Gregor, France.

Routledge frontiers of political economy

Civil Society, the Third Sector and Social Enterprise

Governance and democracy

**Edited by Jean-Louis Laville,
Dennis R. Young and Philippe Eynaud**

Routledge
Taylor & Francis Group

LONDON AND NEW YORK

First published 2015
by Routledge
2 Park Square, Milton Park, Abingdon, Oxfordshire OX14 4RN

by Routledge
711 Third Avenue, New York, NY 10017, USA

First issued in paperback 2016

Routledge is an imprint of the Taylor and Francis Group, an informa business

British Library Cataloguing in Publication Data
A catalogue record for this book is available from the British Library

Library of Congress Cataloging in Publication Data
Civil society, the third sector and social enterprise: governance and
democracy / edited by Jean-Louis Laville, Dennis Young, and Philippe
Eynaud.
    pages cm. – (Routledge frontiers of political economy)
    1. Nonprofit organizations. 2. Civil society. 3. Political participation.
    4. Democracy. I. Laville, Jean-Louis. II. Young, Dennis R. III. Eynaud,
    Philippe.
    HD2769.15.C58 2015
    306.3'4–dc23   2014043681

ISBN 13: 978-1-138-67350-2 (pbk)
ISBN 13: 978-1-138-01331-5 (hbk)

Typeset in Times New Roman
by Wearset Ltd, Boldon, Tyne and Wear

Contents

Figures

Tables

Contributors

Editors

Philippe Eynaud is currently an associate professor at Panthéon Sorbonne University and a researcher in Gregor. He has experience in nonprofit management and information systems and works in social innovation, nonprofit governance, NGO Internet strategy, solidarity economy and new forms of solidarity. He has been a steering committee member of a European consortium on Innovative platform for social services (Call identifier FP7-SSH-2011-3). He has contributed to various books. In 2011, he was guest editor for a special issue of *Voluntas* on CSO governance with Kari Steen-Johnsen and Filip Wijkström. He is a member of the editorial committee of the French revue *Politiques et management public* and a member of the SITES (Science, Innovation et Techniques en Société) Laboratoire d'Excellence. He is a member of the Faculty Team of *EDEN*, European Institute for Advanced Studies in Management. In 2008 he received an award for best thesis in information systems in France. He graduated in Business Administration at Université Panthéon Sorbonne Paris I (2007).

Jean-Louis Laville graduated in economics before obtaining his PhD in Sociology from the Institut D'études Politiques in Paris and his "Habilitation à diriger des recherches" (Qualified Doctoral Dissertation Supervisor) from Paris X. He is a professor at the Conservatoire National des Arts et Métiers (Cnam, Paris), holds the Chair of Solidarity Economy, is a researcher in Lise (Cnam-CNRS) and Ifris, and coordinates investigations on social innovation for the SITES (Science, Innovation et Techniques en Société) Laboratoire d'Excellence. He is a founding member of the EMES network (www.emes. net). He contributes to several academic reviews and journals. He is a member of the international scientific board for *Sociologia e politiche sociali* and is on the editorial committees of *Sociologia del lavoro*, *Sociologie du travail*, *Voluntas*, *Économie et solidarités* and the journal of the International Center of Research and Information on the Public, Social and Cooperative Economy (CIRIEC). He is the European coordinator of the Karl Polanyi Institute of Political Economy and a member of the Association Internationale des

Sociologues de Langue Française, within which he is co-responsible for the research committee on economic sociology. His books have been translated into Italian, Portuguese, English, Spanish and Japanese. He co-edited *The Third Sector in Europe* with Adalbert Evers in 2004 and *The Human Economy* with Keith Hart and Antonio David Cattani in 2006.

Dennis R. Young is a professor of Public Management and Policy at Georgia State University. He holds an MS and a PhD from Stanford University. He helped establish the Mandel Center for Nonprofit Organizations at Case Western Reserve University and was the center's director from 1988 to 1996. He held the Bernard B., and Eugenia A. Ramsey Chair of Private Enterprise and was director of the Nonprofit Studies Program at Georgia State University from 2005 to 2013. A former president of the Association for Research on Nonprofit Organizations and Voluntary Action (ARNOVA), he received this organization's Award for Distinguished Achievement and Leadership in Nonprofit and Voluntary Action Research in 2004. He has written many articles and written and edited several books, including *Financing Nonprofits: Bridging Theory and Practice*, *The Music of Management*, the *Handbook of Nonprofit Economics and Management* (co-edited with Bruce A. Seaman), *Corporate Philanthropy at the Crossroads* (co-edited with Dwight Burlingame), and *Economics for Nonprofit Managers* (co-authored with Richard Steinberg). He was the founding editor of the journal *Nonprofit Management and Leadership* and is the current and founding editor of the journal *Nonprofit Policy Reform*. He was recently listed in the *Nonprofit Times* "Power and Influence Top 50."

Authors (Chapters 1–13)

Carlo Borzaga graduated in Sociology at the University of Trento, where he became professor in 2001 and is currently the dean of the Faculty of Economics. He was vice-president of the EMES network (www.emes.net) and is currently a member of the EMES Board of Directors. Since 1997, he has been the president of EURICSE (European Research Institute on Cooperative and Social Enterprises), University of Trento. He acts as consultant for national and international organizations and public bodies, among them the OECD and the European Commision (DGV).

Rosanna de Freitas Boullosa is an architect and urbanist (UFBa/Brazil), PhD in Public Policy (IUAV/Italy), professor at the Federal University of Bahia, Brazil, and researcher at the National Council for Scientific and Technological Development of Brazil. She is leader of the research group Innovation and Learning in Public Policy and Social Management and national coordinator of the Observatory on Social Management Education. Her main research themes are theory of public policy, public policy evaluation, social management and public action.

Stéphanie Chatelain-Ponroy is a professor at the Conservatoire National des Arts et Métiers (Cnam, Paris). She received her PhD from the University of Paris 12 in 1996 and obtained her "Habilitation à diriger des recherches" in 2008 from University of Paris Dauphine. She has written about 20 articles in academic and professional journals. Her research topics include the development and implementation of management control systems and practices and performance management and measurement systems, with special reference to public organizations.

Sara Depedri received her PhD in Law and Economics at the University of Siena, Italy in 2008. She is a senior researcher at Euricse (European Research Institute on Cooperative and Social Enterprises) in Trento, Italy. She teaches Economics of Welfare systems and Economics for Social Enterprises at the University of Trento. Her research concerns theoretical and empirical analyses on social enterprises, with special focus on self-regarding motivations, governance systems, human resource management practices and vulnerable workers' inclusion. Her publications include articles and book chapters on job dynamics and empirical studies on social enterprises.

Gemma Donnelly-Cox is the academic director of the Centre for Nonprofit Management at Trinity College Dublin. She has an MPhil in Management from Templeton College, University of Oxford and completed her DPhil in Management at Said Business School, University of Oxford. She also has a BA in History and Politics from the University of Waterloo, Ontario. She is a member of the Board of Directors for several nonprofit organizations including the Association for Research on Nonprofit Organizations and Voluntary Action (ARNOVA). She is a co-editor of the Nomos Book Series on European civil society, an editorial board member of Nonprofit Policy Forum and the program coordinator for the European Institute for Advanced Studies in Management.

Bernard Enjolras is research director at the Institute for Social Research and director of the recently formed Norwegian Centre for Research on Civil Society and the Voluntary Sector. He holds a PhD in Sociology from the Université de Québec à Montréal (2006), a post-doctoral certificate of achievement as Senior Fellow in Policy Studies, The Johns Hopkins University, Baltimore, USA (1995) and a PhD in Economics from the Université de Paris I – Panthéon Sorbonne (1994). He is the editor of *Voluntas*.

Genauto Carvalho de França Filho is a professor at Federal University of Bahia and researcher at CNPq (the Brazilian National Council for Scientific and Technological Development). He has experience in administration, with emphasis in organizational studies, and works in economic solidarity associations, the third sector, the popular economy and new forms of solidarity. He graduated in Business Administration from the Universidade Federal da Bahia (1991) and was awarded Masters in Business Administration from Universidade Federal da Bahia (1993) and doctorate in sociology from Université de Paris VII (2000).

Lars Hulgård is a professor of social entrepreneurship at Roskilde University, where he also serves as president of the EMES European Research Network (www.eme.net), chair of the research group Social Innovation and Organizational Learning, chair of RUC innovation – Roskilde University's platform for innovative collaboration between the university, enterprises and organizations – and a researcher, teacher and consultant in social innovation, social work, social policy, social entrepreneurship, co-production in social service, social enterprise and capacity building. He has been on the executive committee of the National Association on Social Policy and president of the Danish Sociological Association. He was a visiting scholar at Minda de Gunzburg Centre for European Studies, Harvard University; in 2004, at University of California, Riverside, in 1998; and at Mannheimer Zentrum für Europäische Sozialforschung, University of Mannheim, in 1992. He is an advisor on donation policies for numerous foundations.

Christopher J. Koliba is an associate professor in the Community Development and Applied Economics Department at the University of Vermont and the director of the Master of Public Administration (MPA) Program. He holds a PhD and an MPA from Syracuse University's Maxwell School of Citizenship and Public Affairs. His research interests include governance networks and complex adaptive systems, organizational learning and development, action research methods, civic education and educational policy. His current research program focuses on the development of complex adaptive systems models of regional planning, watershed governance, food systems, transportation planning and smart grid energy networks.

Florentine Maier is an assistant professor at the Nonprofit Management Group at WU Vienna (University of Economics and Business). She studies the spread of business thinking and business methods into the nonprofit sector. Her research on this topic has been published in *Voluntas*, *Business Research* and numerous book chapters.

Michael Meyer is a professor of Nonprofit Management and vice-rector for human resources at WU Vienna (University of Economics and Business). Since 1989 he has held various academic positions, including as an assistant professor of Marketing and Cultural Management and as a researcher in multidisciplinary projects. His areas of specialization and current research are managerialism in NPOs, organizational theory and professional careers.

Marthe Nyssens is a socio-economist and professor at the Catholic University of Louvain, where she is the co-ordinator of a research team on third-sector and social policies within the Centre Interdisciplinaire de Recherches Travail-Etat-Société (www.uclouvain.be/CIRTES). Her work focuses on conceptual approaches to the third sector (cooperatives, associations, social enterprises, etc.), both in developed and developing countries, as well as on the links between third-sector organizations and public policies. She teaches on nonprofit organizations, social policies and development theories. She conducts research and studies for national, regional and European government units. She was the coordinator of the project "The Socio-economic Performance of Social Enterprises in the Field of Integration by Work." She is a founding member of the EMES network (www.emes.net). She has been widely published in journals and books, both in French and in English.

Francie Ostrower is a professor in the Lyndon B. Johnson School of Public Affairs and the Department of Theater and Dance at the University of Texas at Austin. She is (founding) director of the university's Portfolio Program in Arts and Cultural Management and Entrepreneurship and is a senior fellow at the RGK Center for Philanthropy and Community Service and an affiliated scholar at the Urban Institute.

Francesca Petrella is an economist and associate professor at Aix-Marseille University. She is member of the Laboratoire d'Economie et de Sociologie du Travail, a multidisciplinary research center located in Aix-en-Provence. She is also the co-director of the Masters Degree in Social Economy at Aix-Marseille University and teaches nonprofit organization approaches, organizational theory and social policies in Europe. Her research work concerns the evolution of nonprofit governance forms and public–nonprofit interactions in the field of personal social services (mainly childcare services and home care services for the elderly) and she is a member of the EMES network (www.emes.net).

Marta Reuter has a PhD in Political Science from Humboldt University Berlin. She has a post-doctoral position in the Political Science department at Stockholm University and is also affiliated with the Stockholm Centre for Organizational Research (SCORE). Her research interests include the political agency of civil society organizations and the processes related to the transnationalization of civil society.

Anne Salmon is a professor of sociology at Lorraine University, Metz. She holds a master in philosophy, a PhD in sociology and a "Habilitation à diriger des recherches." Her research interests are in ethics and economics. Her publications include work on ethics and the new economic order, social responsibility, sustainability and the moralization of capitalism.

Bruce R. Sievers is a visiting scholar and lecturer in Political Science at Stanford University and adjunct professor at the Institute for Nonprofit Organization Management at the University of San Francisco. He is a senior fellow emeritus with Rockefeller Philanthropy Advisors. He received a PhD in Political Science from Stanford University and studied at the Freie Universitaet Berlin as a Fulbright Scholar. He was the founding executive director of the California Council for the Humanities and CEO of the Walter and Elise Haas Fund, a private foundation in San Francisco. In 2002, he received the "Outstanding Foundation Executive" award at the National Philanthropy Day celebration in northern California.

Kari Steen-Johnsen is a senior researcher at the Institute for Social Research in Oslo. Her fields of expertise are civil society, organizational change, the impact of the network society on civil society organization and mobilization, and social capital. She holds a PhD in Sociology from the Norwegian School of Sport Sciences.

Samuel Sponem is an associate professor at HEC Montréal. Previously he was assistant professor at the Conservatoire National des Arts et Métiers, Paris, and he received a PhD in management accounting from the University of Paris Dauphine. His work focuses on the use and diffusion of management control systems. He has also worked on the role of management controllers in multinational companies and on the introduction of performance measures in nonprofit organizations (associations and universities). He has published articles on these topics in journals including *European Accounting Review*, *Critical Perspectives on Accounting*, *Management Accounting Research*, *Finance Contrôle Stratégie*, *Comptabilité Contrôle Audit* and *Politiques et Management Public*.

Melissa M. Stone is a professor of Nonprofit Management at the Humphrey School of Public Affairs, University of Minnesota. Her teaching and research focus on governance of CSOs and cross-sector partnerships as policy implementation tools. Stone has published widely on these topics and holds a PhD in Organizational Behavior from Yale University.

Filip Wijkström is a professor in Business Administration at Stockholm University with a specialization in the management of public and nonprofit organizations. He has conducted qualitative as well as quantitative research, taught at both Masters and undergraduate level and supervised PhD candidates in Civil Society Studies since the early 1990s. Earlier research and international cooperation has included extensive cross-disciplinary and comparative efforts on the role and extent of the nonprofit sector in society. Currently, civil society strategy, governance and management as well as cross-sector activities and organizational hybridity are central topics in his research and teaching.

Authors (Chapter 14)

José Coraggio is a professor at the Universidad Nacional de General Sarmiento, Buenos Aires, Argentina.

Philippe Eynaud is an associate professor at the Sorbonne Graduate Business School, Paris, France.

Adriane Ferrarini is a professor at the Universidade do Vale do Rio dos Sinos, São Leopoldo, Brazil.

Genauto Carvalho de França Filho is a professor at the Federal University of Bahia, Brazil.

Luis Inácio Gaiger is a professor at the Universidade do Vale do Rio dos Sinos, São Leopoldo, Brazil.

Isabelle Hillenkamp is a researcher at the Institut pour le Développement, Marseille, France.

Kenichi Kitajima is a professor at Rikkyo University, Tokyo, Japan.

Jean-Louis Laville is a professor at the Conservatoire National des Arts et Métiers (CNAM, Paris), European coordinator for the Karl Polanyi Institute of Political Economy, and a researcher in Lise (CNRS-Cnam) and Ifris.

Andrea Lemaître is a researcher at the Catholic University, Louvain, Belgium.

Youssef Sadik is a professor at the University Mohammed V Rabat, Morocco.

Marilia Veronese is a professor at the Universidade do Vale do Rio dos Sinos, São Leopoldo, Brazil.

Fernanda Wanderley is a professor at the CIDES, Universidad Mayor de San Andrés, Bolivia.

Introduction

Jean-Louis Laville, Dennis R. Young and
Philippe Eynaud

With the hundredth anniversary of the start of World War I, it has become popular to speculate on how the world would be different now if Archduke Franz Ferdinand had not been assassinated in Sarajevo. The interdependencies and treaties connecting European countries at that time underwrote a chain of events over which governments lost control, leading to the Great War. Some speculate that had World War I not occurred, the twentieth century would have been spared World War II, the Bolshevik revolution, the Cold War and much of the collateral damage associated with these great events. Europe might have evolved towards a unified and democratic society under an enlightened and decentralized Austro-Hungarian regime at peace with England, the US and a less autocratic, expansive and brutal Russia.

We will never know the implications of this alternative history. But it is clear that some very fundamental factors were at work in the events of 1914 that changed the world forever. Three of these factors and their interplay – governance, democracy and civil society – are the subject of this book. In 1914, governance in continental Europe was largely a system of autocracies linked by military treaties and royal family relationships. Woodrow Wilson pronounced World War I to be the war that would make the world safe for democracy. Clearly that was never achieved. Democracy was emergent and modelled on the American, French and British experiences. Civil society was a vague concept reflecting the empowerment of the masses, whether in socialist or communist forms, in cooperative and labor movements, or in the American experience of social movements and associational life as described by de Tocqueville in the nineteenth century (Tocqueville, 1996). What is striking in the twentieth century is that some authors such as Mauss continue to believe that alternative forms of social and economic organization (cooperatives, mutual societies, associations) may be the way to democratize the economy from inside in order to achieve a more humanistic and cohesive society (Mauss, 1997).

Of course, today's world is far different from that of 1914. While autocracy prevails in many places, democracy is fuller and more strongly rooted throughout the world; and civil society and the nonprofit sector have come to play critical roles in the social, economic and political life of most countries. Nonetheless, strengthening civil society, governance and democracy remains crucial. For Fukuyama (2006), history was supposed to come to an end when an emerging universal consensus on democracy eliminated ideological conflicts. It is now obvious that much remains to be done to achieve this goal. Governance is still problematic as regional and global institutions such as the United Nations, the European Community and the International Court of Justice help inch society towards a system of economic, social and political regulation and moderation, and as nations continue to face serious flaws and tensions in the internal functioning of their democratic institutions. Furthermore, the planet as a whole faces major global issues: financial crises, climate change, increasing inequality of wealth and income, rising populism and religious fanaticism. Global capitalism is incapable of effectively addressing these issues. Therefore, new and innovative forms of organization emerging in different cultural contexts and a pluralistic economy must be identified. Fair trade, solidarity-based finance, social currency, community supported organic farming, free software, creative commons communities, local energy cooperatives, and sustainable communities that recycle and renew their resources are all examples of what can be done to better integrate the economy with civil society. All these initiatives involve new forms of entrepreneurship embedded in citizenship. Worldwide, civil society has exhibited a spectacular increase in both the number and the roles of its organizations. Yet civil society organizations (CSOs) or associations are very diverse and must be understood through different conceptual lenses.

The first part of this introduction reviews the characteristics of the two most important conceptualizations of CSOs – as a third sector and as social enterprise. The second part highlights how the governance of CSOs has generally been analyzed in the international literature. The third part then explains the specific contributions of this book: the development of a broad understanding of governance, which strongly integrates inter-organizational, intercultural and institutional considerations. In particular, we argue that three factors are especially important for developing a new level of understanding of contemporary governance and democracy: commons, the public sphere and substantive rationality.

The economic approach to CSOs: from the third sector to social enterprise

Following the seminal article by Coase (1937), which highlighted that certain transaction costs can explain the formation of economic enterprises, Williamson (2002) defined an organization as a "governance structure" that allows the reduction of transaction costs. The new institutional economy, as introduced by Coase and further developed by subsequent authors including Williamson, confers to the organization a theoretical status that was not previously recognized by orthodox economic science. From the start, neoclassical economics emphasized idealized maximizing behavior by producers and consumers, leading to equilibration of demand and supply through price setting in the free market. Nevertheless, market failures attributable to imperfect competition and externalities were progressively acknowledged. As a result, the state and the firm emerged as coordinating structures alternative to the market. This new institutional economy stipulates that the execution of contracts among agents requires an operating governance structure, which reduces the costs of transactions, be they coordination costs due to the collect of information and negotiation, or motivation costs attributable to the incentive mechanisms affecting how individuals behave.

The third sector as a collection of nonprofit organizations

Since the 1970s, neoclassical economists have reflected on an apparent paradox: the presence of nonprofit organizations inside markets driven by the quest for profit. They explain this phenomenon by the nature of the particular goods and services produced by nonprofits, including their relational character. In particular, since the precise characteristics of many nonprofit services are unclear before the transaction takes place, particularly acute trust and quality issues arise, as exemplified in the case of care for elderly people or young children where third-party purchasers (e.g., parents) are not always present to observe the quality of care. The market may thus fail in domains where even public services provided by government are not always suitable substitutes.

Going deeper into the argument, when certain agents have more information than others, a condition called *information asymmetry*, they can use their information advantage in transactions to the detriment of their contractual partners. Thus producers can often take advantage of their superior information to mislead consumers. As a consequence, market transparency is replaced by opacity, which is damaging to exchange because it leads to consumer dissatisfaction or reluctance to engage in otherwise desirable transactions. In short, information asymmetry favors some actors over others and destabilizes their relationships to one another. The risk of this condition is especially strong in a service economy, where it is more difficult to evaluate quality *ex ante*. Unlike the quality of goods, the quality of services exists only during consumption, as the result of a co-production between the service provider and the user. The more personalized the service, as in care services, the more prominent is this condition. Services such as home care for elderly people or young children are emblematic because the information necessary to judge quality is especially difficult to obtain.

According to third-sector theory as articulated by Hansmann (1980) and others, the comparative advantage of nonprofit organizations is related to the assurance that nonprofit criteria offer to consumers. In particular, the "non-distribution of profit constraint," which precludes distributing surplus revenues to owners or managers, is a key protection to consumers. This protection derives from two main arguments: the mitigation of adverse selection and moral hazard.

Concerning adverse selection, the exclusive ownership of information by service providers makes it difficult for consumers to distinguish among providers based on prices and uncertain perceptions of quality. In particular, users lack trustworthy indicators to guide them in their choices. For example, when dual-income families require service providers to take care of their parents, they often feel guilty and reluctant to call on "strangers," as if this meant that they were neglecting or "abandoning" their elders. Faced with this discomfort, they may be reassured by high prices, which they take as a signal of high quality. However, ill-intentioned service providers may take advantage of this situation to increase their margins by selling low-quality services for the same price as high-quality ones. Nor is this situation resolved by the presence of lower-priced, lower-quality providers. Even here, bad service providers can drive good providers from the market, because spending money to train staff or ensure the monitoring of services adds to costs, which can disadvantage responsible producers in a highly competitive market context. Eventually, the market runs the risk of contracting instead of growing as users withdraw from it. There are thus various situations, which can be grouped under the general heading "adverse selection," where bad services end up chasing good ones away, a situation characterized by Akerlof (1970) as the "market for lemons."

To address this problem, providers can make quality perceptible through "signals" accessible to consumers. In particular, Hansmann (1980) argued that the non-distribution of profit constraint is such a signal of trust. This is a primary argument justifying the existence of nonprofit organizations in contemporary market-based economies.

The problem of "moral hazard" arises when one of the stakeholders in a transaction takes an action that other stakeholders can neither observe, control nor constrain. For instance, in the case of childcare, absent parents have no real control over service delivery. They can only surmise the results of the service based on imperfect information. The service provider can thus exert less effort or care than agreed upon in the terms of the contract. Even when both parties are present, such opportunistic behaviors can occur, for example when the user is in a state of dependency or when unexpected circumstances occur. Thus, a home care provider can easily take advantage of the weakness of an elderly user, especially if the health of that user deteriorates and requires still more assistance.

Moral hazard can also develop when a transaction requires major investment of time or other resources, for instance when the user has to make substantial effort in order to investigate the adequacy of services. Here too, the service provider may exploit the situation and fail to properly fulfill his or her commitments. This is known as the "hold-up" issue. If the user has made an "irretrievable investment," he or she may hesitate to change service providers, even if he or she is no longer satisfied with the service. This issue is exacerbated in a quasi-rent situation where a scarcity of service providers results in demand exceeding supply. This gives excessive power to existing suppliers, who are empowered to choose solutions and methods that best serve their own interests. Their rationing of services dissuades users from changing service providers because they are unsure of finding better service somewhere else. In this way, information asymmetries lead to market power, reduced transparency, competitive supply, and mobility of buyers and sellers.

Finally, moral hazard may involve third parties such as service funders. For example, funding authorities often cannot prevent the misappropriation of their funds or the "creaming off" of users by service providers who select the "easiest" (least costly) users and leave aside those for which the cost of intervention is too high – either because their pathology is difficult to address or because their geographic location entails high transportation costs. In such instances, Krashinsky (1986) breaks down transaction costs into two categories, coordination costs (concerning information, decision and control) and motivation costs (related to the incentives for individuals to fulfill their obligations).

Economics literature on the nonprofit sector is thus a continuation of the neo-classical tradition, which examines the *raison d'être* of organizations in a market economy. While this tradition remains faithful to rational-choice theory – according to which economic phenomena can be explained as an aggregation of individual rational behaviors, which reflect optimization under constraints based on complete and transitive preferences – it nevertheless acknowledges that the free market is not always the most efficient resource-allocation mechanism. It even recognizes the existence of other organizational modes better adapted than the market to some circumstances. Moreover, this literature recognizes that organizations are not all identical nor are they only capital enterprises. In particular, the special value resulting from absence of profit redistribution is recognized as an asset for organizations in services where information, trust and personalization of services are decisive. As Badelt sums it up, it is precisely this constraint of profit non-redistribution that can overcome informational asymmetries (Badelt, 1990). Be it adverse selection or moral hazard, nonprofit organizations are specifically supposed to provide safety to the consumer because financial surplus resulting from these behaviors cannot be used to reward shareholders.

The third sector, beyond nonprofit

Other theories of the third sector are less concerned with the non-distribution of profit constraint. Instead, they relate the third sector to the public or semi-public nature and characteristics of goods and services, in particular the externalities, that it generates for society as a whole. For instance, childcare services generate positive externalities by facilitating the access of women to employment and training. Likewise, they reduce gender inequality, which is particularly acute in domestic care. As a consequence, childcare services generate positive externalities by reducing uncompensated work and unemployment compensation expenses. Similarly, home care services can generate positive externalities such as job creation for women with reduced family responsibilities or reduction of public expenses where the maintenance of elderly people at home is less expensive than their placement in institutional facilities. Home care services are both individual and quasi-collective services. They are personally targeted to the consumer while also having broader effects on society through positive externalities, which are complex and multidimensional.

Economists address this problem by prescribing the "internalization of externalities." As explained by Pigou (1932), services with positive externalities are under-produced as compared to the social optimum. In many cases it is possible to resolve this problem through bilateral negotiation resulting in payment of monetary compensation by the beneficiaries of positive externalities to the producers of those externalities. However, such solutions become impractical in the case of multilateral collective externalities. In this case, the parties responsible for the positive externalities can be subsidised proportional to the social benefit produced. Thus in the case of services which are both individual and quasi-collective, marked by the extent and the complexity of their related externalities, it is often justified to rely on taxation for funding.

Likewise, intervention by public authorities is encouraged for strictly collective goods and services. These refer to non-rival goods and services (for which consumption by one individual does not hinder consumption by any other individual – as in the case of environmental protection) and non-excludable goods (where the producer cannot prevent consumption by those who do not contribute to the funding – as in the instance of a highway without toll). For quasi-collective and collective services, neoclassical economics thus supports the legitimacy of public funding. However, the theory does not necessarily imply that government should or will respond to demand for all such goods.

This is the point made by Weisbrod in the context of public choice theory, which addresses political decisions based on rational choice. Weisbrod (1975) focuses on the propensity of the state to satisfy the median voter. He argues that this results in an "excess demand" for public goods by those citizens whose preferences for such goods exceed those of the median voter. This condition is especially pronounced when the preferences of citizens within a political jurisdiction are highly heterogeneous. Thus voluntary or associative responses adapted to peoples' needs arise in reaction to the state's neglect of minority groups. Minority demands, which are not directly accommodated by public authorities, thus lead citizens to create third-sector organizations dedicated to the particular services they desire.

From the third sector to social enterprise

The forgoing economic approach to the third sector is a theory of "institutional choice" which highlights users' trust for the services provided by nonprofit organizations and associations, as well as externalities that lead to the provision of services by third-sector organizations for minority groups that are neglected by the state.

These conceptualizations of the role of the third sector are "demand theories." They detail the reasons why users and donors select nonprofit organizations and associations. As such, they postulate their prior existence, allowing for choices to be made in their favor. Yet they do not provide an explanation of the process of establishing these organizations. To address this lacuna, some scholars have addressed the "supply side" by studying the motivations of entrepreneurs and the involvement of stakeholders in voluntary and associative structures.

More broadly, Young (1981, 1983, 1986) approached entrepreneurs as actors seeking autonomy and spaces of creativity, as well as material and other goals.

Motivation to establish new associative forms lies in these objectives, along with religious motivations for groups wishing to promote their beliefs, increase the number of their members and expand their audiences. Young (1983) provides a typology of motivational types for entrepreneurs engaging in organizations for ideological, personal and other reasons. Social purposes are implied as motivators for social entrepreneurs and social enterprise and an important criterion for their economic engagement, even within the business sector.

In contrast to entrepreneurial theories, stakeholder theories stipulate that the aims of an enterprise depend on the configuration of property rights of stakeholders who retain those rights and who determine the objectives of the organization. This view allows for social enterprises to avoid dominance by financial investors. Thus social enterprises may not be controlled by such investors but by other types of stakeholders whose goals may not include the accumulation of capital. As Hansmann (1980) and Gui (1991) emphasize, there are as many potential forms of property rights as types of stakeholders, among which, besides investors, are workers and consumers. Nonetheless, stakeholder control implies the selection of an associative form through which stakeholders can exert their rights.

The association form does not, however, in itself guarantee that stakeholders will deliver a service of quality. Indeed, Ben-Ner and Van Hoomissen (1991) argue that the best way to overcome information asymmetry lies in the control of supply by actors (stakeholders) on the demand side. Users and funders, who might otherwise be poorly informed, can overcome their information deficits by becoming governing members of the organization. However, as conditions may not allow for every stakeholder to be a member, representative members may be required. The efficiency of the latter arrangement may be tenuous, especially where the service is non-rival, i.e., when quality does not vary according to beneficiary – as in the case of a day nursery where the treatment given to the children cannot easily be differentiated. Here, some stakeholders may "free ride" at the expense of other stakeholders. In many cases, however, stakeholders recruit professionals to administer the organization, or such initiative may also arise from professionals themselves. Being conscious of the information problems that stakeholders face, professionals (acting as entrepreneurs) can take the lead in conceiving and organizing a service, allowing them to address stakeholder demands as well as their own goals.

The governance of CSOs

First, what is governance? One reflexively thinks of governance as the function of government, but it is a far broader and more fundamental concept than that. The *Oxford Dictionary and Thesaurus* indicates that to govern is to "rule or control" but this raises the question of how governance works. Obviously governance applied to government or to specific organizations can operate in a variety of ways, through different systems of authority, rules and decision-making regimes. Further insight can be gained from interpreting governance in an engineering context. How do control mechanisms work to guide the operations of machines or electrical or mechanical systems? The interesting thing about governance in the engineering context is that it is generally based on the concept of "feedback and correction." For example, the governor in a steam engine measures the speed at which the engine is running, compared to some desired or standard speed, and then adjusts the flow of steam so as to close the gap (reduce the error) between the desired and actual performance. A thermostat works on the same feedback principle: a desired room temperature is set, actual temperature is measured, and the thermostat turns the furnace on or off so as to reduce the error between the desired and measured temperatures. Once the desired temperature (or speed) is reached, the governor assures the maintenance of that standard by making appropriate adjustments as deviations occur.

This engineering view of governance is easily applied to organizational or political systems, though with alternative possible results. A system of government is based on authority and those in authority act according to the information they receive and the conditions or standards they wish to achieve or maintain. Presumably, some systems of political governance are better than others at maintaining the desired control. Autocracies may receive precious little or distorted feedback from constituents until society overheats, sometimes to the point where control is lost. Democracies may produce loud, frequent, robust, though perhaps confusing, feedback and may have slow and complex corrective mechanisms to reduce the errors between what constituents desire and what they are actually experiencing. Similarly, organizations may be autocratically run without sufficient feedback from members to guide leaders' decisions, or they may be governed democratically, producing a cacophony of feedback and ineffective responses by leaders of limited authority and skill.

Another implication of the engineering metaphor of governance is that feedback can be positive or negative. In this context, so-called "negative" feedback is generally a good thing – identification of errors indicating that the organization or society is off course and requires correction. On the other hand, "positive" feedback can feed on itself through governance mechanisms that amplify the errors, leading to loss of control. Indeed, such positive feedback loops are the basis of the mathematics of chaos theory. One can certainly envision situations where this occurs in societies or organizations. Autocratic regimes receive information indicating disapproval of their performance which leads them to stifle dissent, which further increases dissent until a boiling point is reached beyond which the system ceases to function. This can happen in a democratic regime as well if an unpopular faction takes control. Presumably, however, a democratic regime has a better chance of avoiding this scenario because of its richer flow of feedback information and its multiple means of adjustment. This applies at both societal and organizational levels. Moreover, civil society, in the form of multiple, diverse organizations and networks, itself constitutes a critical part of the feedback loop in democratic societies, providing conduits for societal preferences, expressions of dissatisfaction and levers of political influence to induce course corrections in public policy and administration.

In summary, various understandings of the governance of CSOs reflect the generic notion of control and achieving efficiency and effectiveness evoked by the engineering paradigm.

The disciplinary approach

Berle and Means (1991) worried about the rise of the large corporation and the emergence of a powerful class of professional managers. They warned that such uncontrolled power could endanger the democracy of the United States. Based on the necessity of countervailing power in the firm, their thesis has opened the door to a stream of research in corporate governance related to transaction cost theory. In this research tradition, governance emerges as a function that allows an efficient balance between market and hierarchy to be achieved (Williamson, 1979, 2002). Governance is also a means for share-holders to control managers. To do so, shareholders have fostered the develop-ment of the audit. Accordingly, governance can be seen as the management of the management (Pérez, 2003).

As a result, CSOs have moved into an era of so-called *managerialism*, i.e., a "system of description, explanation and interpretation of the world based on management categories" (Chanlat, 1998). This new era is marked by the centra-lity of the notion of performance, by the importance of instrumental rationality and by the emphasis on concepts of auditability and responsibility. In this narrow paradigm, individuals are viewed abstractly, i.e., as economic objects without any affect, history or culture. As such, they are engaged in an instrumental project, which values a single "technical" logic (Chanlat, 1998, p. 61). This is supposed to guarantee the effectiveness and efficiency of wage-earning mana-gers. In conformity with this firm governance model, internal mechanisms for the governance of CSOs aimed at disciplining their executives have thus been devised. The reasoning behind this is grounded in the aforementioned theory of the neo-institutional economy. It takes into account informational asymmetries favoring managers and seeks their reduction through signals (e.g., reports) provi-ded by the organization's administration, which thus becomes a major control tool for stakeholders.

Behavioral and evolutionary approaches

These first conceptions regarding the governance of the third sector say little about the creation of value, the identification of development opportunities, or the sustainability of activities and their adaptation to contingencies. These gaps have led to alternative approaches, more focused on internal competencies and innovation. Two main approaches can be distinguished: behavioral and evolutio-nary economic theory. The behavioral approach depicts the firm realistically as a coalition of individuals and/or of groups with diverse political interests in situa-tions of cooperation or conflict, but also as a locus for organizational learning. In contrast, in evolutionary theory, the firm is defined as a set of evolutionary capacities (Nelson and Winter, 1982, 2002), i.e., knowledge acquired through collective learning and accumulated in organizational routines. In the tradition of Schumpeter, this approach puts emphasis on innovation-based competition. Focus is on cognition, and the role of administration is approached in strategic terms through the imbrication of stakeholders into the firm's operations, allowing them to bring additional information. This inclusion of stakeholders is clearly relevant to the governance of CSOs and social enterprises.

The chapters in Part I of this book testify to increased complexity in the analysis of third-sector governance. Moreover, given the "blurring of frontiers" (Evers and Laville, 2004) and hybridization between the private nonprofit and the public sectors, the very notion of "sector" must be put into a new perspective (Steen-Johnsen, Eynaud and Wijkström, 2011).

The public approach

The rise of CSOs as economic actors has generated expectations of financial transparency. These expectations derive from budgetary restrictions advocated by major international institutions (e.g., the World Bank, International Monetary Fund and others) and supported by Western governments. In the context of tension over public resources, where states are required to reduce deficits and liabilities, stewardship of CSOs has become a key concern, resulting in pressures for CSOs to professionalize their managements. Furthermore, governance became a buzzword in the 1990s in the public management field. The popularity of this concept may be related to the multiplicity of its definitions. Indeed, the notion of governance reflects many changes that have occurred in recent decades. For example, Rhodes posits that governance is a process that "refers to self-organizing, inter-organizational networks characterized by interdependence, resource exchange, rules of the game and significant autonomy from the state" (Rhodes, 1997, p. 15). But the authors of this way of thinking perceive changes occurring in a particular institutional context: "Governance is a concept that tries to make sense of the changing nature of the state" (Kitthananan, 2006, p. 6). That is, the state has shifted from an era of government to an era of governance (Richards and Smith, 2002).

This twofold origin (the corporate world and the public sector) has consequences for the legitimation of the third sector. In the new configuration of the state reflected in the shift from government to governance, the third sector has a special role to play. Specifically, organizations in the third sector are expected to pursue conditions for the professionalization and democratization of the welfare provision system (Fazzi, 2009). Alternatively, the evolution of the corporate governance model supports the rise of the social enterprise modality of the third sector. Indeed social enterprises can sometimes be seen as corporate cousins – corporations that are hybridized by adding a social goal.

Interdisciplinary perspectives

The forgoing evolutionary thinking about the governance of CSOs establishes the ground for Part II of this book. Here we address the issue of how governance of society as a whole is changing and the role that civil society is playing in this change. One of the classical views of CSOs is that they can serve as "schools of democracy." This is one of the themes in Part II: how civil society can strengthen citizenship and consequently societal governance – through new forms such as networks, participatory forums and hybrid organizational forms, and through opportunities to "practice" democracy within CSOs themselves. Our authors also argue in the reverse direction. As associations seek to promote and respond to social change, they themselves must adapt their governance structures to be appropriately sensitive to, and representative of, the citizenry at large. Several of our authors examine a variety of new organizational forms and strategies that allow civil society to take a stronger role in societal governance through such diverse approaches as multi-stakeholder governance; collective ownership of nonprofits; social purpose cooperatives; social management through "para-economies" that acknowledge cultural differences, equality and individual autonomy; "design thinking" to facilitate interactive policy formation with government; and new holistic institutional approaches to volunteerism and the building of social networks and social capital.

In order to fully appreciate the contributions of the new multidisciplinary approaches to organizational and societal governance, it is helpful to return to the characteristics of the already quoted seminal contributions of Coase and Williamson, whose works helped to establish institutional theory as an expansion of standard neoclassical economic theory. These scholars moved beyond the neoclassical paradigm without violating the axiomatic assumption of rational choice initially developed to analyze market logic (Nyssens, 2013, p. 56). While their versions of rationality are limited and procedural, they remain optimization-based. They see organizations as logical results of individual interests converging towards equilibrium. The contributions of other disciplines in social sciences go beyond this perspective, ascribing special behaviors to enterprises and institutions themselves.

The embeddedness debate

Granovetter (2000) was one of the first to express concern over the weakness of an approach to institutions based solely on effectiveness and efficiency. He questioned the Hobbessian logic adopted by Willamson (1979) according to which institutions are no more than mere "hierarchies" compensating for the market's inability to address opportunism.

According to Granovetter, by neglecting the interactions of the key actors, neo-institutional economics fails to account for social structure. By rejecting this atomized conception of economic activity, Granovetter develops the concept of embeddedness within personal relations networks. Specifically, individual choices are made relative to the choices and behaviors of other individuals and to the personal ties prevailing in networks, these latter being defined as regular sets of contacts or social relations among individuals or groups of individuals.

Embeddedness can be approached from different angles. The "relational" aspect is focused on "personal relations" and the "structural" one on the "structure of the general network of these relations." The structural aspect focuses on segments of the social structure in the larger social context. In this approach, far from being simply the solution to efficiency issues, institutions are products of human history. An institution can thus not be entirely grasped without studying the process through which it evolved. Indeed a variety of historical paths are possible. For example, an institution may result from the crystallization of certain personal relations. Granovetter studied the example of the American electricity industry (Mcguire *et al.*, 1993), which now appears to be very stable and "natural," but could have taken a radically different shape. Thus, the institution as it exists nowadays cannot be fully understood in terms of efficiency. Other factors must be taken into account, in particular personal relations networks. Network analysis must thus be used to capture the explanatory factors underlying institutional formation. Indeed, institutions can be defined, according to Granovetter, as "fixed social networks."

Moreover, network analysis should not eclipse the contexts in which networks are located. Accordingly, neo-institutional sociology has studied from a phenomenological standpoint the relation between economic action and the cultural order. The latter is seen as a cognitive reference framework contributing to the shaping of action logics subordinated to the practices of a social context that defines the identities and possible or preferable choices of the actors involved. This research orientation studies social institutions as symbolic systems which give sense and collective values to entities and particular activities by integrating them into wider schemes according to which social actors are able to order reality and make their experience of time and space more meaningful.

This anti-utilitarian and constructionist institutionalism highlights the influence of cultural interpretations on the daily behaviors of economic actors. In this way, it focuses on systems of meaning and the symbolic framework, and on the cultural repertoires intertwined with social practices. Economic action is channelled by routines related to beliefs, by roles, by scenarios, and even by myths. Institutions establish cognitive and normative regularities (Rizza, 2004, p. 95). Organizations are dependent on institutionalized action models that are legitimate and socially acceptable. Organizations are embedded in contexts characterized by the presence of institutions with a continuously normative influence. This influence depends on legitimacy criteria. Such criteria define appropriate methods of operation and the chances of success. Di Maggio and Powell (1983) illustrate this with the notion of an "organization field" consisting of different actors (enterprise, public organizations, associations, trade unions, etc.) that provide reference standards and promulgate beliefs that influence different dimensions of organizational life.

The contributions of economic and neo-institutional sociology help to clarify the relationship between enterprise and institution. In particular, these conceptual traditions criticize the assumption of market-based choice optimization and the pretence that the market modulates private interests held by strategic agents. This assumption is reductive and precludes definition and study of "good governance" and "accountability" in CSOs.

The institutional framework

In order to compare the institutional structures of for-profit enterprise and civil society organizations, we begin with Table I.1, which outlines the basic dimensions on which these forms differ.

One point to note is that restraint of profit distribution does not mean that "nonprofit organizations do not, in effect, have owners" as argued by Glaeser (2003, p. 1), or at least leaders who make decisions about profits. On the contrary, Petrella (2008) posits that individuals who control the organization have the obligation to reinvest residual profits into the organization in order to advance its mission. Ultimately, residual profit benefits key beneficiaries (Gui, 1991): for example recipients of services, workers in work integration programs, and paid managers. Therefore, even if the redistribution of profit to individuals is legally forbidden in CSOs, residual benefits are allocated nevertheless. This realization helps us to understand the diversity of CSOs and why it is important to identify the stakeholders who control the allocation of benefits.

Chapter 5 by Koliba, which offers a network-oriented approach to the third sector, effectively adapts Granovetter's model relating individuals to organizations. We think that this analysis of reticular embeddedness must be extended to the study of cultural embeddedness. In the field of organizational studies, Powell and Di Maggio put strong emphasis on this point in a neo-institutional sociological framework.

The departure point of organization studies is that all productive action assumes segregation of duties through the breakdown of work into component

Table I.1 Institutional structures

	For-profit enterprise	*Civil society organization*
Decisions	Decision-making power proportional to the share of capital held	Decision-making power from participation in activities
Goals	Maximization of the return on investment and financial value	Sharing common goals
Members	Shareholders	Stakeholders
Ownership rights on residual profit	Distribution of residual profit	No distribution of residual profit

tasks on the one hand and the integration of individuals into groups for the achievement of collective goals on the other hand. Therefore, a tension emerges between differentiation and integration, as noted by Durkheim (1893). Resolving this tension has long been a goal of organizational studies. First, the scientific work organization claimed the capacity to define the most rational structure in order to maximize efficiency. Later, during the 1950s, contingency theories embraced the idea that efficiency was dependent on context, which meant that organizations had to adapt to their environments. Burns and Stalker (1961), Woodward (1956), and Lawrence and Lorsch (1973) posited that the environment had a strong influence on a firm's choices. Contingency analyses have provided new insights: in particular, solutions could be found locally by adjustment to external constraints. This meant that management solutions were no longer universal. However, a major weakness of this idea is the way that it conceived external constraints. In particular, it implied that the environment is the main factor affecting organizational performance. Various criticisms have been levelled at this way of thinking. Chanlat (1998) lists them as follows: excessive formalism, occultation of political processes, pseudo-neutralism, and technicist bias, the latter of which assumes that the environment is determined by technology. We can add to this list the lack of historical perspective, which precludes an understanding of how the current state of an organization is affected by its origins.

By the end of the 1970s, the limits of the foregoing contingency framework were being addressed by the sociological institutionalism school of thought, especially by extending beyond instrumental rationality to the notion of "social conveniences." Attentive to forms, procedures and symbols, sociological institutionalism introduced the notions of legal regulation, agreements and norms as means to shape behaviors.

If CSOs seek to address social demands, their integration into an institutional framework contributes to their normalization. This is less the consequence of an inevitable adjustment to environmental pressures (as suggested by contingency theory) than coercive or mimetic effects that help to ensure socially acceptability. The new sociological institutionalism calls this institutional isomorphism, i.e., a binding process that leads one unit to act in the same way as other units facing the same environmental conditions. Enjolras has built on Powell and Di Maggio to analyze institutional isomorphism in the case of associations. Enjolras argues that isomorphism can be coercive through political influence, mimetic in offering uniform solutions, and normative in the dissemination of standards (Enjolras, 1996).

Sociological institutionalism spans systems of symbols, cognitive models, and moral models which provide signification frameworks to guide human action. It challenges the explanation of structures based on efficiency. For a better understanding of organizational dynamics, it highlights the reproduction phenomenon and the spreading of models embedding particular behaviors. As a result, it argues that the border between public and private models is gradually blurring for a large number of CSOs.

However, sociological institutionalism does not simply postulate isomorphism. It has opened the door to the understanding of actors' roles in the transformation of the institutional framework. It distinguishes itself from contingency analysis by focusing on cultural practices, symbols and routines. Sociological institutionalism also examines the way institutions are able to modify themselves. Lawrence and Suddaby (2006) have called this "institutional work." Social actors are not only dependent on an established framework; they can also take affirmative action through the creation, preservation or weakening of the institutional framework.

According to Di Maggio (1988, 1991), institutional work assumes awareness on the part of the actors. They are capable of reacting to the present and future institutional conditions they face. Through reasoning and practical action, their institutional innovations are related to resources and potentialities in the fields in which they are located. In the 1990s and 2000s, studies of institutional work were mainly based on empirical evidence on firms and the business sector (Lawrence and Suddaby, 2006). As a result, the terminology of institutional entrepreneurship is better suited to organized actors working for their own interests. Nonetheless, institutional work and institutional entrepreneurship are relevant concepts though they require revisiting for application to CSOs. For example, Wijkström and Reuter (Chapter 7) coin the term "norm entrepreneurs," indicating that some CSOs function as primary sources of governance norms – through a process of meta norm-entrepreneurship – by negotiating "the very rules of the game" in society.

From interdisciplinarity to interculturality

In summary, the institutional structure of civil society is endowed with a democratic potential of its own. Therefore, the topic of CSO governance interfaces with the question of democratic governance. Governance in CSOs cannot be assessed only on the basis of value creation. Assessment must also deal with the capacity of governance to stabilize and foster the evolution of society and its political regimes. Even if associations play a modest role in that matter, it is important to identify – internally and externally – the risks and opportunities provided by them relative to the democratization of society.

Several scholars have proposed theoretical frameworks to support this perspective, including Ostrom, Habermas, Polanyi and Ramos. Our own perspective in this book is based on the foundations established by these authors, on their practice of interdisciplinarity, and on the perspective of an intercultural epistemology. Thanks to them, it is possible to enlarge the scope of CSO studies and to supersede an implicit Western-centrism; the latter is currently reflected in the international research literature by a disparity between the amount of Anglo-Saxon cited references and references cited in other language contexts.

From commons to deliberative governance

Ostrom (1990) addresses third-sector goods in terms of their rivalry and excludability. She defines the commons as consisting of both rival and non-excludable goods. Because of their vulnerability to free riders, common resources are subject to depletion. This is the case with fishing areas or irrigation systems, for example. In her third-sector approach to this problem, Ostrom overcomes the dualism of market and state by showing that sustainable governance is possible through collective and self-organized action. Heuristically, her approach bridges economics and sociology.

From an economics perspective, Ostrom stipulates that individuals are best placed to create the relevant institutions to support their interaction and reduce uncertainty, and that surviving institutions are the ones with adaptive efficiency. However, Ostrom "sociologizes" her approach by introducing the social conditions of rules, which take into account the particular norms of each community and the communication among individuals. Hence, there is a close relationship between "reciprocity norm, democratic management, and active participation for producing several resources" (Dardot and Laval, 2014, p. 151). This makes it no longer necessary to identify signals likely to reduce informational asymmetries but rather to build, through deliberation and action, particular institutions. This is a crafting process that is deeply sociological and political (Dardot and Laval, 2014, pp. 137–175). The process assumes that the people involved in the commons are able to define by themselves the rules they will use. But this inventiveness is linked to the depth of their deliberation.

From deliberative governance to the public sphere

It is precisely on this point that we propose to make the connection with Habermas's thesis about politics. The relevance of his conceptual framework is based on the richness of his work perspective and the way he draws on deliberation. Habermas belongs to a philosophical tradition rooted in Europe. In particular, he contributes to the critical theory defined by Marx in 1843 as the "clarification produced by the present time on its own struggles and aspirations" (Marx, 1971, p. 300). This critical theory, characterized by a desire to foster emancipation, challenges the Frankfurt school's concept of domination as articulated by its emblematic authors including Adorno, Horkheimher and Marcuse and by sociologists such as Bourdieu.

Habermas's innovation is his stand against perspectives that suppress emancipation (Habermas, 1981, p. 116). As stated by Rancière, critical theory has locked itself in a "radical critique of a radically immutable situation" (Rancière, 2003, p. 365). To escape this paralysis, Habermas rejects the belief in inevitable domination in favor of the idea that "there is an insurmountable tension between capitalism and democracy" (Habermas, 1998, p. 379). While recognizing the importance of power and money, he highlights the role of democratic resources by including in his political analysis the study of the public sphere (Habermas,

1962) and by acknowledging the necessity of pluralism, which leads him to analyze the link between associations and democracy (Habermas, 1992). This is an important step in the study of CSOs because it leads to a fresh new vision: rather than viewing CSOs merely as private organizations, Habermas's perspective allows us to appreciate their public dimension.

From public dimension to substantive rationality

The clear separation made by Habermas – as well as Arendt – between the public sphere and the economic sphere leads Habermas to emphasize the role of CSOs dedicated to advocacy and protest activity. Such demarcation between policy on the one hand and the economy on the other hand calls for further examination. According to Fraser (1990, pp. 56–80), this demarcation is an impediment to understanding that socio-economic equality serves as a precondition for parity in public participation.

There is broad support for Habermas's view that associations embrace and articulate, in the political public sphere, social issues that derive from the private realm (Habermas, 1997, p. 394). But how can this be done only by associations with no private economic activities and no links with public organizations? The presumed prevalence of such CSOs is not consistent with empirical evidence. Rather it is more relevant to re-examine all CSOs in the light of their communications activities, organizational characteristics and power relations, relative to their involvement in public issues.

In this perspective, Polanyi asks us to avoid what he refers to as the economistic fallacy, i.e., the troublesome conflation of economy and market implied by Smith (1776) when he describes man's propensity to barter, truck and exchange one thing for another. Smith's description reveals indifference to man's social evolution over the long term. In particular, we have become accustomed to minimizing the importance of the last ten thousand years and thinking about them as just a prelude to the real history of our civilization. Economic anthropology usefully challenges this view and allows new insights into modern society. Thus, Polanyi (1944) posits in *The Great Transformation* that four main principles drive and explain economic behaviors: market, redistribution, reciprocity and householding. Each of these principles is associated with a different institutional model: the market itself for the market principle, centrality for redistribution, symmetry for reciprocity, and closed groups for domestic administration or householding. Accordingly, the analysis of CSOs must adopt the concept of hybridization as a way to fully understand what is occurring on the ground, for example such phenomena as income generated from the sale of services; corporate sponsorships; public subsidies related, for example, to social goals or to increasing volunteering; and various forms of in-kind support for CSOs.

To sum up, a CSO involved in commercial activities will not be driven by return on capital or by certain legal requirements and it will combine market principles with those of reciprocity and redistribution. Thus, CSOs mix different economic principles. A private company may also do this, for example when receiving grants. However, an association distinguishes itself by denying dominant power to shareholders in its legal statute and by rejecting a market-oriented perspective. Generally, prioritization is the result of a particular history and not solely dependent on features of a specific legal form. In this respect, both Polanyi's approach and Mauss's are relevant to establish the basis for a plural economy (Laville, 2006, pp. 77–83) by embracing a diversity of economic principles.

Polyani's historical perspective has found its way into international scholarship. In particular, the theoretical social management approach and the new organization science proposed by Guerreiro Ramos retreat from formal rationality (considered as utilitarist and only relevant to the market) in favor of substantive rationality. According to Serva (1997), and reported by Cançado, Pereira and Tenório (2011), substantive rationality and the theory of communicative action can be reconciled "because the two theories have as [their] starting point the human emancipation regarding the constraints of self-realization imposed by contemporary society and constitute a case of complementarity" (Serva, 1997, p. 22).

Chapter 13 of this volume, by França Filho and Boullosa, raises awareness of the issues at stake. The book concludes with a chapter meant to demonstrate the heuristic capacity of an intercultural approach to studying social enterprise. This last chapter provides a glimpse of the possible avenues that could be opened by an intercultural CSO research program.

Conclusion

Overall, it seems fair to expect that changes in civil society itself will be reflected in societal governance writ large. As civil society becomes more complex and as it responds to economic, political and social pressures, it also becomes more prominent as party to the democratic process. Our authors explore the various nuances and ramifications of this development in the framing of public policy, the delivery of public services, the definition of the public interest, and the functioning of government itself. Just as the boundaries within civil society, and between civil society, government and business, have become blurred, the notion of societal governance as a distinct and exclusive function of government per se has clearly become less salient. Indeed, societal governance has become a more diffuse and amorphous phenomenon but perhaps also more democratic and possibly more effective in addressing the ever more complex local and global issues of the twenty-first century.

While we are now far removed from 1914, the world of 2015 and beyond brings many other challenges. Woodrow Wilson's quest to make the world safe for democracy is still a bit beyond our grasp, but the evolution of governance at the nexus of democratic government and civil society brings with it the promise for a future better in many respects than what we have experienced over the past century.

References

Akerlof, G. A. (1970). The market for "lemons": Quality uncertainty and the market mechanism, *The Quarterly Journal of Economics*, 84(3), pp. 488–500.

Badelt, C. (1990). Institutional choice and the nonprofit sector, in Anheier, H. K. and Seibel, W. (eds) *The Third Sector: Comparative Studies of Nonprofit Organizations.* Berlin: Walter de Gruyter, pp. 53–64.

Ben-Ner, A., and Van Hoomissen, T. (1991). Nonprofits in the mixed economy: A demand and supply analysis, *Annals of Public and Cooperative Economics*, 62, pp. 519–550.

Berle, A. A., and Means, G. C. (1991). *The Modern Corporation and Private Property.* New Brunswick, NJ: Transaction Publishers.

Burns, T., and Stalker, G. (1961). *The Management of Innovation.* London: Tavistock.

Cançado, A. C., Tenório, F. G. and Pereira, J. R. (2011). Gestão social: reflexões teóricas e conceituais [Social management: theoretical and conceptual reflections], EBAPE.BR, 9(3/1), Rio de Janeiro, September, pp. 681–703.

Chanlat, J. F. (1998). *Sciences sociales et management.* Paris: Eska.

Coase, R. (1937). The nature of the firm. *Economica*, 4 (16), pp. 386–405.

Dardot, C., and Laval, P. (2014). *Commun.* Paris: La Découverte.

Di Maggio, P. J. (1988). Interest and agency in institutional theory, in Zucker, L. G. (ed.), *Institutional Patterns and Organizations: Culture and Environment.* Cambridge, MA: Ballinger, pp. 3–22.

Di Maggio, P. J., and Powell, W.W. (1983). The iron cage revisited: Institutional isomorphism and collective rationality in organizational fields, *American Sociological Review*, 48(42), pp. 147–160.

Durkheim, E. (1893/2007). *De la division du travail social.* Paris: Félix Alcan, repr. Paris: PUF.

Enjolras, B. (1996). Associations et isomorphisme institutionnel, *RECMA*, 261(59/3).

Evers, A., and Laville, J. L. (2004). Social services in social enterprises: On the possible contributions of hybrid organizations and a civil society, in Evers, A., and Laville, J.-L., *The Third Sector in Europe*, Cheltenham, UK, and Northampton, MA: Edward Elgar.

Fazzi, L. (2009). The democratization of welfare between rhetoric and reality: Local planning, participation, and third sector in Italy, *Journal of Civil Society*, 5(2), pp. 187–203.

Fraser, N. (1990). Rethinking the public sphere: A contribution to the critique of actually existing democracy, *Social Text*, 25–26, pp. 56–80.

Fukuyama, F. (2006). *The End of History and the Last Man*, Free Press; Reissue edition, 464 pages.

Glaeser, E. (2003). *The Governance of Not-for-profit Organizations.* Chicago and London: University of Chicago Press.

Granovetter, M. (2000). *Le marché autrement.* Paris: Desclée de Brouwer.

Gui, B. (1991). The economic rationale for the third sector, *Annals of Public and Cooperative Economics*, 62(4).

Habermas, J. (1962/1995). *The Structural Transformation of the Public Sphere: An Inquiry into a Category of Bourgeois Society.* Cambridge, MA: MIT Press.

Habermas, J. (1981). L'actualité de W. Benjamin. La critique: prise de conscience ou préservation, *Revue d'esthétique*, 1.

Habermas, J. (1992). L'espace public, 30 ans après, *Quaderni*, 18(Autumn): *Les espaces publics*, pp. 161–191.

Habermas, J. (1997). *Droit et démocratie*. Paris: Gallimard.

Habermas, J. (1998). *Théorie de l'agir communicationnel*. Paris: Fayard.

Hansmann, H. B. (1980). The role of nonprofit enterprise, *Yale Law Journal*, 89, pp. 835–898.

Kitthananan, A. (2006). Conceptualizing governance: A review, *Journal of Societal and Social Policy*, 5(3).

Krashinsky, M. (1986). Transactions costs and a theory of the nonprofit organization, in Rose-Ackerman, S. (ed.) *The Economics of Nonprofit Institutions*. New York: Oxford University Press, pp. 114–132.

Laville, J.-L. (2006). Plural economy, in Hart, K., Laville, J.-L. and Cattani, A. D. *The Human Economy*. Cambridge: Polity Press, pp. 77–83.

Lawrence, P., and Lorsch, J. (1973). *Adapter les structures de l'entreprise*. Paris: Editions d'organization (French translation).

Lawrence, T. B., and Suddaby, R. (2006). Institutions and institutional work, in Clegg, S. R., Hardy, C., Lawrence, T. B., and North, W. R. (eds) *Handbook of Organization Studies*, 2nd edition. London: Sage, pp. 215–254.

Marx, K. (1971). Letter to Ruge, in Engels, F., and Marx, K., *Correspondance*, vol. 1, *1835–1848*. Paris: Editions sociales, p. 300.

Mauss, M. (1997). *Ecrits politiques: Textes réunis par Marcel Fournier*. Paris: Fayard.

Mcguire, P., Granovetter, M., and Schwartz, M. (1993). Thomas Edison and the social construction of the early electricity industry in America, in Swedberg, R. (ed.), *Explorations in Economic Sociology*. New York: Russell Sage Press, pp. 213–248.

Nelson, R. R., and Winter, S. G. (1982). *An Evolutionary Theory of Economic Changes*. Cambridge, MA: Harvard University Press.

Nelson, R. R., and Winter, S. G. (2002). Evolutionary theorizing in economics, *Journal of Economic Perspective*, 16(2/spring), pp. 23–46.

Nyssens, M. (2013). Les analyses économiques des associations, in Hoareau, C., and Laville, J.-L., *La gouvernance des associations*. Toulouse: Eres.

Oliver, C. (1991). Strategic responses to institutional processes, *Academy of Management Review*, 16, pp. 145–179.

Oliver, C. (1992). The antecedents of deinstitutionalization, *Organization Studies*, 13, pp. 563–588.

Ostrom, E. (1990). *Governing the Commons*. Cambridge: Cambridge University Press.

Pérez, R. (2003). *La gouvernance de l'entreprise*. Paris: La Découverte.

Petrella, F. (2008). Organizations non lucratives et partenariats: Avantages et risques dans le cas des services de développement local en Belgique, in Enjolras, B. (ed.) *Gouvernance et intérêt général dans les services sociaux et de la santé*. Brussels: Peter Lang.

Pigou, A. C. (1932). *The Economics of Welfare*, 4th edition. New York: St Martins Press.

Polanyi, K. (1944/2001). *The Great Transformation: The Political and Economic Origins of Our Time*, 2nd edition. Boston: Beacon Press.

Rancière, J. (2003). Ethique de la sociologie, in *Les Scènes du peuple*. Paris: Horlieu.

Rhodes, R. (1997). *Understanding Governance : Policy Networks, Governance, Reflexivity, and Accountability*. Buckingham and Philadelphia: Open University Press.

Richards, R. O., and Smith, M. J. (2002). *Governance and Public Policy in the United Kingdom*. New York: Oxford University Press.

Rizza, R. (2004). Néo-institutionnalisme sociologique et nouvelle sociologie économique: quelles relations?, in La Rosa, M., and Laville, J.-L. (eds), *La sociologie économique européenne. Une rencontre franco-italienne*, *Sociologia del lavoro*, special supplement no. 93, bilingual text, Milan: France Angeli, pp. 76–98.

Serva M. (1997). A racionalidade substantiva demonstrada na prática administrativa, *Revista de Administração de Empresas*, 37(2).

Smith, A. (1776). *An Inquiry into the Nature and Causes of the Wealth of Nations* 1, 1st edition. London: W. Strahan.

Steen-Johnsen, K., Eynaud, P., and Wijkström, F. (2011). On civil society governance: A new field of research, *Voluntas*, special issue on civil society organization governance, September, pp. 1–11.

Tocqueville, A. (1996). *Democracy in America*. Ware, UK: Wordsworth Editions.

Weisbrod, B. A. (1975). Toward a theory of the voluntary nonprofit sector in a three sector economy. In Phelps, E. S. (ed.) *Altruism, Morality and Economic Theory*. New York: Russell Sage Foundation, pp. 171–195.

Williamson, O. (1979). Transaction-cost economics : The governance of contractual relations, *Journal of Law and Economics*, 22, pp. 233–261.

Williamson, O. E. (2002). The theory of the firm as governance structure: From choice to contract, *Journal of Economic Perspectives*, 16(3), pp. 171–195.

Woodward, J. (1956). *Industrial Organization: Theory and Practice*. Oxford: Oxford University Press.

Young, D. (1981). Entrepreneurship and the behaviour of nonprofit organizations: Elements of a theory, in White, M. (ed.), *Nonprofit Firms in a Three-Sector Economy*, Washington, DC: Urban Institute.

Young, D. (1983). *If Not For Profit, For What?: A Behavioral Theory of the Nonprofit Sector Based on Entrepreneurship*, Lexington Books; 30th Anniversary Digital Reissue with new front matter and commentaries by leading scholars Georgia State University Library Digital Archive, 2013. http://scholarworks.gsu.edu/facbooks2013/1/.

Young, D. (1986). Entrepreneurship and the Behavior of Nonprofit Organizations: Elements of a Theory, in Michelle White (ed.), *Nonprofit Firms in a Three-Sector Economy, Urban Institute Press*, 1981; reprinted in Susan Rose-Ackerman (ed.), The Economics of Nonprofit Institutions, Oxford University Press, pp.161–184.

Part I

Introduction to Part I

Jean-Louis Laville, Dennis R. Young and
Philippe Eynaud

This book examines governance, civil society and democracy across a full spectrum of societal structures, recognizing that governance is changing at all levels. The first part of the book starts with a traditional focus on the governance of CSOs though not too narrowly on the governing boards of these organizations per se. Throughout these first five chapters, the themes of change, complexity and blurring boundaries predominate. CSOs are discovered to embrace an increasing variety of complex organizational forms, a hybridization of traditional forms that challenge existing modes of governance and call for new approaches. This complexity also manifests itself at the interface of civil society and government, as traditional modes of collaboration are challenged by public policies demanding greater accountability and CSOs are sometimes forced to take a more adversarial posture. The nature of feedback between government and civil society changes as a result, altering governance at both levels. At the very least, the "boundary-spanning" role of nonprofit governing boards becomes increasingly important, changing the character of internal governance of CSOs over time. The modern environment of public accountability is also found to affect the style of civil society organization governance. CSOs necessarily become more rationalized and business-like in nature, possibly squeezing out some of the democratic character traditionally associated with nonprofit governance.

But things are not as simple as that; indeed, our authors find several different styles of nonprofit governance continuing to operate side by side in the population of CSOs, some more democratic, some more managerialist than others. Going further, the character of CSOs themselves is found to be evolving, with the boundaries between one CSO and another becoming less distinct. Thus the focus of CSO governance is moving from the domain of organizational governance to one of governing networks of CSOs as collectives. This indeed is a new frontier: new kinds of governance structures seem to be needed to provide both internal governance of CSO clusters and appropriately framed feedback between civil society clusters and the public sector. Finally, the evolution of civil society governance from traditional board governance of individual organizations to boundary-spanning and network governance is seen to have profound implications for societal governance as a whole. For example, some of our authors observe that as societies become more democratized through technology, globalized networking and economic development, the nature of the social contract itself changes, with greater expectations placed on government for accountability, performance, transparency and fairness. This in turn underwrites another feedback loop between citizens and CSOs, with expectations that the latter will become more democratic and responsive.

Research literature and trade publications intended to guide practice on the governance of CSOs have historically focused on the role of the board of directors or trustees as the key organ for steering the direction of the organization, ensuring its financial sustenance, overseeing staff, and taking ultimate responsibility for its performance and integrity. Moreover, as the chapters in Part I explain, the central thrust over the past half-century has been to model CSO governance on governance in the corporate business sector, emphasizing authority at the top (residing in the board), hierarchical control and top-to-bottom accountability. This trend has been reinforced by resource providers including government and institutional donors as well as trustees drawn from the business sector, who demand accountability for their funding and require performance metrics to help them determine if the organization is accomplishing its mission.

Even in the business sector, however, the traditional corporate governance model has been severely challenged in recent years, as failures in accountability have contributed to the collapse of major corporations in the midst of financial and economic crises and as information technology has made conventional forms of communication and control obsolete. Certainly for CSOs, the corporate model of governance was never a perfect fit. In particular, CSOs are in many ways more complex than business corporations, and not entirely amenable to top-to-bottom, metric-oriented control. CSOs have no overriding criterion analogous to profit with which to judge their performance. They have no owners analogous to stockholders in a business, but rather engage many different stakeholder groups, each with some legitimate claim to the guidance of the organization. Nor do they operate entirely in the marketplace, instead deriving their support from multiple sources ranging from charitable donations and volunteer efforts, to government subsidies and tax benefits, to fees and commercial revenues. All these factors complicate the issue of how they are best governed, and they help explain why the nature of nonprofit governance has always been contentious and complex.

The chapters in the first part of the book take us on a tour of evolving thought on CSO governance. Chapter 1 by Donnelly-Cox focuses on a key dynamic of the contemporary environments of CSOs – the blurring of boundaries between civil society, government and business. One consequence of this blurring has been the hybridization of CSOs themselves, as they take on characteristics of organizations associated with other sectors, especially business. This in turn has important implications for CSO governance. For example, as business practices and market focus become more integral to CSO operations, governance is likely to reflect the corporate model more closely and favor the legal form of the foundation over the association form. Moreover, in the larger scheme of things, hybridization reflects new thinking about the role of CSOs in society as a whole – requiring a refocusing of internal governance to set new missions and programmatic directions. Finally, a changing role for CSOs is likely to be reflected in public policy, including changes in tax exemptions, requiring CSO governance to give new attention both to resource acquisition issues and to advocacy efforts aimed at influencing policy reformulation itself. As Donnelly-Cox observes, these developments in hybridization will require CSO governance to maintain a tenuous balance between efficiency of operations and democratic decision-making.

Meyer and Maier's analysis in Chapter 2 acknowledges the growing dominance of the managerial, corporate model, but also describes parallel discourses in CSO governance that have long been a part of the overall debate and may indeed again become more prominent as CSOs attempt to address their contemporary and future challenges. These latter discourses – domestic, professionalist, grassroots and civic governance – are based on alternative institutional logics, and they capture various unique aspects of CSOs including voluntarism, cooperative culture, civic engagement and professional service. The authors consider these discourses as they map out different possible scenarios of future CSO governance that integrate the alternative logics into the dominant corporate (managerialist) regime in different possible combinations over time.

Chapter 3, by Chatelain-Ponroy, Eynaud and Sponem, challenges the historical preoccupation with board governance by observing that in France, as in many other countries, governance of associations is shared in some manner between the board and the general assembly of organizational members from which the board is usually elected. The general assembly reflects the discourse of civic (democratic) governance considered by Meyer and Maier. Through their survey of French CSOs, Chatelain-Ponroy, Eynaud and Sponem find that governance is shared by the board and the assembly according to several different regimes. In particular, the authors identify three different styles of governance – emphasizing coercion, coaching or democratic decision-making – and six clusters of CSOs in which these styles dominate for the board or the assembly respectively. At the very least, studies of CSO governance such as this, which attend to the role of assemblies, contribute an important and neglected piece to the contemporary literature on CSO governance. Such study also challenges conventional thinking that CSO governance is synonymous with board governance.

Chapter 4 by Ostrower and Stone recognizes that CSO governance is not exclusively about internal control of the organization but is also about the organization's connection with its external environment. The boundary-spanning function of CSO governing boards has long been recognized in the literature but has been largely neglected in recent years. Now, however, in an era of horizontal relationships and decentralized and collaborative decision-making stimulated by the revolution in communications technology, the boundary-spanning function of governing boards is increasingly critical. In fact, Ostrower and Stone find CSO environments to have become substantially more complex, dynamic and multi-faceted, with fuzzy boundaries and multiple intersecting components including economic (resource), public policy, legal and regulatory, community and normative elements. In this context, boundary spanning itself is multi-faceted, with boards serving as buffers, mediators, representatives, information gatherers, translators and advocates for their organizations. Ostrower and Stone report on the results of two surveys of CSOs in the US, one broadly representative of the nonprofit sector and the other focusing on the particularly interesting case of nonprofit charter schools. The authors find considerable variation among CSOs in their emphasis on the different dimensions of boundary spanning and the accountability regimes they entail. Nonetheless, the authors identify a problematic general pattern of stronger focus on vertical accountability (e.g., to funders and regulators) and less on outward or horizontal accountability (e.g., to community and peer networks), raising critical questions for practice as well as research on how CSO governance is adapting to the changing environments in which CSOs are now immersed.

The first four chapters of Part I focus primarily on the governance of individual CSOs in a changing environment. Chapter 5 by Koliba moves our attention to governance of key aspects of the environment itself by focusing on the governance networks in which CSOs are commonly and increasingly enmeshed, and indeed in which they are integral components. These cross-sector networks are primary means through which the boundary-spanning role of individual CSO governance is executed; moreover, the governance of the networks themselves is increasingly consequential in its own right. Koliba identifies five key types of governance networks – grants and contract networks, partnership networks, advocacy networks, intergovernmental networks and regulatory networks – and the different roles that CSOs play in these networks, respectively as contracted agents or grantees; partners; peers; external interested parties; and third-party regulators. Koliba also examines how accountability is executed among organizational participants in these networks, through three alternative frames of reference – market, democratic and administrative. The result of Koliba's review is a rich research agenda on network governance issues and the growing importance of networks to the governance of CSOs and the contributions of CSOs to the governance of the networks themselves.

In Chapter 6, Borzaga and Depedri examine the particular case of social enterprises as studied in the European research tradition. Here, social enterprises are understood as private organizations engaged in ongoing productive activity in the economic marketplace, thus relying on paid work while maintaining autonomy and permitting a degree of economic risk-taking. However, at the societal level, social enterprises are also seen to arise from groups of citizens with objectives of service dedicated to the community. As such, they are supposed to ensure that decision-making is not based primarily on returns to capital and the distribution of profits. Accordingly, Borzaga and Depedri focus on multi-stakeholder cooperatives that engage workers, users and volunteers as governing members. In particular, the involvement of workers in the ownership structure of the firm is seen to reduce the risk of opportunistic behaviors resulting from information asymmetries between management (the employer) and workers (agents) by combining these two roles. Borzaga and DePedri put this proposition to the test empirically by investigating Italian social cooperatives.

The final chapter in Part I, by Wijkström and Reuter, makes the leap to societal governance by considering how CSOs can influence the nature of societal governance as a whole through their capacities to serve as exemplars of governance practice and through their normative powers to influence societal values. These authors view CSOs as sources of ideas and values that can ultimately shape the nature of societal governance by "developing, defining and defending normative principles of governance" For example, CSOs can lead the way on such issues as what it means to be a citizen by establishing and demonstrating norms that embody the concept and values of citizenship. This chapter helps set the stage for Part II, which is primarily concerned with the broader issues of societal governance and its connections to civil society.

In summary, governance of CSOs is essentially inseparable from governance of the society in which CSOs operate. Addressing the problems of societal governance in order to enable society to cope with contemporary issues such as poverty and prosperity, disparities of wealth and income, environmental degradation and climate change, public health and social conflict, must start here. The problems of societal governance are of course much larger and broader than those of CSOs. But CSOs provide a special window through which principles and practices of governance may be understood, developed and disseminated into the wider arena of governance at the level of societies as a whole. The chapters of Part I offer a modest and preliminary stepping stone into that broader arena.

1 Civil society governance

Hybridization within third-sector and social enterprise domains

Gemma Donnelly-Cox

Introduction

The world of civil society organizing is becoming increasingly interesting. Amidst financial meltdowns, big societies and shrinking states, and growing expressions of citizen discontent, the civil society organizational landscape is being redrawn. Indeed, the very notion of civil society as a distinct societal space is contested. There is a rising number of legitimate ways to organize and niches in which to locate. While there are many factors that are bringing about civil society change, there are trends that seem to be particularly pervasive.

First, a move can be identified from the idealized modelling of distinct societal sectors, where business, state, voluntary and family are separate and distinct, to the notion of sector blurring. While it has been recognized for quite some time that there is a great deal of interpenetration of sectors (Brodkin and Young, 1989 and 2014), models based on the societal sectors construction continue to be used and useful (see for example Wijkström, 2011, and Wijkström and Lundström, 2002; for an overview, see Alcock, 2010). Nonetheless, it seems that the sharp demarcation is fading. With the blurring of boundaries, there is a blending of previously segregated actors and activities – and therefore also of organizations. Whereas it was once possible to map distinct locations for various types of organizing onto a sector map, organizations now span sectoral boundaries (Billis, 2010; Dees and Anderson, 2003; Laville and Nyssens, 2001). This has been going on for a long time (Billis, 1991; Powell, 1987, 1990) – but it is now perhaps accelerating, especially with the development of social enterprises that seem to transcend sectors (Dees and Anderson, 2003).

Second, for over three decades scholarship has placed an emphasis on identifying the distinctiveness of the nonprofit form, the role of sector and the definitive functions of civil society, and with this emphasis has come a questioning of whether particular roles and functions are best served, or possibly only served, within a civil society organizing domain (Frumkin, 2002; Galaskiewicz and Barringer, 2012). When boundaries blur, so too does the clarity of roles and functions. If civil society does not have definitive roles and functions – or, at least, if it can be conceived that those roles and functions may be fulfilled within other spheres – then there are new choices as to how, and where, activity is organized to fulfill those functions. This leads to a range of new organizing possibilities. For example, there are new legal forms of organization such as L3Cs (low-profit limited liability companies) in the US, CICs (community interest companies) in the UK (Brakman Reiser, 2010) and social cooperatives in Italy (Defourny, 2001) that seek to combine the civic benefits of civil society organizations and the commercial capabilities of private-sector entities. In the US, self-regulatory models such as the "B Corporation" have emerged, where a framework is developed to create a blended organizational form that can operate under existing nonprofit law (Brakman Reiser, 2010: 619). Increasingly complex intersectoral partnerships engage state agencies, private funders and social enterprise service deliverers. There is great hope for cross-sectoral networks to address some of society's "wicked problems" (Koopenjan and Klijn, 2004) – problems, such as homelessness, that feature complexity, uncertainty and conflict (Rhodes and Donnelly-Cox, 2014) – more effectively and sustainably.

Third, whereas understanding the "for what and for whom" of civil society has been the major goal of the sector-defining research programs (for example Salamon *et al.*, 2000), the combined force of blurring sector boundaries and contested roles and functions leads to the question of what organizations and what stakeholders should be of concern when speaking of civil society. Why should states designate one group of organizations as tax exempt if others can (and in particular if they do) serve the same function? Why should organizations that carry out specific functions that serve the public good be required to adopt one legal form if another proves to be more effective?

In their landmark work on the reshaping of civil society, Borzaga and Defourny (2001) dealt with some of these core issues through their documentation of the emergence of third-sector and social enterprise domains within civil society. This chapter builds on their work and examines the current transformation of civil society through the phenomenon of "hybridization." Specifically, the focus is on the collection of organizational forms described as hybrids, their manifestations within third-sector and social enterprise domains of civil society, and their implications for governance. Hybrids are organizations that combine blends of organizing "properties" (Perry and Rainey, 1988), typically with two or more "sectoral characteristics" (Smith, 2014: 2), sometimes straddling rather than residing within any one sector. While the blurring of sectoral boundaries that has preceded and has been accelerated by hybridization is being examined carefully and with some concern for its possible effects (see for example Dees and Anderson, 2003; Honingh and Karsten, 2007; Hwang and Powell, 2009; Jones, 2007), there is evidence that benefits outweigh risks (Brandsen and Karré, 2011) and that hybrids will come to represent the "new normal" of civil society organizing (Brandsen *et al.*, 2005; Evers, 2005). Hybrids are increasingly viewed as a positive force in organizing, with qualities that include sustainable organizational and business practices (Hoffman *et al.*, 2012) and capacity for change and innovation (Jay, 2013). As societal institutions catch up with hybrid experimentation (Brakman Reiser, 2010), the choice of legal entities available is increasing (Kelley, 2009) and both external (Osborne, 2010) and internal (Low, 2006) governance challenges are being addressed. In this chapter, following Steen-Johnsen *et al.*, "internal governance" relates to the operation of the organizational board in the control of the organization and "external governance" refers to the processes and institutional mechanisms for societal-level regulation (2011: 555–556).

Within civil society, Borzaga and Defourny's work (2001) provides a useful platform for studying hybridization. It allows for identifying patterns of hybridization within the third-sector and social enterprise domains and for drawing out governance implications. Thus the exploration of hybridity that follows is framed within their domains. It is preceded by a brief discussion of the origins of the study of organizational hybridity and the development of a sector-framed hybrid literature.

The meanings of hybridity

The term "hybrid organization" has been used in a number of different ways. In structural organization theory, it is commonly used to describe combinations of ideal-type forms, without any reference to sector. A hybrid is simply one that combines characteristics of various structure approaches, purposely tailored to specific needs. One common hybrid type is the combination of the functional and divisional structures. Used in rapidly changing environments, such hybrids are viewed as providing greater flexibility than either "purer" form (Daft *et al.*, 2010). However, "hybrid" has also been applied as a pejorative label to indicate a problem in organizing. Through the late nineteenth century and the early twentieth, it was regularly used to demarcate illegitimate formations or constructions, as in this use in the social work literature in the 1920s: "Hybrid organizations that attempt to blend medicine and religion have brought religion as a therapeutic measure so into disrepute that one scarce dares to mention it for fear of being misunderstood" (Hospital Social Service Association of New York City, 1921: 136). While concerns about the challenges of hybrid forms have not gone away, in the general management literature the emphasis is on risk management (for example Miller *et al.*, 2008) and in the civil society literature, those concerns are regarded as somewhat overstated (see Brandsen and Karré, 2011) and the focus is moving increasingly to the range of hybrid options that are available (Battilana, 2012; Galaskiewicz and Barringer, 2012; Haigh and Hoffman, 2012; Herranz *et al.*, 2011; Jäger and Schröer, 2013; Jolink and Niesten, 2012; Pache and Santos, 2012; Rhodes and Donnelly-Cox, 2014). In this chapter, the particular use of the term hybrid organization within the public-sector literature is taken as the point of departure. The following discussion of that literature investigates hybridity as a function of blurring and overlap of sector boundaries and the consequent implications for organization form and design.

Hybridity in the public-sector literature

The blending of core organizing properties, such as formal goals, decision-making processes and organizational structure (Perry and Rainey, 1988: 185), that are associated with more than one societal sector was raised as an issue of organization and public administration in the early 1970s (Wamsley and Zald, 1973). Comment on the "dangers and opportunities" presented by "public enterprise ... the New York Port Authority, foundations, and the like, that are neither purely public nor purely private" (Baratz, 1970: v) signaled interest in the governance and organization of these entities, and the 1980s saw increasing description and explanation of organizing practices in the public-sector domain that were not purely public. Writers pointed to "organizations that overlap" (Perry and Rainey, 1988: 184) when there is, for example, public ownership and private funding, or vice versa. Organizations such as public-sector science laboratories which are "part public, part private" were described as "intermediate forms" (Emmert and Crow, 1987: 55). Through and beyond the 1990s, the discussion of hybrid organizations focused increasingly on the integration of market logic into public service delivery. For example, hybrids were defined as "organizations that combine a public orientation with a market orientation" (Joldersma and Winter, 2002: 83).

Within the public-sector literature, discussion of hybrids thus incorporated both sectoral and organizational dimensions. Hybrids were seen to arise within the public and private spheres and in particular in the overlapping space at their borders. When hybrids were discussed at the organizational level, writers often used the device of a continuum of organizing types (Kickert, 2001). For example, Perry and Rainey's work was concerned with developing a continuum of public–private hybrid types that reflected the different properties of goals, decision processes and structures in each type at particular points on a continuum. Lan (1992) contributed to evidence for public–private distinctions that result in hybrids residing on a "complex, multidimensional continuum" (Lan, 1992: 6).

Hybridity in the civil society literature

Throughout the 1980s, civil society scholars were noting the changing relations between civil society and the state and the blurring of sector boundaries (see, for example, Ostrander and Langton, 1987; Brodkin and Young, 1989 and 2014). In 1990, Kramer predicted the implications that changing sectoral relations would have for organizing in the third sector: "future theory-building must somehow take into account the blurring of sectoral boundaries, their overlapping and inter-penetration, as well as the existence of hybrid organizations" (1990: 261). More sustained discussion of these matters did not develop until a decade later. A point of crossover from a primarily public-sector hybridity literature to one that engaged with civil society appeared in a 2001 paper concerned with the governance of social service delivery. Kickert presented an organizing conundrum in the provision of public goods such as healthcare, education, social care and social housing. He noted that in Europe, they are often delivered by "judicially 'private' organizations, the intermediary layer of social, voluntary, nonprofit organizations ... which fit neither in the strictly public realm of state action nor in the strictly private realm of commercial relationships" (Kickert, 2001: 136). The implications for governance of public service delivery, and for civil society, of this hybrid realm were explored in a literature on hybrids that focused on civil society. Contributors (for example Evers, 2004; Brandsen *et al.*, 2005; Evers, 2005; Brandsen and Hout, 2006; Koppell, 2003) noted emerging patterns of organizing within civil society for delivery of public services. Defining hybrid organizations as "heterogeneous arrangements, characterized by mixtures of pure and incongruous origins, (ideal)types, 'cultures,' 'coordination mechanisms,' 'rationalities,' or 'action logics'" (Brandsen *et al.*, 2005: 750), they argued that while they were focused on organizing within civil society, the hybrids under study were arrangements where there was such a mix of mechanisms and logics that there was "no longer a clear match with any single type" (Brandsen and Hout, 2006: 549).

Across the civil society literature concerned with hybridization, one pervasive theme is explaining why the phenomenon has emerged. For the most part, the causal factor is seen to be external to civil society. Changes in the state, the role of the state and its relationship with civil society are cited as important factors. For example, "The basic argument is that hybridization represents the impact of the changing role of the state and the adaptive response of nonprofit organizations to an increasingly uncertain funding and political environment" (Smith, 2010: 220). A civil society organization is forced to structure in new ways as a response to its changing relationship with the state. Thus hybridization can be understood in terms of one sector's relation to another; changes in one sector domain precipitates changes in another. However, the agency of organizational decision-makers is not neglected. Smith comments that nonprofit organizations should see hybrid structures as a strategic choice rather than an intermediate form of organizing – as "helpful for nonprofit organizations as they strive to respond to a rapidly changing environment and create sustainable and effective organizations" (Smith, 2010: 227).

The development of a civil society hybridity literature did not focus exclusively on the border between civil society and the public sector. Another strand focused on the realm of the overlap between civil society and the private sector. While the former focus emerged out of a literature concerned with the delivery of public service, the latter evolved within the burgeoning field of social entrepreneurship and social enterprise. In the sections that follow, Borzaga and Defourny's (2001) conceptualization of third-sector and social enterprise is employed to frame the two domains of civil society. In the third-sector domain, hybrid organizations that are mainly (though not exclusively) found in the public-sector borderlands are described. Defourny's (2001) exposition of the transition from third sector to social enterprise is used to discuss this latter approach to hybridization. In these domains, metaphors used within the public-sector literature – in particular, the sector sphere and the continuum – reappear. Emphasis is placed on presenting the "organizational properties" as well as the sector dynamics of hybridization (Honingh and Karsten, 2007).

Hybridity and the third sector

Within the third-sector literature, there are many explanations for and categorizations of hybrids. Two dominant approaches are profiled in this section. The first, the "rooted organizations" approach, helps to explain the gradual adoption by third-sector organizations of characteristics from other sectors. The second, the "hybrid third sector" approach, makes the case that hybridity has always been present and is a defining characteristic of the sector. Each approach provides some insight into internal and external governance issues. What unites these approaches is that, for the most part, the additional characteristics adopted are taken on as a result of the relationship between the civil society organization and the state. There are exceptions that emphasize adoption of business principles: for example, Cooney defines hybrid organizations as "nonprofit social service organizations that combine business enterprises with a social purpose mission" (Cooney, 2006: 145).

Rooted organizations

This perspective on the development of hybrid organizations is interesting in that it presents third-sector entities both as highly path dependent (Sydow and Schreyögg, 2013) and as capable of acquiring new core characteristics. These organizations, over time, take on "significant" characteristics from other sectors but have clearly emerged from and are embedded in a single sector. Therefore, a third-sector hybrid will differ from a public- or private-sector hybrid due to the impact of its founding origins. Billis proposes that hybrid organizations have "'roots' and primary adherence to the distinctive principles – the 'rules of the game' – of just one sector" (2010: 3). He argues that governance and operational principles reflect the identity of the sector of origin throughout the development of the organization. A third-sector hybrid is certainly not a random collection of heterogeneous elements but rather an identifiable third-sector organization that has become elaborated by the elements of other sectors.

This way of explaining the existence and development of hybrid organizations is very useful for making sense of the evolution over time of a hybrid entity. For example, many service-providing third-sector organizations were initially established as membership organizations. The rooted approach could be used to view a third-sector organization that was founded as a national membership association with democratic governance. Initially, it gets pulled towards the public sector when it applies for and secures state grants and adopts the accounting and reporting procedures that meet public-sector reporting requirements. Over time, it takes on state contracts for delivery of public services that are clearly in the interest of its members. An Extraordinary General Meeting is called at which leadership convinces the membership to agree to the appointment of public-sector representatives and co-option of functional experts onto its board, which heretofore was composed entirely of elected members. As it adapts its practices and procedures, organizational and governance structure, it becomes a third-sector–public-sector hybrid. Eventually the decision is taken to move from associational status to becoming a company limited by guarantee without share capital, as this is the "business-like" legal form with which the state is willing to contract over the long term. In addition to advocating on behalf of its members, it now offers services that are funded by the state and provided to a client set defined by the conditions of its contract, not by its membership. The organization's associational roots are reflected in its membership's representative role on the governing board, the retention of a council of elected members, and a regional structure that reflects its membership as well as its client distribution. It retains core characteristics of its roots but also incorporates public- and private-sector organizing principles.

The rooted organization perspective affords insight into the evolution of hybrids and patterns of adaptation. It provides the foundations for a contingency perspective on hybrid organizing. Whereas there may be no one best way to develop a hybrid organization, some paths may prove more beneficial than others, given the particular requirements of the case at hand.

This perspective also provides insight into the governance issues that may arise during an organization's evolution. While the emergence of these hybrids is at least in part a function of systematic changes in societal governance, in which the functions of the state are taken on by civil society, these changes have knock-on effects on organizational governance. From a civil society perspective, long-standing norms of democratic governance have, in the evolution of these third-sector hybrids, been transformed into corporate governance. While this kind of transformation meets the approval of some stakeholders – largely those outside civil society – in that it confers legitimacy and demonstrates accountability to funders, to donors and to society at large, other stakeholders are disenfranchised by such a transformation.

Further, a rooted approach may be useful for identifying the challenges that arise as institutionalized mechanisms are disrupted, as "the combination of characteristics and objectives present in a hybrid organization generates conflict of interests" (Thomasson, 2009: 364). For example, a hybrid with roots in exclusively serving its own members that takes on contractual obligations for universal service delivery creates a fundamental dissonance for its stakeholders. These, and the other adaptations described above, bring about fundamental clashes in sector logics and create a set of contradictory requirements for an organization (Skelcher and Smith, 2014). Such trade-offs (Steinberg, 2012) may result for example from conflicting internal and external demands, such as internal pressures for democratic governance and external rationalizing or managerialist pressures (Maier and Meyer, 2011; Hwang and Powell, 2009). As a rooted hybrid continues to adapt to changing requirements, the organization may grow increasingly ambiguous about whether any outcome may be regarded as a success or a failure, given the multiple organizing logics reflected in its makeup (Jay, 2013). Overall, we see a picture of organizations exposed to multiple tensions (Sanders and Mcclellan, 2014).

The hybridized third sector

The rooted approach takes sector identity as a core element of organizing. It does not easily accommodate those organizations that, at their establishment, explicitly incorporate logics of two or more sectors. Rooted organizations evolve and adapt about their core essence. In contrast, there is a second distinct approach to third-sector hybridization which argues that hybridization replaces the distinctiveness previously associated with the sector metaphor. To speak of the third sector is to acknowledge a space of hybridized activity, a mix of ways of organizing, in which all organizations operating within it are, by definition, hybrids. Hybridity is synonymous with third sector; it is a "hybrid domain ... that is, organizations in this sector emerge as hybrid types between the pure actors we know as bureaucracies, enterprises, and families or clans" (Brandsen *et al.*, 2005: 751). Whereas the rooted organization approach sees fundamental conflicts of logics as a function of the divergence from the roots, in the hybridized third sector there is a "mix of pure, but incongruent, contradictive and conflicting behavioral rationalities" (van der Wal and van Hout, 2009: 225). Contradiction is the rule rather than the exception.

This perspective does not dispense entirely with the context of a sector map but rather positions the sectors differently when explaining what hybridization is. Rather than sectors per se, the context for the hybrid third sector is a set of pure organizing domains. Third-sector organizations draw on all three in their pursuit of mission. They are united – whether the activity is advocacy, community action, service delivery or political engagement – in seeking to care for others. Care supersedes commercial or policy agendas as the motivating force within the hybridized third sector (Brandsen *et al.*, 2005).

While the focus of the domain is care, the driver of the hybridization is, largely, the state and changes within the state, the "political trends and fashions like the privatization, decentralization and deregulation of public services" (Brandsen and Karré, 2008: 2). Whereas the conceptual model of the hybridized third sector is central, it is worth noting that the focus for analysis has been, almost exclusively, policy fields (Brandsen and Karré, 2011) such as housing, social welfare and education and the policy context in which these hybridized entities operate. It would be interesting to see whether this model is applicable to organizations operating largely outside policy domains, such as human rights non-governmental organizations or development agencies.

To summarize, the two models of third-sector hybridization presented here are positioned within the concept of the third sector offered by Borzaga and Defourny (2001). Rooted hybrids sit largely in the borderlands between state and third sector, with deep roots reaching back into the third sector. The hybridized third-sector model complements the essence of Defourny's third sector (2001), with the state playing the major role in governing the operating environment. These models of third-sector hybridization provide insight into the changing governance of society. Third-sector hybrids take on the organizational characteristics that are required for them to legitimately fill social service delivery roles and demonstrate accountability.

Social enterprise hybridization

Within the third-sector hybrid literature discussed above, the sector metaphor provided an image of spheres of civil society, commercial activity and public-sector activity. Hybrid organizations were seen as being located in the overlaps between these spheres. The overlap that commanded most attention in this literature was that of the public and civil society spheres. The focus was on third-sector organizations that become more like public-sector organizations as they adopt public-sector regulatory and service delivery systems. It might be expected, then, that in the literature on social enterprise hybrids, the metaphor of sphere remains but shifts to the private sector and the commercial arena. However, while there is a clear accent on the benefits that can be gained from organizations becoming business-like, there is limited emphasis on the sector "space." Rather, the dominant metaphor is one of a continuum. At each end of the continuum is an ideal-type organizational form: typically, purely commercial at one end and purely voluntary at the other. Hybrid forms occur at any point along the continuum. Organizations at various points on the continuum exhibit different mixes of private and voluntary characteristics. This distinction is marked in Defourny (2001), with a set of four commercial/entrepreneurial characteristics and a set of five social characteristics. A second point of distinction between the third-sector and social enterprise hybrid conceptualizations is the explanation for how hybrids come about. Rather than falling into hybridity over time, or being that way as a function of sector overlap, social enterprise hybrids are purposely constructed. Their mix of voluntary and commercial characteristics is selected by their founding entrepreneurs so that they are vehicles fit for a social purpose. A third distinction, which is more explicit in some of the North American social enterprise literature and rather implicit in Defourny, is sustainability (Van Huylenbroeckt, 2009).

Fit-for-purpose organizations

Thus the social enterprise literature generally uses the term "hybrid" to classify organizations that combine business practices and methods with social goals, without great emphasis on sector. Indeed, choice of sector becomes one of the founding decisions for the entity – would it better serve its social mission as a nonprofit or as a commercial organization? In some but certainly not all of this literature, the hybrid organization is assumed not to distribute profits. Borzaga and Defourny (2001) include cooperatives and emphasize the Italian social cooperative form. Other writers dispense with the sector concept in their definition, for example defining hybrids as "the entities through which social entrepreneurs carry on their affairs" (Kelley, 2009: 340). Yet the notion of "sector" does sneak back in, as choice of vehicle requires the selection of a legal entity. Kelley points to a "legally challenging trend: hybrid organizations formed as for-profits even though their purpose is essentially charitable" (2009: 341). This creates a dual mandate of sustained profit-making and measurable social outcomes. A recent characterization of hybrid organizations in the social enterprise sphere is "for-benefit organizations" – "organizations that generate earned income but give top priority to an explicit social mission" (Sabeti, 2011: 99). Proponents of the for-benefit organization assume that the corporate form will be the core of the entity (Billitteri, 2007).

Within the social enterprise literature, the explanations for hybridization tend to either ignore or at least put less emphasis on a sectoral logic and to leave the public sector out of the equation altogether. There are a few exceptions. For example, the call for a "tri-value" model of social enterprise is based on the premise that the public sector has been incorrectly excluded from many social enterprise models (see Herranz *et al.*, 2011). At least one attempt has been made to incorporate public, private and nonprofit within a continuum model (see Crossan *et al.*, 2011). Usually, though, the focus is on the organization and the form through which it can best achieve its objectives. Thus hybridization in social enterprises may be understood as a structural choice directly related to goal achievement: "Increasingly we are turning to business methods and structures in our efforts to find more cost-effective and sustainable ways to address social problems and deliver socially important goods" (Dees and Anderson, 2003: 16). While Dees and Anderson wrote on "sector-bending" (2003), they did not linger on sector but rather on modes of organization and development most suited to producing social and financial returns. This approach is pragmatically focused on identifying how best to secure desired outcomes. Many of the contributors are concerned with building fit-for-purpose social ventures – these writers are grappling with the challenges of how to design and build social enterprises that can do both the social and the business functions well (Sabeti, 2011; Brewster, 2009; Cooney, 2006). The focus is on how to fit these together depending on what it is you want to do. This is reflected in the growing literature on the appropriate legal form for social enterprise (Brewster, 2009; Kelley, 2009; Sabeti, 2011). We find within the social enterprise literature examples of organizations that are incorporating conflicting logics from the outset (Pache and Santos, 2012).

As with the other two approaches, there are challenges. Multiple stakeholders have contrasting conceptions of value. How best to evaluate outcomes is a constant concern. And the underlying challenge of creating both social and financial value is recognized, by some authors at least, as a fundamental hybrid problem (Kelley, 2009).

Discussion, implications and conclusions

This chapter has presented the three conceptualizations of civil society hybrids within the Borzaga and Defourny (2001) framework encompassing the third sector and social enterprise. Their third-sector concept embraces both the rooted organization and hybrid third-sector perspectives on hybridity and assists in drawing out the strengths and limitations of each.

Rooted hybrids are characterized by continuous adaptation to a changing environment, in which they inevitably become increasingly hybridized – whether due to their responses to the demands of the environment or due to the agency they exert in their attempts to manage it. The rooted organization approach helps to understand what happens when organizations depart from embedded sector organization logics. It could be very useful for a detailed study of organizing logics and the factors that are related to their change. Overall, however, it is grounded on the assumption that sectors have boundaries and that the distinctions between them must be understood if we are to understand hybrids.

Hybrids in the "hybridized third sector" are complex entities that reflect the complexity of their environment. The approach can be applied to the study of third-sector organizations in public policy domains. The study of public value creation, the engagement of actors in policy fields and the evaluation of policy outcomes are all topics that would correspond with this approach.

Hybrids on the social–commercial continuum are truly heterogeneous entities, with their core organizing properties selected on the basis of being fit for purpose. Observing the ongoing development of hybrids is useful for understanding some of the trends in favored organizing forms that have been identified by other organization scholars. For example, observations regarding the rise of the foundation form and the decline of the associational form in Swiss civil society (Von Schnurbein and Schönenberg, 2010) can be understood as a response to the challenges of multi-stakeholder governance in rooted hybrids. The preference for the foundation form can be explained, from a rooted hybrid perspective, as reducing internal pressures for democratic governance and responding to external rationalizing or managerialist logics. An alternative response to the challenges of multi-stakeholder governance is discussed in this volume in Chapter 6, in Borzaga and Depedri's work on Italian social cooperatives. We see in differing patterns of hybridization that there are many approaches to reaching a balance between efficiency objectives and democratic needs.

Finally, there is an open opportunity for theorizing hybridity. While in this chapter the notion of hybridity as embedded within the third sector and social enterprise (Borzaga and Defourny, 2001) has supported discussion of hybrid patterns and governance issues, there is much further to go. Smith (2014) argues that hybridity's isolation from nonprofit theory needs to be addressed; Skelcher and Smith (2014) use institutional theory to frame a comparative cross-national analysis of hybrids. Further, Jolink and Niesten (2012) illustrate the utility of agency theory, transaction cost economics and the resource-based view. Each of these organization theory perspectives addresses both the internal organizational dynamics of the hybrid and the environmental context in which it operates.

Hybrid organizations arise for many different reasons – as reactions to external pressures; as opportunistic responses to a change in operating conditions; as entrepreneurial efforts to create more fit-for-purpose organizations. Whatever the driver, they are, by definition, more complex forms than pure types. Whether pushed or pulled into hybridity, these organizations raise interesting opportunities and challenges for governance at both the societal and organizational levels.

References

Alcock, P. 2010. A Strategic Unity: Defining the Third Sector in the UK. *Voluntary Sector Review*, 1, 5–24.

Baratz, M. S. 1970. *The American Business System in Transition*, Crowell.

Battilana, J. and Dorado, S. 2012. Building Sustainable Hybrid Organizations: The Case of Commercial Microfinance Organizations. *Academy of Management Journal*, 53, 1419–1440.

Billis, D. 1991. The Roots of Voluntary Agencies: A Question of Choice. Nonprofit and *Voluntary Sector Quarterly*, 20, 57–70.

Billis, D. 2010. *Hybrid Organizations and the Third Sector: Challenges for Practice, Theory and Policy*, Palgrave Macmillan.

Billitteri, T. J. 2007. Mixing Mission and Business: Does Social Enterprise Need a New Legal Approach? Highlights from an Aspen Institute Roundtable, Nonprofit Sector Research Fund, The Aspen Institute.

Borzaga, C. and Defourny, J. 2001. *The Emergence of Social Enterprise*, Routledge.

Brakman Reiser, D. 2010. Governing and Financing Blended Enterprise. *Chicago–Kent Law Review*, 85, 619–656.

Brandsen, T. and Hout, E. v. 2006. Co-management in Public Service Networks. *Public Management Review*, 8, 537–549.

Brandsen, T. and Karré, P. 2011. Hybrid Organizations: No Cause for Concern? *International Journal Of Public Administration*, 34, 827–836.

Brandsen, T., van de Donk, W. and Putters, K. 2005. Griffins or Chameleons? Hybridity as a Permanent and Inevitable Characteristic of the Third Sector. *International Journal of Public Administration*, 28, 749–765.

Brewster, B., Henning, N., Reyna, E., Wang, D. E., Welch, M. D. and Hoffman, A. J. 2009. *Hybrid Organizations: New Business Models for Environmental Leadership*, Greenleaf.

Brodkin, E. Z. and Young, D. 1989 and 2014. Making Sense of Privatisation: What can we Learn from Economic and Political Analysis?, in Kamerman, S. B. and Kahn, A. J. (eds) *Privatization and the Welfare State*, Princeton University Press.

Cooney, K. 2006. The Institutional and Technical Structuring of Nonprofit Ventures: Case Study of a U.S. Hybrid Organization Caught Between Two Fields. Voluntas: *International Journal of Voluntary and Nonprofit Organizations*, 17, 137–161.

Crossan, D., Ibbotson, P. and Bell, J. 2011. The Hologram Effect in Entrepreneurial "Social Commercial" Enterprises. *Journal of Small Business and Enterprise Development*, 18, 655–672.

Daft, R. L., Murphy, J. and Willmott, H. 2010. *Organization Theory and Design*, Southwestern Cengage Learning.

Dees, J. G. and Anderson, B. B. 2003. Sector-Bending: Blurring Lines Between Nonprofit and For-profit. *Society*, 40, 16–27.

Defourny, J. 2001. From Third Sector to Social Enterprise, in Borzaga, C. and Defourny, J. (eds) *The Emergence of Social Enterprise*, Routledge.

Emmert, M. and Crow, M. M. 1987. Public–private Cooperation and Hybrid Organizations. *Journal of Management*, 13, 55.

Evers, A. 2005. Mixed Welfare Systems and Hybrid Organizations: Changes in the Governance and Provision of Social Services. *International Journal of Public Administration*, 28, 737–748.

Evers, A. and Laville, J.-L. 2004. Social Services by Social Enterprises: On the Possible Contributions of Hybrid Organizations and a Civil Society, in Evers, A., and Laville, J.-L. (ed.) *The Third Sector in Europe*, Edward Elgar.

Frumkin, P. 2002. *On Being Nonprofit: A Conceptual and Policy Primer*, Harvard University Press.

Galaskiewicz, J. and Barringer, S. N. 2012. Social Enterprises and Social Categories, in Gidron, B. and Hasenfeld, Y. (eds) *Social Enterprises: An Organizational Perspective*, Palgrave Macmillan.

Haigh, N. and Hoffman, A. J. 2012. Hybrid Organizations: The Next Chapter of Sustainable Business. *Organizational Dynamics*, 41, 126–134.

Herranz, J., Council, L. R. and McKay, B. 2011. Tri-Value Organization as a Form of Social Enterprise. *Nonprofit and Voluntary Sector Quarterly*, 40, 829–849.

Hoffman, A. J., Badiane, K. K. and Haigh, N. 2012. Hybrid Organizations as Agents of Positive Social Change: Bridging the For-profit and Nonprofit Divide, in Golden-Biddle, K. and Dutton, J. E. (eds) *Using a Positive Lens to Explore Social Change and Organizations: Building a Theoretical and Research Foundation*, Routledge.

Honingh, M. and Karsten, S. 2007. Marketization in the Dutch Vocational Education and Training Sector. *Public Management Review*, 9, 135–143.

Hospital Social Service Association of New York City. 1921. Hospital Social Service.

Hwang, H. and Powell, W. W. 2009. The Rationalization of Charity? The Influence of Professionalism in the Nonprofit Sector. *Administrative Science Quarterly*, 54, 268–298.

Jäger, U. and Schröer, A. 2013. Integrated Organizational Identity: A Definition of Hybrid Organizations and a Research Agenda. *VOLUNTAS: International Journal of Voluntary and Nonprofit Organizations*, 1–26.

Jay, J. 2013. Navigating Paradox as a Mechanism of Change and Innovation in Hybrid Organizations. *Academy of Management Journal*, 5, 137–159.

Joldersma, C. and Winter, V. 2002. Strategic Management in Hybrid Organizations. *Public Management Review*, 4, 83–99.

Jolink, A. and Niesten, E. 2012. Recent Qualitative Advances on Hybrid Organizations: Taking Stock, Looking Ahead. *Scandinavian Journal of Management*, 28, 149–161.

Jones, M. B. 2007. The Multiple Sources of Mission Drift. *Nonprofit and Voluntary Sector Quarterly*, 36, 299–307.

Kelley, T. 2009. Law and Choice of Entity on the Social Enterprise Frontier. *Tulane Law Review*, 84, 337–377.

Kickert, W. J. M. 2001. Public Management of Hybrid Organizations: Governance of Quasi-autonomous Executive Agencies. *International Public Management Journal*, 4, 135–150.

Koopenjan, J. and Klijn, E.-H. 2004. *Managing Uncertainties in Networks*, Routledge.

Koppell, J. G. S. 2003. The *Politics of Quasi-government*, Cambridge University Press.

Kramer, R. 1990. Nonprofit Social Service Agencies and the Welfare State, in Anheier,

H. K. and Seibel, W. (eds) *The Third Sector: Comparative Studies of Nonprofit Organizations*, Walter de Gruyter.

Lan, Z. and Rainey, H. G. 1992. Goals, Rules, and Effectiveness in Public, Private, and Hybrid Organizations: More Evidence on Frequent Assertions about Differences. *Journal of Public Administration Research and Theory: J-PART*, 2, 5–28.

Laville, J.-L. and Nyssens, M. 2001. The Social Enterprise: Towards a Theoretical Socioeconomic Approach, in Borzaga, C. and Defourny, J. (eds) *The Emergence of Social Enterprise*, Routledge.

Low, C. 2006. A Framework for the Governance of Social Enterprise. *International Journal of Social Economics*, 33, 376–85.

Maier, F. and Meyer, M. 2011. Managerialism and Beyond: Discourses of Civil Society Organization and Their Governance Implications. *VOLUNTAS: International Journal of Voluntary and Nonprofit Organizations*, 22, 731–756.

Miller, P., Kurunmäki, L. and O'Leary, T. 2008. Accounting, Hybrids and the Management of Risk. *Accounting, Organizations and Society*, 33, 942–967.

Osborne, S. 2010. *The New Public Governance? Emerging Perspectives on the Theory and Practice of Public Governance*, Routledge.

Ostrander, S. A. and Langton, S. 1987. *Shifting the Debate: Public/Private Sector Relations in the Modern Welfare State*, Transaction Books.

Pache, A.-C. and Santos, F. 2012. Inside the Hybrid Organization: Selective Coupling as a Response to Conflicting Institutional Logics. *Academy of Management Journal*, DOI 10.5465/amj.2011.0405.

Perry, J. L. and Rainey, H. G. 1988. The Public–Private Distinction in Organization Theory: A Critique and Research Strategy. *Academy of Management Review*, 13, 182–201.

Powell, W. W. 1987. Hybrid Organizational Arrangements: New Form or Transitional Development? *California Management Review*, 30, 67–87.

Powell, W. W. 1990. Neither Market nor Hierarchy: Network Forms of Organization, in Staw, B. M. and Cummings, L. L. (eds) *Research in Organizational Behavior*, 2, 295–336.

Rhodes, M. and Donnelly-Cox, G. 2014. Hybridity and Social Entrepreneurship in Social Housing in Ireland. *VOLUNTAS: International Journal of Voluntary and Nonprofit Organizations*, 25, 1–18.

Sabeti, H. 2011. The For-Benefit Enterprise. *Harvard Business Review*, 89, 98–104.

Salamon, L. M., Hems, L. C. and Chinnock, K. 2000. *The Nonprofit Sector: For What and for Whom?* The Johns Hopkins Center for Civil Society Studies.

Sanders, M. L. and McClellan, J. G. 2014. Being Business-like While Pursuing a Social Mission: Acknowledging the Inherent Tensions in US Nonprofit Organizing. *Organization*, 21, 68–89.

Skelcher, C. and Smith, S. R. 2014. Theorizing Hybridity: Institutional Logics, Complex Organizations, and Actor Identities: The Case of Nonprofits. *Public Administration*, DOI 10.1111/padm.12105.

Smith, S. R. 2010. Hybridization and Nonprofit Organizations: The Governance Challenge. *Policy and Society*, 29, 219–229.

Smith, S. R. 2014. Hybridity and Nonprofit Organizations: The Research Agenda. *American Behavioral Scientist*.

Steen-Johnsen, K., Eynaud, P. and Wijkström, F. 2011. On Civil Society Governance: An Emergent Research Field. *VOLUNTAS: International Journal of Voluntary and Nonprofit Organizations*, 22, 555–565.

Steinberg, R. 2012. *What Should Social Investors Invest in, and With Whom?* Indiana University Press.

Sydow, J. and Schreyögg, G. 2013. *Self-reinforcing Processes In and Among Organizations*, Palgrave.

Thomasson, A. 2009. Exploring the Ambiguity of Hybrid Organizations: A Stakeholder Approach. *Financial Accountability and Management*, 25, 353–366.

van der Wal, Z. and van Hout, E. T. J. 2009. Is Public Value Pluralism Paramount? The Intrinsic Multiplicity and Hybridity of Public Values. *International Journal of Public Administration*, 32, 220–231.

Van Huylenbroeckt, G., Vuylsteke, A. and Verbeke, W. 2009. Public Good Markets: The Possible Role of Hybrid Governance Structures in Institutions for Sustainability, in Beckmann, V. and Padmanabhan, M. (eds) *Institutions and Sustainability: Political Economy of Agriculture and the Environment: Essays in Honour of Konrad Hagedorn*, Springer.

von Schnurbein, G. and Schönenberg, D. 2010. Legal Forms of Civil Society Organizations as a Governance Problem: The Case of Switzerland. *International Journal of Not-for-profit Law*, 12, 90–101.

Wamsley, G. L. and Zald, M. N. 1973. *The Political Economy of Public Organizations: A Critique and Approach to the Study of Public Administration*, Lexington.

Wijkström, F. 2011. "Charity Speak" and "Business Talk": The Ongoing (Re)hybridization of Civil Society, in Wijkström, F. and Zimmer, A. (eds) *Nordic Civil Society at a Cross-Roads: Transforming the Popular Movement Tradition*, Nomos.

Wijkström, F. and Lundström, T. 2002. *Den ideella sektorn. Organizationerna i det civila samhället*, Sober Förlag.

2 The future of civil society organization governance

Beyond managerialism

Michael Meyer and Florentine Maier

Introduction

Since the 1980s, CSOs have become increasingly business-like (Dart, 2004). In terms of governance, this development has entailed the adoption of corporate, managerialist forms (Alexander and Weiner, 1998) modelled after business corporations, with a governing board that has management expertise and is responsible for setting the strategic agenda and a managing director who is responsible for implementing it. Often those boards are self-perpetuating and only loosely coupled with the NPO's constituencies. To a large extent, this shift has occurred at the expense of democratic forms of governance, which are increasingly seen as too slow and inefficient.

The present chapter investigates how this trend may continue in the near future, aiming to both contribute ideas that sensitize the debate on CSO governance and suggest ways in which democratic values may survive in a predominantly managerialist era. This is done in four steps. First, a conceptualization of governance is provided, and the characteristics of managerialist governance – in contrast to alternative notions of domestic, professionalist, grassroots, and civic governance – are analyzed. The second step is a closer look at the history and societal context of managerialist governance. Third, two future scenarios are proposed, involving either the development of managerialism into a total hegemony or the proliferation of multiple discourses of governance. In the conclusion, conditions for realizing those scenarios and avenues for further research are discussed.

Five discourses of CSO governance

A governance system comprises elements of organizational structure that ensure accountability (Stone and Ostrower, 2007) and safeguard stakeholder interests (Speckbacher, 2008). Accordingly, each CSO has a governance system of some kind. It may be more or less successful in protecting stakeholder interests, and it may do a good or not so good job at fulfilling the requirements stipulated by various theoretical approaches to governance. This chapter outlines five discourses of governance that can be found in CSOs, in accordance with previous research carried out by the authors of the chapter.

In 2008 and 2009, a research project on CSO governance was conducted in Austria (Maier and Meyer, 2011). In this project, groups of two or more representatives of 16 CSOs were interviewed. They were sampled for maximum variety, to capture as wide a range of understandings of organizing and governance as possible. The CSOs under investigation were between seven and about 450 years old, had between zero and almost 19,000 employees, and between zero and 30,000 volunteers. Areas of activity covered were culture and arts, social services, sports, emergency and relief, environment, international activities, professional associations, political organizations, labor unions, religious congregations and associations, health services, and recreation and social clubs. Interviews were semi-structured, following a funnel-shaped structure. The first question was: "If you think back to a decade ago, what has changed in your organization and what has stayed the same?" This was followed by increasingly narrow questions, with the final questions designed to test assumptions developed in previous stages of the research and to ask about suggestions for further sampling. Interviews took 90 minutes on average. Transcripts were analyzed jointly by both authors. The identification of discourses was achieved, first, by isolating those text passages in which speakers distinguished between different ways of organizing, and, second, by analyzing these sections for the discourses employed. Third, after initial categories had become somewhat stable, the remaining text passages that did not involve distinctions between ways of organizing were coded to confirm and further enrich initial understandings. To further corroborate validity, a summary of preliminary findings was sent to all interviewees, who were asked for feedback.

The findings pointed to five distinct understandings of organizational governance: (1) managerialist, (2) domestic, (3) professionalist, (4) civic, and (5) grassroots governance (see Table 2.1). These understandings are based on diverging normative assumptions. In what follows, they shall be discussed by answering three questions about the accountability these governance systems aim to ensure (Stone and Ostrower, 2007): "Who is the organization accountable to?," "How should accountability be ensured?" and "What kind of performance is the organization accountable for?".

1   *Managerialist discourse* emulates the practices of large for-profit corporations. Donors, funding institutions and sometimes volunteers are the primary addressees of governance, since their role is viewed as most similar to that of shareholders in for-profit corporations. The most important governance mechanism is the interplay between executives and the governing board. The latter is responsible for strategic matters and for supervising executives, who, in turn, are given rein in operative matters. It is taken for granted that the organization must have an explicit mission and that the criterion for assessing performance is the efficient and effective achievement of that mission, or of the goals derived from that mission. The origins of managerialist governance discourse in CSOs can be found in the US and the UK of the 1980s, when neoliberal political reforms and a shift of stakeholder

Table 2.1 Discourses of CSO governance

	Managerialist	Domestic	Professionalist	Civic	Grassroots
Addressees of governance	Funders	Beneficiaries	External peers	Active members	Activists
Governance mechanisms	Boards, executive directors	Personal relationships, feelings	Peer assessments, comparison with other organizations	Elections, votes, checks and balances, adherence to formal rules	Domination-free discussion, consensus-seeking, organizational openness
Performance criteria	Effective and efficient achievement of an explicit mission	Achievement of an implicit mission	Professional standards, peer evaluation	Mass support	Adherence to rules of grassroots democracy

Source: authors' own compilation, based on Maier and Meyer 2011.

expectations towards business-like forms caused CSOs to formalize, stream-line and professionalize. This trend has spread to other countries, spurred by similar political and ideological forces. Nevertheless, a number of altern-ative discourses are still relevant.

2   In practice, the most influential one of these alternative discourses is perhaps *domestic discourse*. It is based on informal mechanisms. Since every organ-ization has an informal as well as a formal structure, domestic elements can arise in every organization. Domestic governance centers on the image of the organization as one big family. It is believed that because beneficiaries are the weakest and neediest of all stakeholders, the organization is prim-arily accountable to them. To ensure this accountability, the organization uses paternalist methods. There are no mechanisms to directly involve bene-ficiaries in governance. Instead, service providers are expected to learn about the needs of beneficiaries through personal contact, to empathically internalize those needs, and to let these experiences guide them in their decision-making processes. Governance mechanisms are thus based on feel-ings and personal relationships. Performance is not defined by explicit cri-teria, let alone assessed formally. Instead, members share an implicit understanding about their goals and performance norms. In academic dis-cussion, domestic governance typically serves as a foil (in the sense of "bad governance" or "lack of governance") to be contrasted with forms of "good" – often equated with managerialist – governance. In fact, governance fail-ures in CSOs are mostly due to overreliance on informal, personal, "feeling-based" mechanisms.

3   Another important discourse of governance is that of *professionalism*. Pro-fessionalist elements are often found in CSOs active in research, medicine or education, but also in fields where voluntary labor is predominant, such as sports, firefighting, paramedics or arts. In professionalist governance, the norms and standards of the profession are the central point of reference. The primary addressees of governance are peers working in the same profession, but operating outside the organization, who represent these standards. Peers monitor whether the organization conforms to professional standards, either by directly evaluating the organization against these standards, or by compar-ing organizations within the field. Accreditations or inspections by authori-ties are forms of direct evaluation. Participating in competitions or closely observing the activities of other organizations in the field are characteristic behaviors. Professionalist CSOs typically provide complex services, the quality of which is not transparent to outsiders, and operate in areas where management by output criteria only would provoke unwelcome effects.

4   *Civic discourse* prescribes that the CSO must be a member-based organiza-tion, i.e., an association or a cooperative. Democratic participation rights lie at the core of this discourse. It is assumed that CSOs are primarily account-able to their active members. Accordingly, elections, votes and rules of representation are important governance mechanisms. An intricate system of checks and balances, as well as a comprehensive set of formal rules, the

adherence to which is strictly monitored, are important parts of civic governance. It is believed that the best indicator of good performance is the fact that the CSO enjoys broad support among its members. Performance criteria are therefore figures such as the number of members; the number of works councils and organized businesses (in the case of unions); or election results (in the case of political parties).

5   Finally, there is *grassroots governance*. Building on ideals of the 1960s social movements, among others (Polletta, 2004), this discourse centers around autonomy and consensual decision-making. The organization is primarily accountable to members who contribute their work. Unlike in civic governance, it is not representation but direct participation in decision-making that counts. Members have to align with all decisions made in the organization, and, in principle, every member is entitled to question all decisions. The organization tries to keep external dependencies, e.g., on funders, to a minimum. Grassroots democracy provides many mechanisms to ensure accountability, such as rules for domination-free discussions (e.g., lists of speakers, time limits for speech, rules for bias-free language) and various methods for finding consensus. Grassroots organizations adhere to the principle of openness: everyone who is interested can participate and contribute his or her view. Since organizations that practice grassroots democracy often aspire to radical societal change, which, however, comes about slowly, if at all, mission achievement would not be a feasible performance criterion. Instead, adherence to principles of grassroots democracy is the primary performance criterion: it is deemed a success that the organization demonstrates the possibility of egalitarian and consensual cooperation here and now. In its pure form, grassroots governance can be found in niches of civil society. Its broader potential to provide legitimacy and to mobilize people has recently been demonstrated, not so much in CSOs, but in social movements such as the Tunisian and Egyptian revolutions and the Occupy movement.

The societal context of managerialist governance

Since the 1980s, views on "good governance" have shifted in favor of managerialism, mainly at the expense of grassroots and civic discourses. While domestic discourse has been widely discredited, professionalist discourse seems to be somewhat successful at putting up resistance, at least in its homeland areas such as education, healthcare, social work, etc. The rise of managerialist governance can be seen in line with the corporate takeover of markets and public spheres (Crouch, 2012), and as part of a societal development towards "post-democracy" (Crouch, 2004). This means that governance systems no longer primarily draw their legitimacy from the democratic participation of stakeholders, but from their ability to produce results. Such a governance system can entail participatory methods, but only if they are superior to other methods in terms of efficiency and effectiveness. Developments towards post-democracy can manifest themselves in manifold ways in CSOs. A typical pattern is the shift of responsibilities and authority from elected representative bodies, or from full assemblies, to executive managers or management teams that have been selected not through democratic elections but through business-like recruitment and selection. It should be noted that such changes are usually not initiated because actors are hostile to democratic beliefs and principles, but because democratic forms are considered to deliver results of insufficient quality, speed or efficiency, or to have degenerated into a burden for the constituencies to whom they were originally intended to give a voice. In other words, the intentions behind governance reforms in CSOs are usually benign, but the consequences may nonetheless be serious.

What makes these consequences even more serious is the role that CSOs play in third-party governance, for instance when governments contract with CSOs to deliver services or otherwise act on their behalf. The main concern here is delivery at an appropriate cost and quality (Brudney *et al.*, 2005: 395). Democratic governance in such arrangements is often weak (Evans, Richmond and Shields, 2005; Justice and Skelcher, 2009: 739). Hardly anyone would argue that CSOs should live up to democratic ideals if they want to participate in macro governance.

Regarding this tendency, a stark contrast to discourses that proliferated from the late 1960s to the early 1980s can be observed. At that time, it was quite legitimate to consider democratic participation as the primary criterion for "good governance" (without anyone using that term), while a certain level of economic efficiency was simply considered a necessary precondition. Democracy was thought to enable people to realize their true selves in contributing to the common good. This ideology inspired many CSOs in the fields of culture, social services and the alternative economy (e.g., cooperatives) to follow the social-democratic plea for a "democratization of all spheres of life."

Today, in publications about governance in CSOs, it is regularly stated that their main aim is to ensure efficient and effective mission achievement. Democracy is only valuable if it helps to reach that aim. Such views seem to be based on a broad societal consensus. A major grassroots revolution of excluded stakeholders who demand more influence is not in sight. Small donors, members and clients seem quite happy to play the role of consumers who choose among available alternatives and whose influence is limited to the exit option. They willingly leave decision-making to managers and other experts. A possible interpretation of this state of affairs is that most people already have their hands full trying to handle the increasing opportunities, risks and responsibilities in their lives. Thus they turn towards managers for leadership and for vital products and services (Blühdorn, 2007).

The future of CSO governance

Against this background, possible future scenarios shall now be outlined. We expect an increasing number of CSOs to embrace elements of managerialism. What remains open to speculation is the qualitative dimension of further managerialization. Hence we shall draw up two scenarios, one envisaging the rise of managerialism to total hegemony, the other the establishment of managerialism as a backbone of CSO governance that coexists with alternative discourses.

Scenario A: managerialism as total hegemony

The rise of managerialism to total hegemony would mean that economically efficient and effective mission delivery becomes the unquestioned and only legitimate purpose of CSO governance. Such a development would not be limited to a quantitative spread of managerialism, but would include qualitative transformations, as they have always characterized the history of managerialism (Boltanski and Chiapello, 2005). The managerialism we know today differs from that between the 1940s and 1970s (Herman, 2006: 37–42). While older forms of managerialism focused on mass production, direct control, and the manipulation of people similarly to that of machines, today managerialism emphasizes autonomy and empowerment. Managerialism is remarkably good at assimilating the critiques mounted against it, as in, for instance, post-Fordist managerialism, which addresses the critique that hierarchies are inimical to innovation and hinder organizations from adapting to changing environments. Several signals indicate that an assimilation of ideas from alternative discourses might be underway. Superficial elements of those discourses are integrated into managerialism under the overarching imperative of efficiency and effectiveness. What remains of them are empty forms, merely symbolic acts that leave power structures of managerialism intact.

In the case of civic discourse, assimilation can be observed in many cases of web-based activism: in campaigns orchestrated by public relations experts, millions of supporters are mobilized to create an image of community support that legitimizes the organization's claims (Tatarchevskiy, 2011). Many symbolic actions can be used to create such an image, e.g., supporting an online campaign by submitting your email address, "liking" something on Facebook, etc. (ibid.: 309f.). Further action, however, is left to professional staff. Such processes remain widely passive, despite their colorful masquerade of community involvement (ibid.: 310). The difference between staged and real civic governance is that "members" are reduced to the role of donors and symbolic supporters but are excluded from organizational decision-making, for example by electing board members. A case in point is the campaigning organization Avaaz. Individuals can make donations and sign petitions, and Avaaz regularly polls its supporters to see what their interests are and how it can reflect them. However, supporters have no institutionalized right to participate in decisions at Avaaz, let alone run for office as a board member. In fact, little information is publicly available about how Avaaz's board of directors is composed, which suggests that it is self-perpetuating.

An assimilation of grassroots discourse can be observed in cases where platforms are provided that give people the chance to express their views, but that have no decision-making power. Common examples are open discussion forums, or blogs with a "comments" function. Face-to-face meetings for information and consultation purposes can also work this way.

Professionalist governance is integrated into managerialism when tools such as certifications and evaluations are employed for pure marketing purposes. Care is taken to commission agencies that will not be too critical or exercise any substantial power over the organization. Their only task is to provide confirmation of quality for legitimation purposes.

Attempts to integrate domestic governance into managerialism began long ago. The "how-to" literature on leadership, teamwork, and organizational culture bears ample evidence to this fact: leaders should show as much concern for people as for production; teams need teambuilding; organizational culture should be engineered to implant the organization's mission and values deep into the hearts and souls of its members. However, in contrast to real domestic discourse, all of this should happen under the guidance of managerialism, for the purpose of maximizing efficiency and effectiveness.

Scenario B: embracing multiple discourses of governance

Our second scenario would be that managerialism continues to gain importance but remains distinct from alternative discourses and coexists with them in manifold relations of mutual support and conflict. If managerialism is understood as an institutional logic, it can be challenged by alternative logics, as institutional environments are pluralistic and offer multiple sources of legitimacy (Friedland and Alford, 1991; Townley, 1997). Managerialist governance thus offers a means of "mediating between organizations and society" and "provides supra-organizational norms which pattern organized social life" (Townley, 1997). Friedland and Alford (1991) identify various institutional logics that resemble the discourses identified in the research at hand and argue that access to different institutional logics is a major source of resistance towards isomorphic pressures.

The new thing about this scenario is that CSOs would recognize alternative discourses more deliberately. They would oppose, balance or momentarily combine them for their purposes and according to their institutional environments, and in this sense embrace their diversity. This would help CSOs to fulfill their polyvalent roles in society, not just as efficient service providers but also as political advocates, schools of democracy, and spaces for community-building.

From our empirical work, we have gathered the – not yet systematically tested – impression that successful CSOs combine the rationalities of several governance discourses (a notion similar to that expressed by, for example, Grandori and Furnari, 2008). Organizations that mainly model themselves after one single discourse, be it managerialist or another, tend to have difficulties with sustainably, with realizing their missions, and with satisfying the expectations of all relevant stakeholder groups. CSOs that combine elements of different discourses into a balanced arrangement seem to have stronger links with a broader range of stakeholders and to be working towards their missions in more effective and durable ways. Reliance on more than one rationality seems to increase CSOs' adaptability to dynamic environments.

For example, a CSO that organizes international student exchanges combines a lively system of civic governance (by being an association with a broad membership base, annual plenary assemblies, and a multi-tier system of elected board members) with a fair dose of managerialism (by systematically training its volunteer board in managerialist approaches). This is complemented by domestic governance that prevails in local grassroots groups, which are responsible for recruiting host families, fostering ties with schools, and organizing the preparation and supervision of exchange students and families.

Another CSO, an advocacy organization for environmental issues, has successfully undergone a growth process that involved shifting from grassroots democracy to governance that combines civic, managerialist and grassroots elements. In its early days in the 1980s, all staff members were part of a plenary meeting that decided by consensus on all matters of the organization. As the organization grew, it became infeasible to integrate everybody into this meeting. For some time, the meeting worked as a circle of up to 18 self-selecting and self-perpetuating representatives. This was perceived as undemocratic, and eventually an elected board of directors replaced this body. At the same time, its size was reduced to a maximum of six persons. Directors are now elected by the associational members of the organization, which include all staff members, as well as external supporters who make up one-sixth of the membership base. The board appoints two executive managers. Relationships between the board and executives follow the managerialist model. However, grassroots democracy, subsidiarity and consensus-seeking are formally acknowledged as part of the organization's philosophy. In setting the strategic agenda, executive management demands strong involvement from the whole team. Only if no consensus on strategy and campaigning priorities can be found on the staff level – and this sometimes happens –is the matter decided by executive managers.

In view of those examples, it seems that embracing multiple discourses of governance means utilizing the strengths of each discourse and combining those elements in loosely coupled ways. Managerialism is most appropriate when it comes to ensuring efficient service delivery, but other worthwhile elements can be gathered from alternative discourses of governance. In what follows, some thoughts are offered on what those elements might be.

Civic governance, with its focus on a broad membership base and majority voting, can draw on the legitimacy of representative democracy. While tedious and anaemic if used as the main mode of decision-making within an organization, it is probably the most legitimate way to reach binding collective decisions. Particularly in case of conflict, majority voting provides a legitimate last resort. For CSOs engaged in political advocacy, civic governance is a way to pre-test propositions by having them undergo an internal voting process, to strengthen their legitimacy by ensuring internal support, and to develop skills by having members practice political decision-making within the organization.

Grassroots governance also has great potential to turn CSOs into "schools of democracy," in particular if combined with civic governance: members prepare decisions through consensus-seeking discussions, and then send delegates to bodies that operate on the basis of civic principles. Grassroots governance prioritizes openness over exclusion: since no formal qualifications, admission approvals or entry fees are required, individuals are given a say that would not be heard otherwise. This makes grassroots governance suitable for experiments in social change and social innovation (e.g., in the case of the hospice movement or associations of people with disabilities). Grassroots structures seem to work well for issues that affect a variety of people directly (e.g., illnesses, regional ecological issues) and for simple issues in cases where it is clear how to address them (e.g., freeing a particular political prisoner, preventing a particular landfill). Grassroots structures require little in the way of financial resources and, due to their openness, can attract time and knowledge resources from a variety of people. With its focus on the power of the better argument, grassroots discourse can reopen debates on matters that have already been closed officially. This can be tedious, but it can also be a corrective to bureaucratic rationalities (e.g., resistance to a construction project that has already received its official construction permit, or petitioning for death-row inmates). Due to its low dependence on external resources and mainstream legitimacies, grassroots discourse leaves the organization relatively free to use unorthodox and controversial advocacy tactics. Some CSOs make use of this fact by forming networks: often, more reputable CSOs take care of uncontroversial issues but, at the same time, support grassroots CSOs that deal with more explosive issues.

Although grassroots and civic governance suffer from the trend towards "post-democracy," faint signals towards their revitalization can be spotted: some CSOs, e.g., the Pirate Parties in various European countries, have recently developed new tools for democratic governance, such as "liquid democracy," also known as delegated voting. These tools uphold the ideals of old civic and grassroots discourse but support them with web 2.0 technology. The feasibility and broad appeal of these innovations remain to be proved, but at least they are a signal that democratic ideals continue to be attractive.

Professionalist discourse is appropriate to ensure legitimacy based on expertise. If tasks are highly complex, if aims cannot be captured adequately with quantitative indicators, and if quality is paramount, methods of professionalist governance stand to reason. Professionalist governance helps to keep key personnel motivated by granting them far-reaching autonomy. This is important in case of paid staff, but also for developing and retaining highly qualified volunteers.

Domestic governance is the discourse that we believe will undoubtedly continue to exist alongside managerialism. As an approach that is firmly anchored in everyone's lifeworld, it is intuitively plausible to many people. For many start-ups and social entrepreneurs, domestic governance is taken for granted. It is extremely efficient in terms of time and monetary resources: resources go directly into core activities; almost nothing is spent on planning and control;

identification is achieved through charismatic persons instead of programs; personal trust is paramount; and there is plenty of room for spontaneity. It will always remain the appropriate governance mode for new ventures that strive to efficiently tackle specific challenges. Rather than worrying about domestic governance being swamped by managerialism, the more common challenge is to defend more sophisticated notions of governance against the everlasting threat of lapsing into the informality and the individual person orientation of domestic governance.

Our scenario of embracing multiple discourses of governance would mean that the vivid game of competing discourses continues but that players become more aware of its rules. They would thus gain the freedom to deliberately choose which discourse they draw on, to make new combinations, or to even undertake the co-construction of new governance discourses (as is perhaps the case with "liquid democracy"). The result might be an enlightened approach to CSO governance, where instead of flocking to the seemingly easy solutions of managerialism, CSOs would be more self-confident in retaining old approaches that suit them or in exploring entirely new modes of governance.

Conclusion

Comparing the two scenarios outlined above, one may wonder what conditions would lead to one or the other. In view of the developments of recent decades, it may be hard to imagine anything but an increasing hegemony of managerialism. Indeed, current trends towards impact-orientation in the provision of public services, together with the growing overload of demands on individuals to juggle the stresses, choices and risks of daily life, make managerialism look like an attractive solution. At the same time, the recent revival of interest in direct democracy, as an act of resistance in the face of adversity, provides a nourishing ground for civic and grassroots forms and for inventing new ways to put old values into practice. Social movements across the world, from Occupy Wall Street to Tahrir Square and Gezi Park, enrich public discourse with ideas about the value and meaning of democracy.

In the development of either scenario, academic research, education and training will play an important part. The questions that researchers ask will set the frame for the types of answers we get. If discussions about CSO governance merely center on looking for the most efficient and effective way to produce tangible outcomes, answers will tend towards managerialism. However, if we ask how participation and inclusion can be strengthened while, at the same time, satisfying basic requirements of efficiency and effectiveness, new knowledge will be generated that supports the development of multifaceted governance arrangements. We would encourage the latter type of questions, not least out of concern for the democracy of macro-governance systems in which CSOs play a part. In particular, we see a need for research on the following issues:

First, to corroborate – or challenge – our argument that CSOs are most successful when they combine various governance discourses in loosely coupled ways that fit their institutional environment, further empirical research would be needed. The distinctive strengths of alternative governance discourses would also need further empirical inquiry.

Second, to clarify the implications of CSO governance for macro governance, it is necessary to revisit the issue of CSOs as "schools of democracy." Historical research indicates that CSOs once fulfilled this function (Skocpol, 2004), but recent data point to the contrary (van der Meer and van Ingen, 2009). To better understand this discrepancy, fine-grained investigations into how governance arrangements contribute to the democratic socialization of members would therefore be necessary (as undertaken, for example, by Unterrainer, Palgi, Weber, Iwanowa and Oesterreich, 2011, on for-profit businesses).

Third, we need more research that investigates tensions between internal democracy and the external democratic role of CSOs in society. Is it really possible, and sustainable, to strengthen democracy in society through CSOs that are not democratically governed themselves?

Finally, we see a gap in the literature regarding the question of how to make organizational democracy work. Evidence on the conditions, possibilities and effects of democratic governance is exceedingly scarce. As a consequence, there is a lack of practitioner-oriented literature on this issue. CSO practitioners who want to develop their governance find plenty of literature on the managerialist model, but hardly anything, especially not in a reader-friendly format, on alternative models, or on how to combine different models into a system that is tailored to the organization's environment and that fits its values.

References

Alexander, J. A., and Weiner, B. J. (1998). The adoption of the corporate governance model by nonprofit organizations. *Nonprofit Management and Leadership*, 8(3), 223–242.

Blühdorn, I. (2007). The third transformation of democracy: On the efficient management of late-modern complexity. In I. Blühdorn and U. Jun (eds), *Economic Efficiency – Democratic Empowerment: Contested Modernisation in Britain and Germany*. Plymouth: Lexington Books, 299–331.

Boltanski, L., and Chiapello, È. (2005). *The New Spirit of Capitalism*. London: Verso Books.

Brudney, J. L., Fernandez, S., Ryu, J. E., and Wright, D. S. (2005). Exploring and explaining contracting out: Patterns among the American states. *Journal of Public Administration Research and Theory*, 15(3), 393.

Crouch, C. (2004). *Post-democracy*. Cambridge: Polity.

Crouch, C. (2012). *The Strange Non-death of Neoliberalism*. Cambridge: Polity.

Dart, R. (2004). Being "business-like" in a nonprofit organization: A grounded and inductive typology. *Nonprofit and Voluntary Sector Quarterly*, 33(2), 290–310.

Evans, B., Richmond, T., and Shields, J. (2005). Structuring neoliberal governance: The nonprofit sector, emerging new modes of control and the marketisation of service delivery. *Policy and Society*, 24(1), 73–97, doi: 10.1016/s1449-4035(05)70050-3.

Friedland, R., and Alford, R. R. (1991). Bringing society back: Symbols, practices, and institutional contradictions. In W. W. Powell and P. J. Di Maggio (eds), *The New Institutionalism in Organizational Analysis*. London: Sage.

Grandori, A., and Furnari, S. (2008). A chemistry of organization: Combinatory analysis and design. *Organization Studies*, 29(3), 459–485, doi: 10.1177/0170840607088023.

Herman, C. (2006). *Prophets and Profits: Managerialism and the Restructuring of Jewish schools in South Africa.* Human Sciences Research Council.

Justice, J. B., and Skelcher, C. (2009). Analysing democracy in third-party government: Business improvement districts in the US and UK. *International Journal of Urban and Regional Research*, 33(3), 738–753.

Maier, F., and Meyer, M. (2011). Managerialism and beyond: Discourses of civil society organization and their governance implications. *Voluntas: International Journal of Voluntary and Nonprofit Organizations*, 22(4), 731–756, doi: 10.1007/s11266–011–9202–8.

Polletta, F. (2004). *Freedom is an Endless Meeting: Democracy in American Social Movements.* Chicago: University of Chicago Press.

Skocpol, T. (2004). *Diminished Democracy: From Membership to Management in American Civic Life.* Norman, OK: University of Oklahoma Press.

Speckbacher, G. (2008). Nonprofit versus corporate governance: An economic approach. *Nonprofit Management and Leadership*, 18(3), 295–320, doi: 10.1002/nml.187.

Stone, M. M., and Ostrower, F. (2007). Acting in the public interest? Another look at research on nonprofit governance. *Nonprofit and Voluntary Sector Quarterly*, 36(3), 416–438, doi: 10.1177/0899764006296049.

Tatarchevskiy, T. (2011). The "popular" culture of internet activism. *New Media and Society*, 13(2), 297–313.

Townley, B. (1997). The institutional logic of performance appraisal. *Organization Studies*, 18(2), 261–285.

Unterrainer, C., Palgi, M., Weber, W. G., Iwanowa, A., and Oesterreich, R. (2011). Structurally anchored organizational democracy. *Journal of Personnel Psychology*, 10(3), 118–132.

van der Meer, T. W. G., and van Ingen, E. J. (2009). Schools of democracy? Disentangling the relationship between civic participation and political action in 17 European countries. *European Journal of Political Research*, 48(2), 281–308, doi: 10.1111/j.1475–6765.2008.00836.x.

3 Civil society organization governance

More than just a matter for the board

Stéphanie Chatelain-Ponroy, Philippe Eynaud and Samuel Sponem

Introduction

In France in the 1980s, relations were rather harmonious between civil society organizations (CSOs) and the state (Archambault, 2001, p. 205). To begin with, associations accomplished missions that the state did not want to be involved in, while at the same time the state agreed to fund them. Yet recent political and economic changes have disturbed this harmony, leading (in some subsectors) to more adversarial relationships, state direction of programs and loss of funding. During the 1980s and 90s, the decrease in state funding of CSOs was offset by increases in funding from local and regional authorities (Tchernonog, Prouteau, Tabariès and Nogues, 2013). Today, local authorities are also affected by cuts in public spending and are less generous in their financial support and grants to CSOs. As a result, most of the recent regulation of the nonprofit sector enhances instrumental accountability – "an organization's accountability to resource suppliers ... both internal and external to the organization" (Knutsen and Brower, 2010: 589) – at the expense of more comprehensive forms of accountability. Furthermore, a new legal framework (Warsmann, 2009) is helping to drive this trend towards a rational and instrumental accountability. Nowadays the challenge for the French state seems to be moving from a subsidy culture to a new public management culture in its relationships with the nonprofit sector. Two recent parliamentary reports announce a "cultural revolution." The first one refers to the concept of "nonprofit enterprise" (Langlais, 2008) and the second one asks for more assessment and control of subsidised nonprofit organizations (Morange, 2008). Implicitly, these reports encourage CSOs to make their governance similar to those of private companies. In that way, the situation in France is not very different from that in other countries (Maier and Meyer, 2011).

Effective governance is crucial to the viability of civil society organizations (Kreutzer and Jacobs, 2011). However, most of the research on CSO governance emphasizes corporate governance as a model for more effectiveness even if the authors notice its inadequacy to really fit the specificities of the organizations in question (Brown, 2005; Ostrower, 2008). Such research focuses on the role of the board in terms of control and accountability (Bradshaw, 2002; Brown, 2005;

Callen *et al.*, 2003; Herman *et al.*, 1996; O'Regan and Oster, 2005; Ostrower, 2008; Ostrower and Stone, 2010; Taylor *et al.*, 1991; Zimmermann and Stevens, 2008).

Some authors deny that more instrumental accountability is necessarily better (Ebrahim, 2005). They focus on the values shared by the volunteers in a community and point out the importance of expressive accountability (Knutsen and Brower, 2010). They stress the role of governance structures in enabling managers to act as compliant stewards of the organization and as "boundary spanners" in connecting the organization with important players in its environment (Kreutzer and Jacobs, 2011). Other authors emphasize political issues (Richards and Smith, 2002; Rosenau and Czempiel, 1992), public interest (Stone and Ostrower, 2007) and democratic governance (Hoarau and Laville, 2008).

Little existing research explores or criticizes the board-based approach. However, most CSOs are not exclusively board-governed. Different governance bodies oversee CSOs' decisions and daily activities. Alongside the board, other bodies play a major role in the governance of CSOs. Thus, members of CSOs have a legitimate voice during the annual general meeting or general assembly. For this reason, the general assembly has a role to play to support internal democracy and is the body that can approve the CSO budget (Kreuzer, 2009).[1] Funders and economic stakeholders also play a major role in fostering the accountability of CSOs (Szper and Prakash, 2011; Thompson, 2010; Young, 2011).

This diversity of governance bodies requires conceptualizing governance as a complex and multi-layered process involving a wide range of different actors (Steen-Johnsen, Eynaud and Wijkström, 2011). Indeed, the governance of nonprofit organizations can be described as a kaleidoscopic picture drawn from different disciplinary, theoretical and empirical points of view (Maier and Meyer, 2011). Our aim in this chapter is to explore the respective roles of two specific governance bodies (the board and the general assembly) in the governance process.

The research discussed in this chapter explores the context of French CSOs that previously underwent a transformation in their governance. Based on a quantitative survey of 715 French CSOs, we propose a typology of CSO governance styles that reflects a broad view of governance. Our results show that nonprofit governance practices are more robust and diverse than what is accounted for by the conventional, board-centered model (Ostrower and Stone, 2010).

The chapter is organized as follows. After a literature review on governance mechanisms, we describe in the second section the method of data collection and statistical treatments used to construct the typology. In the third section, the styles of governance are analyzed from a theoretical perspective on CSO governance. We conclude by offering suggestions for further research.

Board and general assembly: multiple arrangements in CSO governance

Governance of CSOs occurs at several interrelated levels and involves multiple actors (Stone and Ostrower, 2007). In this chapter we propose a conceptual framework to understand the different dimensions of CSO governance. One way to deal with the complexity of the concept is to investigate the details of the governance bodies' activities and describe the relationships between them. We assert that the prevailing research focus on the board has neglected the importance of core groups in board effectiveness and the crucial role played by the general assembly (Kreutzer, 2009).

An extended view of board roles in CSOs

What roles and responsibilities do boards of CSOs actually fill? This question should be studied through the description of roles and responsibilities in practice (Stone and Ostrower, 2007).

The coercive role of the board

Most contemporary research assumes that the main function of a board is to ensure managerial compliance and to monitor and control management in order to guarantee that it acts in the interests of the organization (Kreutzer and Jacob, 2011, p. 617). This perspective, based on agency theory, was initially developed for for-profit organizations and was then widely adopted in research on CSO governance (Jegers, 2009). It relies on the basic assumption that agents (managers) engage in opportunistic behavior because the principals (board/directors) do not have access to all available information and the board does not share the manager's objectives.

This literature suggests that board effectiveness affects organizational outcomes by mitigating agency problems between board and management (Brown, 2005). It assumes that the role of the board is to ensure managerial compliance and avoid fraud by reinforcing supervision of the directors. The board must also motivate managers through extrinsic motivation systems (rewards and sanctions). In particular, the board must be actively involved in the monitoring of executive directors to ensure that adequate resources are in place, that legal and ethical responsibilities are met, and that the activities of the organization are in line with its mission. In this perspective, the accountability of CSOs is mainly instrumental and result-based (Carman, 2010; Keevers *et al.*, 2012) and the role of the board is mainly coercive (Hoarau and Laville, 2008).

However, this perspective has been criticized. Some authors note that a few of its conceptual assumptions are partly false. For instance, opportunistic behaviors and incongruence are less frequent in CSOs than in for-profit organizations (Kreutzer and Jacobs, 2011): a self-selection process for managers of civil society organizations should attract committed managers, and the differences in objectives between board and management are smaller. Moreover, there are no owners of CSOs to represent and protect. We can thus question whether or not the board in a civil society organization can be considered a "principal" in the classical sense of agency theory (Kreutzer and Jacobs, 2011; Oster, 1995). In such a context, efficient control of manager performance appears difficult to achieve. That is why the board cannot be seen solely as a control body and why other research perspectives are needed.

The "coaching" role of the board

Kreutzer and Jacobs (2011) suggest that stewardship theory could usefully complement agency theory in order to understand governance in CSOs. Stewardship theory assumes that there is a certain level of agreement about organizational goals between managers and principals and that intrinsically motivated managers will act as compliant stewards of the organization because they identify strongly with the organization's mission (Davis *et al.*, 1997). In this perspective, the board must be a "facilitator." It should define and review the mission of the CSO and establish working relationships with staff to support CSO managers. Kreutzer and Jacobs (2011) refer to this collaborative behavior of boards as "coaching." In this perspective, board members are expected to promote the sharing and management of knowledge in order to improve the decision-making process.

The democratic role of the board

The success of nonprofit organizations is also based on philanthropy, volunteerism, a participatory ethos and citizenship engagement (Haeringer, 2008). Therefore, a focus on the internal efficiency of CSOs will not be sufficient to comprehend their governance. One of the roles of the board is to ensure that the basic mission, values and democratic principles are fulfilled and sustained, and the board should allow for the expression of interests by different stakeholders through a democratic form of governance. A democratic perspective on governance suggests that the role of board members is to represent and express the interests of stakeholders (Cornforth and Edwards, 1999).

For a balanced relationship between the various stakeholders, the governance mode must mainly be based on partnership and deliberative process (democratic perspective). This enables a balance in terms of power and involvement between couples such as employees/volunteers, internal/external actors, funders/stakeholders in the field, etc. The partnership perspective also implies a certain level of active democracy in the association and attention to its history (Hoarau and Laville, 2008). This requires all board members to participate in discussions and decisions, the existence of democratic rules, effective counter-powers (which the board can delegate to the management), and a high level of skill on the part of board members (March, 1995). Scholars have shown that a democratic perspective enhances transparency, improves governance accountability (Steffek and Ferretti, 2009), and facilitates expressive accountability (Knutsen and Brower, 2010) based on values and beliefs. Expressive accountability relies on the fact that "organizations perceive themselves accountable ... because of philanthropic values or self-imposed responsibility to the community" (Knutsen and Brower, 2010, p. 601).

Considering the roles of the general assembly

Even though the French law of 1901 does not require convening a general assembly, most associations do it. French local authorities, institutions, and banks actually never contract with an association if it does not organize a general assembly once a year. A significant aspect of our work lies in the fact that we do not limit ourselves (as have previous studies) to the mere analysis of boards and their place in the CSO governance. Thus, we have extended our observations to two other relevant governance bodies: the general assembly and the core group.

Members are the legitimating body of CSOs. The general assembly is the place where members can express themselves. The general assembly should ensure democracy within the organization (Kreutzer, 2009): most of the time in the general assembly, the budget has to be approved and members are informed about activities. The general assembly is sovereign and elects the board. Therefore, the general assembly has the same type of control on the board that the latter has on executive management. In the same way, the general assembly can assume a coaching role vis-à-vis the board.

The existing governance research works that refer to the general assembly mainly point to the democratic role of the board as described above. However, there is no argument made against the governance body having a coercive, coaching or democratic role in the organization.

Following Stone and Ostrower, we argue that we cannot fully understand nonprofit governance "by focusing so exclusively on the board [because] many other stakeholders, including executive directors, staff, volunteers, donors, and beneficiaries, are likely to influence organizational mission, major policies, executive director performance, and external relationships" (Stone and Ostrower, 2007, p. 418). We thus explore the three dimensions – the coercive, coaching and democratic roles – for both the board and the general assembly (see Table 3.1).

Table 3.1 Governance body attributes

Governance mechanism	Dimensions measured
Board	Coercive role
	Coaching role
	Democratic role
General assembly	Coercive role
	Coaching role
	Democratic role

Methodology

For the purpose of describing alternative governance regimes, we adopted an inductive design of research and developed an empirical taxonomy to form distinct homogeneous groups of observations in a descriptive, neutral and exploratory perspective (Meyers *et al.*, 2013). Based on literature review, we defined two sets of characteristics to include in the classification of governance styles: board attributes and general assembly attributes.

A survey was launched in October 2010 at the French national forum of associations (Table 3.2).[2] The questionnaire was administered by email to association leaders (association members with responsibilities related to governance: director, coordinator, president, board, etc.). From the 2,015 responses, 715 observations without missing values were used in our analyses. The associations that took part in our survey constitute a broad sample of different organizational sizes and sectors. For instance, 19 percent of our associations work in the sports sector, 16 percent in the leisure sector, 15 percent in the culture sector and 16 percent in the local development sector. With respect to sector, this sample is almost equivalent to the population of associations in France (Tchernonog *et al.*, 2013).

All measures of our model were based on existing instruments where possible, and all variables were measured using a seven-point Likert scale (1 = disagree, 7 = agree) (see Table 3.3). To improve the quality of the constructs, we first performed an exploratory factor analysis on each construct to reduce the number of items down to the most relevant ones (Hinkin, 1998). In addition, reliability tests (Cronbach's alphas) were computed and demonstrated satisfactory results (see Table 3.3).

We performed a cluster analysis using Ward distance on standardized variables. We obtained a classification in four clusters that differentiates four styles of governance. We describe these clusters using both active variables and complementary illustrative variables. In Table 3.4 the different groups are characterized by means of the ordinal Likert scales that we used to construct the clusters. These means are basic indicators of the variables we measured. The range of these means is 1 to 7.

Results

Board and general assembly roles

For the global sample (Table 3.4), the highest scores are related to the democratic roles of the board (BOD, 6.51) and the general assembly (GA, 6.30). On average, there is a high level of agreement with regard to the democratic role of the board (standard deviation = 0.84). The results are quite close concerning the democratic role of the general assembly (standard deviation = 0.94). A broad consensus exists among the respondents about the democratic role of these two governance bodies measured by their ability to hold debates. Thus it seems that

Table 3.2 Characteristics of the nonprofit organizations studied (%)

		Cluster 1	Cluster 2	Cluster 3	Cluster 4	Average
In which sector is your organization involved?	Humanitarian	10.1	6.1	6.0	8.6	7.6
	Social	32.1	27.9	31.5	20.5	28.1
	Health	10.1	13.0	11.4	8.6	11.0
	Human rights	10.7	9.7	7.4	11.9	9.9
	Education	25.6	32.8	30.9	22.5	28.5
	Sports	28.0	21.1	22.8	31.7	25.9
	Culture	27.4	25.1	28.2	29.8	27.3
What was the total amount of your organization's budget in 2010?	Less than €50,000	17.9	7.8	13.9	32.2	15.7
	Between €50,000 and €500,000	40.5	44.2	44.3	39.0	42.5
	More than €500,000	41.7	48.1	41.8	28.8	41.9
What is the proportion of public funding in your total budget?	No public funding	6.7	5.9	8.7	13.2	7.9
	Up to 50%	40.0	35.3	39.1	34.2	37.1
	More than 50%	53.3	58.8	52.2	52.6	55.0
How many people are employed in your organization as permanent paid staff (more than six months)?*	No paid staff	16.7	16.8	15.8	40.0	21.6
	1 to 5	40.5	30.4	34.2	33.3	34.2
	5 to 50	30.2	38.6	36.7	19.2	32.0
	More than 50	12.7	14.1	13.3	7.5	12.2
How many people are working on the ground as volunteers for your organization?	No volunteers	10.9	16.8	9.5	4.1	11.0
	1 to 5	19.8	13.9	16.7	17.3	16.7
	5 to 50	51.5	55.5	53.6	60.2	55.2
	More than 50	17.8	13.9	20.2	18.4	17.1

Table 3.3 Main measurement definitions

Concepts	Items	Mean	Standard deviation
Coercive role of the board (Board_Coerc) (4 items, $\alpha=0.73$) The items used to measure coercive inclination of the board were adapted from literature on board monitoring in for-profit organizations and in CSO governance (Herman and Renz, 2008; Ostrower and Stone, 2010; Stone and Ostrower, 2007)	The board regularly asks the management team for complementary accounting information	4.56	2.01
	The board controls the manager's activities	4.40	2.19
	The board makes a systematic assessment of the management team's decisions	4.11	2.09
	The board regularly asks the management team for current activities information	4.69	1.97
Coercive inclination of the general assembly (GA_Coerc) (2 items, $\alpha=0.7$) The items used to measure coercive inclination of the GA were adapted from literature on board monitoring in for-profit organizations and in CSO governance (Herman and Renz, 2008; Ostrower and Stone, 2010; Stone and Ostrower, 2007)	The general assembly makes a systematic assessment of the board's decisions	4.43	2.13
	The general assembly ask the management team for complementary information in order to assess the implementation of the CSO's project	4.33	1.97
Coaching role of the board (Board_Coach) (3 items, $\alpha=0.77$) To measure the cognitive inclination of the board we used a multi-item scale that includes both advice-seeking interactions (McDonald et al., 2008) and strategic help provided (McDonald and Westphal, 2010)	The board of the association welcomes discussions and debates around new ideas	5.80	1.40
	The chairman of the association consults the board members regarding the definition of the collective project	6.15	1.46
	The board of the association allows new ideas to be expressed	5.36	1.60

continued

Table 3.3 Continued

Concepts	Items	Mean	Standard deviation
Coaching role of the general assembly (GA_Coach) (2 items, $\alpha = 0.88$) To measure the cognitive inclination of the general assembly we used a multi-item scale that includes both advice-seeking interactions (McDonald et al., 2008) and strategic help provided (McDonald and Westphal, 2010)	The chairman of the association consults the general assembly participants regarding the definition of the collective project	5.30	1.87
	The general assembly participants have a decision role to play in the definition of the global strategy	4.63	2.12
Democratic role of the board (Board_Dem) (5 items, $\alpha = 0.88$)	The board allows contradictory opinions to be heard	6.53	1.01
	The board allows debates and discussion	6.58	0.99
	Deliberations are compliant with the views expressed in the board	6.57	0.93
	Every member has a chance to voice their views in the board	6.68	0.85
	A clear assessment of what is at stake in the association is reported to the board members	6.21	1.27
Democratic role of the general assembly (GA_Dem) (5 items, $\alpha = 0.86$)	The general assembly allows contradictory opinions to be heard	6.35	1.16
	The general assembly allows debates and discussion	6.06	1.36
	Deliberations are compliant with the views expressed in the general assembly	6.48	0.97
	Every member has a chance to voice their views in the general assembly	6.46	1.06
	A clear assessment of what is at stake in the association is reported to the general assembly members	6.14	1.25

Table 3.4 Characteristics of the clusters

Governance	Role	Cluster 1 (n = 168)	Cluster 2 (n = 247)	Cluster 3 (n = 149)	Cluster 4 (n = 151)	Mean	Standard deviation	Min.	Max.
Board	Coercive	5.03***	4.76***	4.00***	3.70***	4.44	1.58271	1.00	7.00
	Coaching	5.40***	5.98***	5.54*	6.06***	5.77	1.20194	1.00	7.00
	Democratic	6.38*	6.53	6.56	6.58	6.51	0.84477	1.00	7.00
General assembly	Coercive	5.55***	3.24***	3.42***	5.88***	4.38	1.81744	1.00	7.00
	Coaching	4.51***	3.86***	6.12***	6.12***	4.96	1.84291	1.00	7.00
	Democratic	6.31	6.06***	6.45*	6.52**	6.30	0.94180	1.00	7.00

Notes
t-test with the mean of other groups ***<0.001; **<0.01; *<0.05.

conflicting perceptions might be expressed (see Table 3.3: BOD=6.53; GA=6.35), that open debates occur (BOD=6.58; GA=6.06) and that deliberations are consonant with the debates (BOD=6.57; GA=6.48).

The lowest scores (Table 3.4) are related to the coercive roles of the board (4.44) and the general assembly (4.38). Those two variables are also characterized by a low level of agreement among respondents (standard deviation: BOD=1.58; GA=1.81). The board and the general assembly do not usually assess the decisions of the core management team (Table 3.3: BOD=4.11; GA=4.43).

The coaching orientation of the governance bodies is situated between these two extremes (Table 3.4: BOD=5.77; GA=4.96). The managers regularly consult the board for definition of the mission (Table 3.3: BOD=6.15; GA=5.30).

A typology in four clusters

The characteristics of the four clusters are summarised in Table 3.4.

These categories give a multidimensional picture of CSOs. Clusters are described using bivariate t-tests (between the mean of the subgroup and the mean of all the other subgroups). The fourfold classification can be summarised as follows:

Cluster 1: control-based governance

The first cluster is composed of 168 observations (23.49 percent). It is the second largest cluster.

This cluster is mainly characterized by a substantial coercive inclination of the board (5.03***), which is higher than in other groups (t-test with the mean of other groups: ***<0.001; **<0.01; *<0.05). The coercive role of the general assembly is also significantly higher than the mean (5.55***). The democratic role of the board is significantly lower than in other groups (6.38*).

Concerning the general assembly, the results are close. The coercive role of the general assembly is dominant and is significantly higher than in other groups (5.55***) at the expense of the coaching role (4.51***).

Thus, both governance bodies are characterized by the significance of the coercive role relative to the other groups. We can consider that in this cluster, governance is mainly *control based*.

This cluster is more involved than any other group in the social sector (Table 3.2: 32.1 percent), the humanitarian sector (10.1 percent) and the sports sector (28.0 percent).

Cluster 2: board-based governance

The second cluster is the largest group, with 247 observations (34.54 percent).

This cluster is distinguished by the minor role played by the general assembly in governance relative to other groups. In this group, the general assembly is less coercive (3.24***), less helpful (coaching role=3.86***), and less democratic

(6.06***) than in any other group. This suggests that the general assembly is generally less involved in the governance structure than in other clusters.

Conversely, the coaching (5.98***) role of the board is higher than in any other group and the coercive role of the board is above the mean of the other clusters (4.76***).

Compared to other groups, in this cluster the board plays a major role in governance. We can call this *board-based governance*. This cluster is more involved than any other groups in the health sector (13.0 percent) and the education sector (32.8 percent). The budgets in this group are higher than in other groups: 44.2 percent of these CSO budgets are between €50,000 and €500,000, and 48.1 percent of them have a budget that exceeds €500,000. The proportion of public funding in these budgets is high: 58.8 percent of the respondents in this group report that their proportion of public funding exceeds 50 percent of their total revenue. The CSOs in this cluster employ more people than other groups: 5 to 50 paid employees (38.6 percent) or more than 50 paid employees (14.1 percent). These CSOs work less with volunteers than other groups (16.8 percent with no volunteers at all, and only 13.9 percent with more than 50 volunteers.).

Cluster 3: participative governance

The third cluster represents 149 observations (20.83 percent).

This group is associated with a low coercive inclination of the board (4.00***) and of the general assembly (3.42***). The general assembly has substantial democratic (6.45*) and coaching (6.12***) roles. The board plays a significant democratic role in governance (6.56, above the mean of the other groups).

This group emphasizes the democratic roles of the two governance bodies and not their coercive roles. Thus this cluster is characterized by *participative governance*.

This cluster is involved in all sectors, with no significant variations from the mean. The budgets in this group are greater than in other groups, largely between €50,000 and €500,000 (44.3 percent). More than in other groups, the respondents work with more than 50 volunteers in the field (20.2 percent).

Cluster 4: general-assembly-based governance

This cluster comprises 151 observations (21.11 percent).

In this cluster the coaching inclinations of the board (6.06***) and of the general assembly (6.12***) are more significant than in other groups. The coercive role of the board is weaker than in any other group (3.70***) but the coercive role of the general assembly is greater than in any other group (5.88***). Finally, the democratic role of the general assembly is stronger than in any other group (6.52**).

This group is thus characterized by a strong involvement of the general assembly in governance, whereas the coercive role of the board is weak. It would appear that where the board does not play a coercive role, this allows stronger involvement of the general assembly.

This cluster is more involved than any other group in human rights (11.9 percent) and culture (29.8 percent). The budgets in this group are smaller than in other groups, many below €50,000 (32.2 percent). 13.2 percent of the respondents in this group have no public funding, a larger proportion than in other groups. More than in other groups, CSOs in this cluster have no paid employees (40.0 percent). Also more than in other groups, the respondents work with a team of 5 to 50 volunteers in the field (60.2 percent).

Discussion and conclusion

The four clusters that emerged from the data can be classified according to two main dimensions (see Figure 3.1): the influence of coercive inclination in the governance process and the respective weights of the board and the general assembly.

Boards of directors carry out essential roles and functions in the governance of CSOs (Enjolras, 2009; Zimmermann and Stevens, 2008). Our results show that the level of monitoring by the board varies. Moreover, it is this dimension that we find the greatest variance in responses in our sample. In cluster 1 (control-based governance), the coercive inclination of the board and of the general assembly is high relative to other clusters. In cluster 2 (board-based

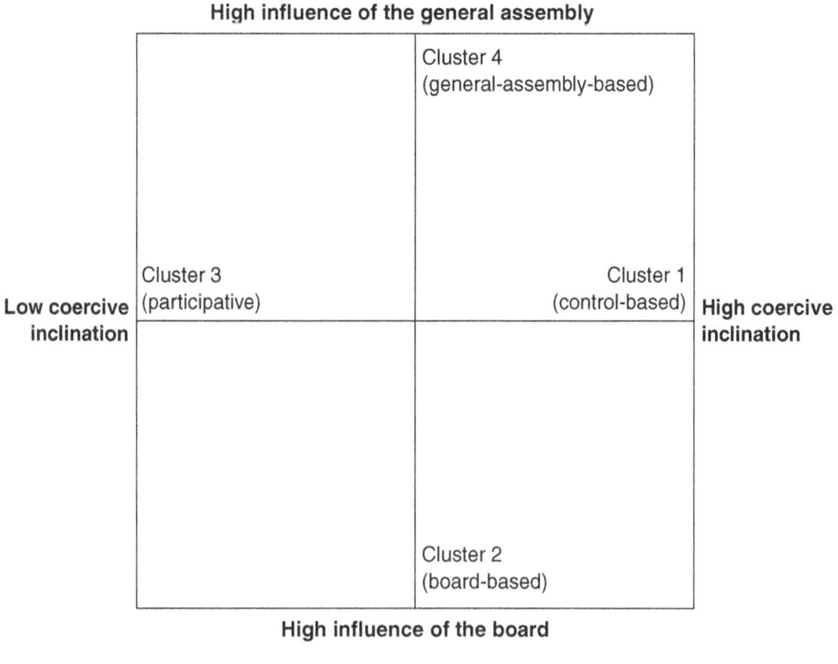

Figure 3.1 Governance styles.

governance), the board plays a major role in both the coercive and coaching dimensions. By contrast, in cluster 3 (participative governance) neither the board nor the general assembly has a coercive inclination. In cluster 4 (general-assembly-based governance), the general assembly plays a significant coercive role while the board does not.

Our results also suggest that the governance model depends on the place and role of the general assembly (Kreuzer, 2009). The relative dominance of the board and the general assembly in governance is the second differentiating factor between CSOs in our sample. Only cluster 2 (board-based governance) can be characterized by a strong board compared to the general assembly. In other clusters, the general assembly seems particularly dominant in the governance process. In cluster 1 (control-based governance), the board and the general assembly share the same weight and coercive inclination in governance. In cluster 3 (participative governance) and in cluster 4 (general-assembly-based governance), the general assembly plays a major role compared to the board.

Our results thus suggest that various governance arrangements are possible. These arrangements depend substantially but not solely on the level of coercive action exercised by the board, as suggested by the literature (Brown, 2005). The relative dominance of the board and the general assembly must also be taken into account in terms of other roles played by these bodies (Brown and Guo, 2010; Miller-Millessen, 2003; Young, 2011; Zimmerman and Stevens, 2008): specifically coaching roles (Kreutzer and Jacobs, 2011) or democratic roles (Cornforth and Edwards, 1999; Haeringer, 2008).

Our main contribution is twofold. First, these results confirm the significant role of the general assembly in governance relative to that of the board (as seen in clusters 3 and 4). We posit that the prevailing focus on the role of the board thus introduces a bias. It overemphasizes the coercive role of the board and offers a distorted picture of overall governance by ignoring the diversity of CSO governance practices. Therefore we argue that a research design should be focused not only on the board but also on the general assembly and the core group. This is required to obtain a more realistic understanding of CSO governance in France and elsewhere.

Second, our results suggest that the coercive role is not always in conflict with the coaching role (Kreutzer and Jacobs, 2011). In fact, the coercive and coaching roles can work together. This result is revealed by including the general assembly in the research design. In the same organization, the different bodies can specialize in different roles: the board can be coercive while the general assembly can be a coach, or the board can have a coaching role while the general assembly is coercive. By enlarging the scope of analysis to different governance bodies (beyond the board), we can observe how the balance of power can be expressed in different places and committees. This opens new avenues for research in nonprofit organization governance.

Enlarging the scope of the field to include the general assembly means also enlarging the scope of the literature review. Thus, the focus of the literature on coercive board mechanisms of governance suggests the dominance of instrumental orientations of nonprofit governance at the expense of more expressive mechanisms of governance (Ebrahim, 2005; Knutsen and Brower, 2010). Considering the relevant role played by the general assembly in governance also suggests a new balance between instrumental and expressive accountabilities. This hedges the risk of CSOs being perceived in academic literature as losing part of their uniqueness by becoming too "business-like" (Van Til, 2009). We argue that the emphasis put on the coercive functions of governance derives from academic preoccupation with the corporate governance model. Indeed, in the corporate model the general assembly does not play the same role as the one we have analyzed in this study.

Notes

1 In France, most CSOs adopt the legal status of "associations." Indeed, in France the law on establishing foundations is very restrictive. They must be recognized as being of public interest. In "associations," there is no legal obligation to have a general assembly; however, Article 9 of the "Loi du 1er juillet 1901 relative au contrat d'association" evokes the role of the general assembly in the dissolution of associations. Moreover, the default template provided by the ministry of the interior to elaborate the statute of associations proposes a general assembly. As a consequence, almost all associations do have a general assembly.
2 Once a year more than 4,000 CSO practitioners, experts and academics meet for the French National Forum of Associations convention in Paris.

References

Archambault, E. (2001). Historical Roots of the Nonprofit Sector in France. *Nonprofit and Voluntary Sector Quarterly*, 30(2): 204–220.

Bradshaw, P. (2002). Reframing Board-Staff Relations: Exploring the Governance Function Using a Storytelling Metaphor. *Nonprofit Management and Leadership*, 12(4): 471–484.

Brown, W. A. (2005). Exploring the Association between Board and Organizational Performance in Nonprofit Organizations. *Nonprofit Management and Leadership*, 15(3): 317–339.

Brown, W. A., and Guo, C. (2010). Exploring the Key Roles for Nonprofit Boards. *Nonprofit and Voluntary Sector Quarterly*, 39(3): 536–546.

Callen, J. L., Klein, A., and Tinkelman, D. (2003). Board Composition, Committees, and Organizational Efficiency: The Case of Nonprofits. *Nonprofit and Voluntary Sector Quarterly*, 32(4): 493–520.

Carman, J. G. (2010). The Accountability Movement. *Nonprofit and Voluntary Sector Quarterly*, 39(2): 256–274, doi: 10.1177/0899764008330622.

Cornforth, C., and Edwards, C. (1999). Board Roles in the Strategic Management of Nonprofit Organizations: Theory and Practice. *Corporate Governance*, 7(4): 346–362.

Davis, J. H., Schoorman, F. D., and Donaldson, L. (1997). Toward a Stewardship Theory of Management. *The Academy of Management Review*, 22(1): 20–47.

Ebrahim, A. (2005). Accountability Myopia: Losing Sight of Organizational Learning. *Nonprofit and Voluntary Sector Quarterly*, 34(1): 56–87.

Enjolras, B. (2009). A Governance-Structure Approach to Voluntary Organizations. *Nonprofit and Voluntary Sector Quarterly*, 38(5): 761–783.

Haeringer, J. (2008). *La démocratie : Un enjeu pour les associations d'action sociale.* Paris: Desclée de Brouwer.

Herman, R. D., Renz, D. O., and Heimovics, R. D. (1996). Board Practices and Board Effectiveness in Local Nonprofit Organizations. *Nonprofit Management and Leadership*, 7(4): 373–385.

Hinkin, T. R. (1998). A Brief Tutorial on the Development of Measures for Use in Survey Questionnaires. *Organizational Research Methods*, January, 104–121.

Hoarau, C., and Laville, J.-L. (2008). *La gouvernance des associations : Economie, sociologie, gestion.* Paris: Erès.

Jegers, M. (2009). Corporate Governance in Nonprofit Organizations: A Nontechnical Review of the Economic Literature. *Nonprofit Management and Leadership*, 20(2): 143–164.

Keevers, L., Treleaven, L., Sykes, C., and Darcy, M. (2012). Made to Measure: Taming Practices with Results-based Accountability. *Organization Studies*, 33(1): 97–120.

Knutsen, L. W., and Brower, R. S. (2010). Managing Expressive and Instrumental Accountabilities in Nonprofit and Voluntary Organizations: A Qualitative Investigation. *Nonprofit and Voluntary Sector Quarterly*, 39(4): 588–610.

Kreutzer, K. (2009). Nonprofit Governance during Organizational Transition in Voluntary Associations. *Nonprofit Management and Leadership*, 20(1): 117–133.

Kreutzer, K., and Jacobs, C. (2011). Balancing Control and Coaching in NPO Governance: A Paradox Perspective on Board Behavior. *VOLUNTAS: International Journal of Voluntary and Nonprofit Organizations*, 22(4): 613–638, doi: 10.1007/s11266–011–9212–6.

Langlais, J. L. (2008). *Pour un partenariat renouvelé entre l'Etat et les associations.* Paris: Ministère de la santé, de la jeunesse, des sports et de la vie associative.

Maier, F., and Meyer, M. (2011). Managerialism and Beyond: Discourses of Civil Society Organization and their Governance Implications. *VOLUNTAS: International Journal of Voluntary and Nonprofit Organizations*, 22(4): 731–756.

March, J. (1995). *Democratic Governance.* New York: Free Press.

McDonald, M. L., and Westphal, J. D. (2010). A Little Help Here? Board Control, CEO Identification with the Corporate Elite, and Strategic Help Provided to CEOs at Other Firms. *The Academy of Management Journal*, 53(2): 343–370.

McDonald, M. L., Khanna, P., and Westphal, J. D. (2008). Getting them to Think Outside the Circle: Corporate Governance, CEOs' External Advice Networks, and Firm Performance. *The Academy of Management Journal*, 51(3): 453–475.

Meyers, L. S., Gamst, G., and Guarino, A. J. (2013). *Applied Multivariate Research: Design and Interpretation*, 2nd edition. New York: Sage.

Miller-Millesen, J. L. (2003). Understanding the Behavior of Nonprofit Boards of Directors: A Theory-Based Approach. *Nonprofit and Voluntary Sector Quarterly*, 32(4): 521–547.

Morange, P. (2008). *Rapport d'information no. 1134 en conclusion des travaux de la mission sur la gouvernance et le financement des structures associatives.* Paris: Assemblée Nationale.

O'Regan, K., and Oster, S. M. (2005). Does the Structure and Composition of the Board Matter? The Case of Nonprofit Organizations. *Journal of Law, Economics, and Organization*, 21(1): 205–227.

Oster, S. (1995). *Strategic Management for Nonprofit Organizations: Theory and Cases.* New York: Oxford University Press.

Ostrower, F. (2008). Boards of Midsize Nonprofits: Their Needs and Challenges. Urban Institute.

Ostrower, F., and Stone, M. M. (2010). Moving Governance Research Forward: A Contingency-Based Framework and Data Application. *Nonprofit and Voluntary Sector Quarterly*, 39(5): 901–924.

Richards, R. O., and Smith, M. J. (2002). *Governance and Public Policy in the United Kingdom*. New York: Oxford University Press.

Rosenau, J. N., and Czempiel, E.-O. (1992). *Governance Without Government: Order and Change in World Politics*. Cambridge: Cambridge University Press.

Steen-Johnsen, K., Eynaud, P., and Wijkström, F. (2011). On Civil Society Governance: An Emergent Research Field. *VOLUNTAS: International Journal of Voluntary and Nonprofit Organizations*, 22(4): 555–565.

Steffek, J., and Ferretti, M. P. (2009). Accountability or "Good Decisions"? The Competing Goals of Civil Society Participation in International Governance. *Global Society: Journal of Interdisciplinary International Relations*, 23(1): 37–57.

Stone, M. M., and Ostrower, F. (2007). Acting in the Public Interest? Another Look at Research on Nonprofit Governance. *Nonprofit and Voluntary Sector Quarterly*, 36(3): 416–438.

Szper, R., and Prakash, A. (2011). Charity Watchdogs and the Limits of Information-Based Regulation. *VOLUNTAS: International Journal of Voluntary and Nonprofit Organizations,* 22(1): 112–141.

Taylor, B. E., Chait, R. P., and Holland, T. P. (1991). Trustee Motivation and Board Effectiveness. *Nonprofit and Voluntary Sector Quarterly*, 20(2): 207–224.

Tchernonog, V., Prouteau, L., Tabariès, M., and Nogues, H. (2013). *Le paysage associatif français mesures et évolutions*. Paris and Lyon: Dalloz Juris éditions.

Thomson, D. E. (2010). Exploring the Role of Funders' Performance Reporting Mandates in Nonprofit Performance Measurement. *Nonprofit and Voluntary Sector Quarterly*, 39(4): 611–629.

Van Til, J. (2009). A Paradigm Shift in Third Sector Theory and Practice: Refreshing the Wellsprings of Democratic Capacity. *American Behavioral Scientist*, 52(7): 1069–1081.

Warsmann, J. L. (2009). *L'optimisation de la dépense publique (Rapport d'information)*. Paris: Assemblée Nationale.

Young, D. R. (2011). The Prospective Role of Economic Stakeholders in the Governance of Nonprofit Organizations. *VOLUNTAS: International Journal of Voluntary and Nonprofit Organizations*, 22(4): 566–586.

Zimmermann, J. A. M., and Stevens, B. W. (2008). Best Practices in Board Governance: Evidence from South Carolina. *Nonprofit Management and Leadership*, 19(2): 189–202.

4 Governing boards and organizational environments

Growing complexities, shifting boundaries

Francie Ostrower and Melissa M. Stone

Introduction

Early research on governing boards, primarily conducted within the US context, focused on boards as mechanisms for dealing with environmental uncertainties through their various boundary-spanning roles (Middleton, 1987). The literature on boards has grown enormously over the past 20 years, but environmental concerns are no longer at the center (Ostrower and Stone, 2006). Elsewhere, we have called for the need to re-integrate elements of the external environment back into research on nonprofit governance, while expanding the guiding conception of the environment (2010). Early board research focused on the funding environment, but also important as evidenced in recent years are the policy, legal and regulatory, community, and normative environments (Ostrower, 2007; Ostrower and Stone, 2010; Stone and Ostrower, 2007). In this chapter, we seek to explore and expand the discussion of the role of the board as boundary spanner in the context of a broader conception of environments. This broader view is further necessitated by changes in organizational environments themselves. As Scott and Davis argue, "The boundaries of today's organizations are no longer stable or fixed, but transitory and flexible, and ... they no longer circumscribe all of the actors and processes of interest" (Scott and Davis, 2007, pp. 382–383). If organizational boundaries and environments are shifting, permeable and far from clearly demarcated, then what does this mean for the role of the board as boundary spanner?

To expand a conceptualization of the environment, we propose that a fruitful approach is to think in terms of accountability environments that encompass but are not limited to resource environments. Accountability environments are multidimensional and arise from different types of pressures from a variety of institutions and stakeholder groups (Benjamin, 2008; Kearns, 1996; Morrison and Salipante, 2007; Ebrahim, 2010). In fact around the globe demands have risen sharply in the last two decades for greater accountability from the sector overall and from specific types of nonprofits (Gugerty and Prakash, 2010; Jeavons, 2010; Morrison and Salipante, 2007).

This chapter begins to develop an understanding of the implications of multiple and potentially competing accountability environments for boards and their role as boundary spanners. Not all stakeholders or all types of accountability, however, command equal attention. A key question concerns to whom boards (which generally enjoy considerable autonomy in the US) choose to hold themselves accountable (Ostrower, 2014). A related issue concerns the differential ability of stakeholders to enforce their accountability claims.

This chapter maps out types of accountability environments and links them to various boundary-spanning tasks and roles based on a more refined understanding of to whom nonprofits may be held accountable and for what. The chapter uses data from recent research to highlight the current state of boundary-spanning activities undertaken by nonprofit boards and compares these findings to the range of boundary-spanning tasks and roles encompassed within accountability environments.

In line with previous work that has emphasized the variable and context-dependent nature of nonprofit boards (Ostrower and Stone, 2010), the chapter argues that the behaviour of boards in the role of boundary spanners will differ among types of nonprofit organizations depending on variations in their accountability environments. Here, it is important to go beyond the characteristics that nonprofit boards share by virtue of their legal status as nonprofits. For example, some nonprofit industries are more highly regulated than others and may be more likely to face clearly defined and enforced accountability rules. Additionally, the advent of hybrid forms means that some types of nonprofits confront boundary issues that are more traditionally associated with governmental and for-profit enterprises. For example, in recent years, many states have passed legislation recognizing special forms of dual-mission social enterprises, such as low-profit limited liability companies. While beyond the scope of this chapter, hybridity and the formation of these dual mission organizations are raising challenging questions about what constitutes accountability environments for organizations that serve the "two masters" of social benefit and profit (Brakman Reiser, 2013), a topic explored in Chapter 1 of this volume.

This chapter is organized as follows. The next section presents literature on boundary-spanning roles, boundaries and accountability environments that relates to important governance and board functions. The second section provides data from recent research that illustrates tension points and differences in how the boards of various types of nonprofit organizations fulfill boundary-spanning roles. The third section explores the implications of these research data for the boundary-spanning roles of boards that face multiple accountability environments and raises questions to guide future research.

Boards and the changing nature of boundary spanning, boundaries and accountability environments

Complementary to the emergence of resource-dependence theory, the initial literature on boundary-spanning roles in organizations emphasized how organizations use these roles to manage critical external dependencies while maintaining autonomy and independence. The focus of this research was on specific organizational positions, such as purchasing agents (Spekman, 1979), or organizational units, such as bargaining units (Kochan, 1975), that were involved in various types of power and exchange relationships with facets of an organization's environment.

The primary functions of boundary spanning were found to include absorbing uncertainty from external environments in order to protect an organization's technical core (Thompson, 1967), processing various types of information from the external environment (Aldrich and Hecker, 1977), and representing the organization to the environment in a favorable light to enhance its legitimacy and attract needed resources (Aldrich and Hecker, 1977; Daft, 1998). Given these functions, specific boundary-spanning roles included:

- buffering (Thompson, 1967);
- mediating or bridging (Daft, 1998);
- representing (Daft, 1998);
- information gathering, processing and translating (Aldrich and Hecker, 1977);
- influencing the environment on the organization's behalf (Pfeffer and Salancik, 1978).

The power of these boundary-spanning positions or organizational units was related to various characteristics of the external environment (e.g., uncertainty, complexity, heterogeneity, concentration of power) and to some extent internal factors, such as the expertise of the boundary spanner and degrees of internal conflict (Aldrich and Hecker, 1977; Kochan, 1975; Spekman, 1979).

The resource-dependence literature introduced boards of directors, both for-profit and nonprofit, as important boundary-spanning units that stood between the organization and its environment and could, more specifically, help an organization manage its resource dependencies (Pfeffer and Salancik, 1978, p. 161). In the nonprofit realm, early research focused on how boards helped manage the organization–environment boundaries by linking the nonprofit to critical financial resources, buffering it from external criticism and aligning the nonprofit with the interests of community elites (for a summary of this literature, see Middleton, 1987). For example, power structure theorists emphasized boards as links to a cohesive upper class, whose members sat on their boards and brought the organizations into alignment with class interests (see, for example, Ratcliff *et al.*, 1979; Salzman and Domhoff, 1983).

The early work on boundary-spanning and on boards as critical boundary spanners was predicated on an assumption that there was a clear demarcation between organizations and their environments and that boundaries between organizations and environments could be fairly easily determined. However, as stated above, there is growing evidence that organizational boundaries are no longer as stable or as fixed as they were (Scott and Davis, 2007) and that distinguishing what is internal to an organization from what is external is increasingly problematic. The fluidity and permeability of organizational boundaries, or the "boundary problem" as Scott and Davis (2007) describe it, is due to several emerging trends, such as the growing use of networks, partnerships and contracting to develop and implement services and products that heretofore had resided within the bounds of a single organization. Additionally, a rise in the number and types of hybrid forms of organization that select elements from for-profit, nonprofit and public-sector entities illustrates the ways in which traditional demarcations are breaking down (Billis, 2010; Scott and Davis, 2007; Smith, 2010). As boundaries become more fluid and less stable, questions of *whether and how* boards are playing various boundary-spanning roles become much more complex.

A focus on accountability environments recognizes the complexities of the boundary problem and is a fruitful approach to answering these questions. Accountability is central to the governance function for organizations in all three sectors. As Brody argues (2002), an independent board (along with the prohibition against distributing profits to private shareholders) is a critical component of nonprofit accountability even though nonprofits lack clear principal–agent relationships, such as those between citizens and public officials or stockholders and managers. In the public and nonprofit sectors, however, there is growing recognition that accountability demands encompass more than vertical chains of principal–agent relationships, including, for example, interest groups, clients, the media, or what are often referred to as "horizontal" or non-hierarchical accountability claimants (Benjamin, 2008; Bovens *et al.*, 2008; Gugerty and Prakash, 2010; Schillemans, 2008).

Many now argue that in fact nonprofits now face multiple accountability demands, such as accountabilities for performance, responsiveness and transparency (Ebrahim, 2010; Kearns, 1996; Morrison and Salipante, 2007), and multiple accountability environments, including elements of resource, institutional and policy contexts. Kearns (1996), for example, distinguishes among four types of accountability (legal, negotiated, discretionary and anticipatory) that differ with regard to the nature of the accountability demands on the nonprofit made by different stakeholders. Ebrahim (2010) elaborates these distinctions, presenting three different types of accountability demand: (1) "upward" to resource suppliers and government regulators, with an emphasis on accountability for the use of funds; (2) "downward" to beneficiaries, communities, networks and professional associations, with a focus on accountability to those whom the nonprofit impacts; and, (3) "inward" accountability to the nonprofit itself, its staff and volunteers, for implementing the mission of the organization. The relative importance of these claims varies along two dimensions – the type of nonprofit and the degree of power dispersion among claimants. Ebrahim argues that the accountability demands of the most powerful actors often garner the most organizational attention. In cases of more dispersed power, significant conflict may arise within the organization regarding how to meet competing accountability demands. For example, funders may hold a nonprofit accountable for implementing a particular approach to service delivery that is in tension with the nonprofit's mission or an approach or priorities advocated by field staff.

We draw on Ebrahim's framework for understanding multiple accountability environments; but we make two modifications. First, we re-label his "downward" accountability as "outward" accountability to reflect more accurately the type of environment he is describing. Second, we divide into two subcategories the kinds of stakeholder groups included in the outward accountability environment. The first subcategory includes direct recipients of programs or products (beneficiaries and communities) and the second encompasses more field-related groups such as networks and professional associations.

Table 4.1 presents a summary of connections between multiple accountability environments and boundary-spanning roles.

Upward accountability (concentrated largely on issues related to the use of funds) involves legal, regulatory and funding stakeholders. The boundary issue is one of managing the power of these stakeholders while maintaining organizational autonomy and external legitimacy. This accountability environment has been the focus of much nonprofit governance research where the boundary-spanning roles of boards typically include buffering the organization from external intrusion, bridging or representing the nonprofit in terms of relationship-building with funders, and even co-opting some of these elements of the external environment through recruitment to board positions.

There are two aspects of the outward accountability environment. The first concerns accountability for the quality of services, programs and products and involves understanding and translating the needs and demands of beneficiaries and communities relative to the nonprofit's mission. The boundary-spanning roles, therefore, primarily include information gathering and processing. The second aspect of the outward accountability environment incorporates the non-profit field more generally, including, for example, networks or partnerships with

Table 4.1 Relationships among accountability environments and boundary-spanning roles

Type of accountability environment and key stakeholders	Boundary-spanning roles	Who performs the role
Upward for use of funds • Legal, regulatory institutions • Resource suppliers	Buffering Bridging Co-opting	Board Executive director
Outward I for quality of services • Beneficiaries • Communities to be impacted	Information gathering and processing	Line staff Executive director/top managers Possibly board
Outward II for norm alignment • Networks • Professional associations • Accrediting agencies	Representational Bridging Influencing external environment	Executive director Possibly board
Inward for implementation of mission • Staff and volunteers	Oversight Mission framing	Executive director Board

which the nonprofit is involved, professional associations, and accrediting agencies, and is much more norm-based. Here the boundary task is to demonstrate that the nonprofit is in alignment with the norms and goals of the networks, professional associations, and accrediting agencies in which they participate. In some cases, being aligned with field-level goals may include advocacy or systems change activities and being held accountable for participation and leadership in these activities. Boundary spanning is likely to include, therefore, representational and bridging roles where organization members (including board members) serve as representatives of the organization and its programs and as bridges between these external groups and the nonprofit.

The inward accountability environment focuses on implementation of the nonprofit's mission. Traditionally, the board not only represents the organization to its external environment but also serves to represent the public looking in; hence, its boundary-spanning role in this type of accountability environment would include oversight of the chief executive officer (CEO) and protection of the assets of the nonprofit in the service of its mission. However, another boundary task within this type of environment includes what Scott and Davis (2007) refer to as cognitive alignment, or creating and maintaining a singular identity throughout the nonprofit that is aligned with its mission. Bridging differences among staff or between staff and top management that concern the core mission would be an example of an important boundary role that the board would play within this type of accountability environment.

Two important points are raised by Table 4.1. First, multiple boundary-spanning roles are associated with these different accountability environments and may become activated at any point in time by external events or by the actions of particular stakeholder groups. Abrupt changes in policy or legal environments may activate buffering roles and potentially an influencing or advocating boundary role. Changes in funding environments may also affect these roles. For instance, increased reliance on government funding appears to diminish the board's role in boundary spanning relative to that of the CEO (see, for example, Guo, 2007; Smith and Lipsky, 1993). Furthermore, Guo's findings suggest that with increased government funding, boards decrease their ability to act as representatives of community interests (2007), thus diminishing their outward, bridging capacities. Second, in virtually all accountability environments, either the CEO or the board (or both) may play important boundary-spanning roles – and in some cases staff may as well. Because we start (as the table illustrates) from an analysis of various types of accountability environments and what each necessitates in terms of boundary spanning, the board becomes only one of several organizational actors that may play those roles. Previous perspectives on board boundary-spanning roles started with board functions and then matched these to various environmental demands, perhaps overstating the uniqueness or singularity of the board's role in boundary-spanning activities.

Illustrations from recent research on board boundary-spanning roles

To this point, this chapter has argued that boards play boundary-spanning roles that are more complex and diverse than suggested by the earlier literature, and that this is partly due to the multifaceted accountability environments in which organizations function. But what boundary-spanning roles do today's boards actually engage in? To shed light on this question, we consider selected findings from two recent US research projects from the perspective of this discussion's focus on boundary-spanning roles. One is the 2005 Urban Institute National Survey of Nonprofit Governance, which includes over 5,100 nonprofit organizations of different sizes and fields of activity (Ostrower, 2007). The other is a statewide survey of Minnesota's charter schools, which we considered to explore the boundary-spanning topic in a distinctive type of nonprofit.

Urban Institute National Survey of Nonprofit Governance

The Urban Institute National Survey of Nonprofit Governance, of which one of the authors served as Principal Investigator (Ostrower, 2007),[1] was the first national representative study of nonprofit governance in the United States. It was administered to a stratified random sample of nonprofits drawn from the Urban Institute's NCCS-Guidestar National Nonprofit Research Database of public charities that filed Internal Revenue Service (IRS) Form 990. Thus all potential sample members had a minimum of US$25,000 in annual receipts, the filing requirement threshold at that time. The sample was stratified by size (measured as annual expenditures) to obtain adequate numbers of large organizations. Thus descriptive analyses are weighted to adjust for differential probabilities of selection by size as well as non-response patterns (except when analyses are already broken down by size). Responses were received from 5,115 nonprofits, for a response rate of 41 percent. The survey was administered by mail, with an online option (for further discussion of sampling and weighting procedures see Triplett and Ostrower, 2007).

From the perspective of the current discussion, the following subset of findings and conclusions from the study are particularly relevant here:

- Significant numbers of boards were not very actively engaged in carrying out roles traditionally ascribed to them, including certain boundary-spanning roles. Low levels of activity in certain areas raise questions about whether the roles have been taken up by the executive director and/or whether boards have been able to adapt to the increasingly complex environments faced by the organizations they oversee.
- There is considerable variation among boards in terms of which roles they actively engage in. From the perspective of the current analysis, additional research is needed to understand how these variations may relate to distinct accountability environments that nonprofits find themselves in.

• It is imperative to attend to the legal, policy and normative environments, as well as the resource environment, when considering accountability and board roles.

In terms of overall prevalence, roles related to upward accountability predominate. The two roles in which a majority of boards were very actively engaged were financial oversight and setting organizational policy (52 percent). Note that these forms of upward accountability are more specifically related to the legal and regulatory environment. The percentage of surveyed boards very actively engaged in fundraising – an activity related to the resource environment – was considerably lower (less than one-third).[2]

The survey also found that among organizations with a paid CEO, over half were very actively engaged in one form of inward accountability, namely evaluating the CEO. However, boards exhibited lower levels of engagement in outward accountability, with no one activity of this type commanding participation by a majority: indeed, less than one-third were very active in community relations or educating the public about the organization.

There were, however, significant variations. First, organizational size was positively associated with engagement in the upwardly accountable roles of financial oversight and fundraising, but negatively associated with the outwardly accountable roles of community relations and educating the public. This raises the question of whether larger organizations are less likely to focus on outward accountability processes per se, or whether that role has shifted to staff. Among the factors positively associated with engagement in multiple outwardly accountable roles were receipt of funding from government and importance placed on certain board recruitment criteria. Second, having a paid professional executive director was negatively associated with board activity in upward boundary-spanning roles of fundraising, the outward role of community relations, and the inward role of monitoring programs. It was positively associated with the upward accountability role of financial oversight and the inward accountability roles of evaluating the CEO and acting as a sounding board for management. This suggests that with professionalization, as indicated by the presence of a paid professional executive director, the board may delegate some of its boundary-spanning activities to the executive director who it then oversees.

Furthermore, the survey found that boards are extremely homogeneous with respect to race and ethnicity, raising questions about boards' ability to represent and bridge to the diverse publics served by nonprofits.

The survey also included a particular focus on practices related to the Sarbanes–Oxley Act that are relevant to upward accountability. The act was passed by the US congress in 2002 and focused on deterring fraud in the business sector. However, it was quickly followed by debates over whether nonprofits should also abide by aspects of the act on a required or voluntary basis. In 2004, the Senate Finance Committee issued a draft paper advocating stronger nonprofit governance, some states proposed or passed regulations, and several professional associations issued guidelines about "compliance" with the act (Ostrower, 2007; Ostrower and Bobowick, 2006).

Findings from the survey support the idea that passage of the Sarbanes–Oxley Act did significantly impact nonprofits: large percentages of respondents with conflict-of-interest policies, whistleblower policies and audit committees had created or revised the policies since the passage of Sarbanes–Oxley. The passage of the Sarbanes–Oxley Act and its aftermath contributed to changing expectations and standards about nonprofit governance (Ostrower, 2007).

In short, nonprofits have been subject to greater pressures to demonstrate upward accountability. More recently, revisions to the IRS Form 990 included additional questions about governance practices. Although these are not necessarily required for tax exempt status, answers are publicly available and that may spur nonprofits to adapt their practices (Fishman, 2010).

Once again, the survey found considerable variations among organizations in terms of the adoption of various accountability practices. At the same time we found wide variability in the percentage of organizations that had adopted various practices, even controlling for organizational size. One striking finding was that nonprofit boards with members that serve on corporate boards were more likely to adopt several Sarbanes–Oxley related policies. This suggests that businesspeople brought upward accountability practices from the corporate sector into the nonprofit world. In contrast, having the nonprofit's CEO as a voting board member was negatively associated with adoption, including having an audit, and having conflict-of-interest, document retention, and whistleblower policies. This further suggests that the blurring of CEO and board roles may be associated with lesser engagement of the board in upwardly accountable functions.

The survey did not find evidence of widespread efforts to influence public policy, a potentially important boundary-spanning role. Only 10 percent were very actively engaged, with another, larger group (over one-fourth) somewhat active. The engagement of boards in outward-looking efforts to influence, in addition to comply with, public policy bears further investigation.

Minnesota's charter schools[3]

Charter schools, first established by state statute in Minnesota in 1991, are public schools and are part of a wider public education reform movement that emphasizes decentralized control to the school level, parental choice, and student outcomes and performance (Finnigan, 2007). At the core of the argument for charter schools, or the "horsetrade" as some term it (Manno *et al.*, 2000), is the agreement that charters will be granted autonomy from bureaucratic regulation in exchange for results-oriented accountability. The argument is that if charters are free from regulatory burden and compliance-focused accountability and are granted more autonomy, then accountability to parents and students for academic results will increase and will improve overall educational standards (Manno *et al.*, 2000; Finnigan, 2007; Shober *et al.*, 2006). This suggests that the core argument for charter schools is to trade an upward accountability focus for more outward accountability so as to improve public education.

Despite the emphasis on accountability to parents and students for educational excellence, charter schools face a dense upward accountability environment composed of legal, regulatory, funding and policy components. For example, individual charter schools must deal with public education mandates at both federal and state levels, and, if they are incorporated as nonprofit entities, charter schools must comply with federal IRS requirements, state nonprofit corporation law, and state charter school governance law. Additionally, charter schools' upward accountability environment includes "authorizers" who are legally responsible for oversight of charter schools; the environment may also include institutional entities such as local school districts or state education agencies or more independent entities such as higher education institutions or nonprofit organizations.

In terms of the outward accountability environment, beneficiaries include parents and students. Accountability to them for quality education and "results" is clearly central to the argument for charter schools. In Minnesota, this accountability is manifested by several legislative mandates: (1) electors of charter school boards must include all parents of the charter's students (as well as staff); (2) charter boards must include at least one teacher, parent, and community representative; (3) boards must comply with the state's Open Meeting Law.

The inward accountability environment includes primarily teachers, who, until 2009, were mandated to be a majority of a charter school's board membership.

Below we report on the results of a governance survey administered in the spring of 2012 to the population of Minnesota charter schools ($n = 150$) via their school leaders through an online survey mechanism.[4] The response rate was 50 percent of the population and, after testing for respondent bias, was representative of the population in terms of size, location and age. The survey replicated several components of the Urban Institute study and was supplemented with 16 interviews with school leaders and board members from several charter schools.

Overall, survey data suggests that charter school boards are focused on the upward accountability environment:

- In terms of board functions and activities, boards are most active in providing financial oversight (87 percent report very active). School leaders report that most have active finance committees (86 percent).
- When asked to choose two groups to whom their boards and they felt most accountable, school leaders reported that their boards felt most accountable to authorizers (56 percent) and that they, as school leaders, felt most accountable to their boards (67 percent). At the bottom of both lists (under 20 percent) were the public at large, taxpayers, the Minnesota Department of Education, and teachers.
- Boards were far less active, however, in the upward accountability role of fundraising.[5] Only 11 percent report that their boards are very active in

fundraising, and when recruiting, executive directors report that an ability to fundraise or donate is not important (only 9 percent and 3 percent respectively report these are very important criteria). Few have active committees for fundraising and development (29 percent).

Boards were active in some inward accountability practices, including planning for the future (73 percent) and evaluating the executive director (69 percent). They were not very active in terms of outward accountability, including influencing public policy (8 percent) or community outreach (11 percent). In line with these findings, executive directors reported that the top two priorities for their boards were financial oversight and planning for the future (86 percent and 44 percent respectively); the bottom two priorities were fundraising and community outreach (0 percent and 5 percent respectively).

The striking lack of activities focused on outward accountability to communities may be driven, at least in part, by the homogeneity of these boards: they are small boards (5–9 members) composed of relatively young (under 50 years of age), white, female members. The largest group on boards is teachers (42 percent), most of whom are employed by the charter school. Board member expertise is primarily in education (60 percent) while far few are employed elsewhere. Sixty-nine percent reported having the most difficulty recruiting people to fulfill the community representative role. Interviewees also reported that it was difficult to recruit people who were not directly related in some way to school staff, students, alumni or current board members.

What do these data indicate about boundary-spanning roles of charter school boards? It appears that these boards are compliance-oriented, with much of their attention focused on buffering their charter school against a powerful and complex upward accountability environment. Their attention to financial oversight activities, use of finance committees, and accountability to authorizers illustrate ways in which these boards may attempt to meet the demands of outside overseers and regulators in order to buffer the school's educational programming (its technical core) from external intrusion.

These boards do perform some representing and bridging boundary-spanning roles to their inward and outward accountability environments. Teachers on the board may represent the school's teachers more broadly; however, this role also causes some degree of conflict for teachers. For example, several reported that they had to balance the role of being a representative of teachers with being a board member making decisions for the good of the entire school. The bridging role was performed by parents on the board who reported that they often were in touch with other parents to gather information or report on board decisions.

It is important to stress, however, that these bridging and representing roles linked board members to a narrow network of charter school relationships. For example, when asked to define "community," most interviewees said that it encompassed current students and their parents, alumni, teachers and staff. Few described "community" as encompassing a broader geographic or cultural reach. Furthermore, bridging or representing the school for fundraising purposes was

extremely rare. Few of these boards have fundraising and development committees, and when recruiting board members, most do not put an emphasis on fundraising ability or business connections. In summary, these boards demonstrate
far less outward accountability to the public at large and communities beyond
the schools' walls. They are not actively engaged in community outreach and
that is not a priority.

Conclusion and implications

The purpose of this chapter has been to re-examine the boundary-spanning role
of boards by expanding the way we think about the environment itself. This in
part involves a call for recognizing multiple environments that include but go
beyond the resource environment to encompass policy, legal and regulatory,
community and normative environments. The chapter argues that the concept of
accountability provides a useful way to frame analyses of these various environments. Accountability claims are mechanisms through which these various
environments enact their diverse influences. Different types of claims made by
more or less powerful actors in these environments elicit different boundary-
spanning roles. To illustrate various accountability environments and board
boundary-spanning roles in a preliminary way, the chapter drew on a national
survey of nonprofit boards and a statewide survey of the boards of a particular
type of nonprofit, charter schools.

The national survey in particular indicated that considerable variations exist
among types of nonprofits. Both surveys call attention to the comparatively more
widespread engagement by boards with upward accountability and inward
accountability activities than with outward accountability activities aimed at the
wider public. The prevalence of upward accountability activities suggests that
much of the boundary spanning done by nonprofit boards involves buffering –
engaging in practices to ensure compliance with laws and regulations in order to
buffer the nonprofit from external scrutiny. The extent to which boards engage
even in these roles, however, seems to vary, for instance by organizational size
and by degree of professionalization. We hypothesize that the even higher percentage of organizations in the charter school board sample actively engaged in
buffering activities (by comparison with the national sample) reflects the high
levels of regulation in their specific environment.

Also noteworthy is the apparent indirect and normative impact of the regulatory environment as suggested by the national survey's findings with respect to
nonprofits' adoption of activities related to Sarbanes–Oxley. Here, an interesting
overlap has occurred between upward and outward accountabilities as expectations are heightened for boards to adopt policies that demonstrate "compliance"
with legal standards that do not necessarily apply to them but that have become
normative expectations for public accountability. Indeed, the normative pressures toward adoption and calls for greater self-regulation by nonprofit professional associations may in part reflect a boundary-spanning co-optation role,
namely to attempt to forestall greater government regulation (see Sidel, 2005).

The relative focus on upward or inward-facing roles versus bridging activities raises questions that deserve further investigation. What has happened to the bridging, representing and information-gathering boundary-spanning roles? These boundary-spanning roles are critical because they transport values, norms and perspectives across boundaries between the nonprofit and elements of its external environments. Three aspects of this question deserve particular attention: (1) why do boards seem less engaged in these roles? (2) are these roles shifting to other actors within the nonprofit? (3) are nonprofits not actively carrying them out at all? For any of these questions, we need to consider their implications not only for the specific organizational functioning of nonprofits, but also for our broader understanding of nonprofits as vehicles for civic expression.

One possibility is that the CEO and perhaps other staff have taken on some outward-reaching roles. If so, then we need to ask what is lost or gained by this arrangement. To what extent do more dominant boundary-spanning roles by staff reflect the character of nonprofits as professionalized service-deliverers (who happen to be nonprofit rather than some other organizational type) but detract from their character as vehicles of civic engagement? We might even ask whether the ability of nonprofits to deliver services that meet community needs may suffer to the extent that the board does not perform strong bridging, representing or information-gathering and -processing roles. Especially troubling in this regard is the high degree of racial and ethnic homogeneity of boards as reported in both studies.

Another possibility is that some outward-reaching roles are being carried out at the level of organizational associations and networks, rather than at the level of the individual organization. As this suggests, analyses of individual organizations needs to be complemented by field-level research. For instance, it may be that nonprofit boards are relying on state and national associations of nonprofits (of which they may be members) to organize policy advocacy efforts about the nonprofit sector. Such research would be particularly timely because evidence suggests that these associations are growing both in the US and around the world, at least partly in response to increased accountability demands and government scrutiny (Gugerty and Prakesh, 2010). Also important would be to ask about the degree to which nonprofits look to associations within their own field of activity to advocate and educate about policy issues relevant to their particular clients, beneficiaries and mission. A question for both types of studies would be to try to assess the extent to which nonprofits and their associations are proactive in this respect, or reactive – turning outward when prompted to do so by a perceived threat directed at the sector's independence.

In addition to the questions just posed, our discussion clearly calls for a research agenda that is more strategically oriented to the environment. For instance, we see a need for comparative studies that focus on the governance activities of organizations that function in different types of accountability environments. In this respect, a particularly interesting line of research involves new social enterprise hybrid forms of organization that incorporate into their very nature dual accountabilities to their social mission and to their investors. Another is a comparative study of organizations in different regulatory (professional or legal) environments. The fruitfulness of this approach, we believe, is illustrated by the comparison of the highly regulated charter schools with the national sample.

Furthermore, we believe it is critical to pursue additional qualitative research that probes the question of to whom board members see themselves as accountable, why, for what and with what consequences. And we need research that is structured to identify specific roles and processes – upward, outward and inward – and then examines whether, how and by whom these roles and processes are being carried out.

Recent years have witnessed ever-growing calls for nonprofits to be more "accountable." Most often those calls are related to upward accountability, and we believe it is important to understand how nonprofits do carry out those roles. But we look to nonprofits to do more than be formally accountable and to boards to hold the organization accountable for more than just behaving in a fiscally prudent and legal fashion. Focusing on accountability environments and how boards – and others in the organization – perceive and respond to these environments will lead to a richer understanding not only of boards but also of how nonprofits today are engaging with the larger society.

Acknowledgments

Previous versions of this chapter were presented at the EMES conference, Liège, Belgium, 1–4 July 2013, and the ARNOVA Annual Conference, 21–23 November 2013, Hartford, Connecticut.

Notes

1 The following findings are drawn from Ostrower 2007.
2 "Fundraising" broadly does not neatly fall within the upward or outward category alone. On the one hand, "fundraising" may be indicative of reliance on funders that brings with it accountability demands to them (upward). On the other hand, "fundraising" may also be indicative of the activity of reaching out to a broad range of external constituents for support (outward). In the future, we hope to include more refined indicators that can better capture and distinguish between fundraising as an outwardly focused activity from potential upward accountability requirements resulting from fundraising.
3 Based on Stone, Zhao and Cureton (2012).
4 For details, please see Stone, Zhao and Cureton (2012).
5 See note 2, however, regarding the outward and upward elements potentially comprised by "fundraising" that call for more refined refined measures to distinguish them in the future.

References

Aldrich, H. and Herker, D. 1977. "Boundary spanning roles and organizational structure," *Academy of Management Review*, 2(2), 217–230.
Benjamin, L. 2008. "How accountability requirements shape nonprofit practice," *Nonprofit and Voluntary Sector Quarterly*, 37(2), 201–223.

Billis, D. 2010. "From welfare bureaucracies to welfare hybrids," in D. Billis (ed.) *Hybrid Organizations and the Third Sector*. London: Palgrave Macmillan, 3–24.

Bovens, M., Schillemans, T. and Hart, P. 2008. "Does public accountability work? An assessment tool." *Public Administration*, 86(1), 225–242.

Brakman Reiser, D. 2013. "Regulating social enterprise," http://web.law.columbia.edu/ sites/default/files/microsites/attorneys-general/Dana%20Brackman-Reiser%20-%20 Columbia%20draft%20for%20March%20submission.pdf.

Brody, E. 2002. "Accountability and public trust," in L. Salamon (ed.) *The State of Nonprofit America*. Washington, DC: Brookings Institution Press, 471–498.

Daft, R. 1998. *Essentials of Organization Theory and Design*. Cincinnati, OH: Southwestern College Publishing.

Ebrahim, A. 2010. "The many faces of nonprofit accountability," in D. Renz (ed.) *The Jossey-Bass Handbook of Nonprofit Leadership and Management*, 3rd edition. San Francisco: Jossey-Bass, 101–121.

Finnigan, K. S. 2007. "Charter school autonomy: The mismatch between theory and practice," *Educational Policy*, 21(3), 503–526.

Fishman, J. 2010. "Stealth pre-emption: The IRS's nonprofit corporate governance initiative," *Virginia Tax Review*, 29, 545–591.

Gugerty, M. K. and Prakash, A. 2010. "Voluntary regulation of NGOs and nonprofits: An introduction to the club framework," in M. K. Gugerty and A. Prakash (eds) *Voluntary Regulation of NGOs and Nonprofits: An Accountability Club Framework*. New York: Cambridge University Press, 3–38.

Guo, C. 2007. "When government becomes the principal philanthropist: The effects of public funding on patterns of nonprofit governance," *Public Administration Review* 67, 458–473.

Jeavons, T. 2010. "Ethical nonprofit management: Core values and key practices," in D. Renz (ed.) *The Jossey-Bass Handbook of Nonprofit Leadership and Management*, 3rd edition. San Francisco: Jossey-Bass, 178–205.

Kearns, K. 1996. *Managing for Accountability: Preserving the Public Trust in Public and Nonprofit Organizations*. San Francisco: Jossey-Bass.

Kochan, T. A. 1975. "Determinants of the power of boundary units in an interorganizational bargaining relation," *Administrative Science Quarterly*, 20, 434–452.

Manno, B. V., Finn, C. E. Jr. and Vanourek, G. 2000. "Charter school accountability: Problems and Prospects," *Educational Policy*, 14(4), 473–493.

Middleton, M. 1987. "Nonprofit boards of directors: Beyond the governance function," in W. W. Powell (ed.) *The Nonprofit Sector: A Research Handbook*. New Haven, CT: Yale University Press, 141–153.

Morrison, J. B. and Salipante, P. 2007. "Governance for broadened accountability: Blending deliberate and emerging strategies," *Nonprofit and Voluntary Sector Quarterly*, 36(2), 195–217.

Ostrower, F. 2007. *Nonprofit Governance in the United States: Findings on Performance and Accountability from the First National Representative Study*. Washington, DC: The Urban Institute, Center on Nonprofits and Philanthropy.

Ostrower, F. 2014. *Boards as an Accountability Mechanism*. Washington, DC: The Urban Institute.

Ostrower, F. and Bobowick, M. 2006. *Nonprofit Governance and the Sarbanes–Oxley Act*. Washington, DC: The Urban Institute.

Ostrower, F. and Stone, M.M. 2006. "Governance research trends, gaps, and future prospects," in W. W. Powell and R. Steinberg (eds) *The Nonprofit Sector: A Research Handbook*, 2nd edition. New Haven, CT: Yale University Press, 612–628.

Ostrower, F. and Stone, M. M. 2010. "Moving governance research forward: A contingency-based framework and data application," *Nonprofit and Voluntary Sector Quarterly*, 39, 901–924.

Pfeffer, J. and Salancik, G. 1978. *The External Control of Organizations*. New York: Harper and Row.

Ratcliff, R., Gallagher, M. and Ratcliff, K. 1979. "The civic involvement of bankers: An Analysis of the influence of economic power and social prominence in the command of civic policy positions," *Social Problems*, 26, 298–313.

Salzman, H. and Domhoff, G. W. (1983). "Nonprofit organizations and the corporate community," *Social Science History*, 7, 205–216.

Schillemans, T. 2008. "Accountability in the shadow of hierarchy: The horizontal accountability of agencies," *Public Organization Review*, 8, 175–194.

Scott, W. R. and Davis, G. F. 2007. *Organizations and Organizing: Rational, Natural and Open System Perspectives*. Upper Saddle River, NJ: Pearson Prentice Hall.

Shober, A. F., Manna, P. and Witte, J. F. 2006. "Flexibility meets accountability: State charter school laws and their influence on the formation of charter schools in the United States," *The Policy Studies Journal*, 34(4), 563–587.

Sidel, M. 2005. "Guardians guarding themselves: A comparative perspective on self-regulation." *Chicago-Kent Law Review*, 80, 803–835.

Smith, S. R. 2010. "Hybridization and nonprofit organizations: The governance challenge," *Policy and Society*, 29, 219–229.

Smith, S. R. and Lipsky, M. 1993. *Nonprofits for Hire*. Cambridge, MA: Harvard University Press.

Spekman, R. E. 1979. "Influence and information: An exploratory investigation of the boundary role person's basis of power," *Academy of Management Journal*, 22(1), 104–117.

Stone, M. M. and Ostrower, F. 2007. "Acting in the public interest? Another look at governance research in nonprofit organizations," *Nonprofit and Voluntary Sector Quarterly*, 36(3), 416–438.

Stone, M. M., Zhao Z. and Cureton, C. 2012. "Toward understanding governance in hybrid organizations: The case of Minnesota charter schools," paper presented at the 2012 ARNOVA Conference, Indianapolis, IN, 15–17 November.

Thompson, J. D. 1967. *Organizations in Action*. New York: McGraw-Hill Book Company.

Triplett, T. and Ostrower, F. 2007. "Sampling, weighting, and variance estimation for the 2005 Urban Institute National Survey of Nonprofit Governance." Appendix D in Ostrower, F. Appendices (Expanded Version, July 2007) to *Nonprofit Governance in the United States: Findings on Performance and Accountability from the first National Representative Study*. Washington, DC: Urban Institute.

5 Civil society organization accountability within governance networks

Christopher J. Koliba

Introduction

Across most of the network governance literature, civil society organizations (CSOs), often synonymous with nonprofit organizations, are acknowledged as critical actors within governance networks, working alongside public-sector and private-sector organizations to carry out policy functions within and across many policy domains. Although governance networks of various shapes and forms have existed since the dawn of modern civilization, appreciation of their existence has only recently emerged (Koliba, Meek and Zia, 2010). It should be noted that the rise of network studies in public administration coincides with the growth of, and interest in, nonprofit civil society organizations. With this rise of interest in networks, a deeper understanding of governance networks has evolved within the growing bodies of empirical studies and theoretical frameworks that have been undertaken by scholars from around the world. Greater understanding is needed of how the unique characteristics of nonprofit organizations contribute to a governance network's performance and accountability structures. Additionally, an explicit examination is needed of the role of nonprofit organizations in bringing accountability to and taking accountability from governance networks. This chapter addresses this need by: (1) defining the types of networks that CSO are engaged in and their roles within them; (2) clarifying the properties of CSOs internal governance mechanisms; and (3) discussing how the internal governance of a CSO impacts, and is impacted by, the externalized governance of the whole network, as well as the other governance mechanisms of their grantors/ contractors, partners or peers. The chapter begins by situating CSOs as critical agents operating within governance networks. An overview of governance network accountability regimes, introduced in previous published works of the author (Koliba, Meek and Zia, 2010; Koliba, Mills and Zia, 2011; Zia and Koliba, 2011; Mills and Koliba, 2013) follows. The place and purpose of nonprofit accountability within the hybridized democratic, market and administrative frames of network governance is examined. Implications for further research and theory development are drawn.

The networked context of governance and the nonprofit sector's role within it

As of 2014, a large volume of literature describing the networked properties of modern governance arrangements has emerged. A summary of this growing literature can be found in a number of stand-alone books (Agranoff, 2007; Agronoff and McGuire, 2003; Goldsmith and Eggers, 2004; Koliba *et al.*, 2010; Koppenjan and Klijn, 2004; Rhodes, 1997) and edited volumes (Gage and Mandell, 1990; Kickert, Klijn and Koppenjan, 1997; Sorensen and Torfing, 2008; Agranoff, Mandell and Keast, 2014). Although this literature applies any number of different modifiers to characterize these network configurations, the "governance" network as a unit of analysis has emerged as one of the more popular constructs to describe these kinds of multi-organizational networks. Governance networks persist within all policy domains (Baumgartner and Jones, 1993) and take on various policy functions (Boviard, 2005). The structures (Koliba *et al.*, 2010; Provan and Kenis, 2007), functions (Agranoff and McGuire, 2003; Bovaird, 2005; Milward and Provan, 2006), accountabilities (Mashaw, 2006; Koliba *et al.*, 2011) and performance (Kenis and Provan, 2009; Koliba, 2013; Turrini *et al.*, 2010) of governance networks has been widely discussed and evaluated. Drawing on a comprehensive synthesis of this literature, the following definition of a governance network is given. Governance networks are

> relatively stable patterns of coordinated action and resource exchanges; involving policy actors crossing different social scales; drawn from the public, private and/or nonprofit sectors and across geographic levels; who interact through a variety of competitive, command and control, cooperative, and negotiated arrangements; for purposes anchored in one or more facets of the policy stream.
>
> (Koliba *et al.*, 2010, p. 60)

Governance networks are structured by and through the use of certain types of policy tools, policy functions, and governance arrangements. Several "macro level" network arrangements may be classified. These macro level network arrangements are described in Table 5.1 as grant and contract networks, partnership networks, advocacy networks, intergovernmental networks and regulatory networks. We will discuss how CSOs play different roles across each type of network structure.

CSOs play integral roles in most types of networks identified in Table 5.1. Within a grant and contract network, nonprofits may play the role of grantee or contractor, following the lead of a government or private foundation granting or contracting entity. Drawing on the Provan and Kenis (2007) model of network governance, the granter or contractor serves as the "lead organization," dictating the terms of the contract. However, after the grant or contract is let, nonprofit agents may have a lot of freedom to execute the terms of the contract as they see fit. In some instances a CSO may play the role of granter, as in the cases when nonprofits are private or community foundations. Tangible examples of CSO

Table 5.1 Types of governance networks enabled by policy tools and functions

Network type	Dominant policy tools	Role of CSOs (nonprofits)	Notes
Grant and contract networks	Grants; purchase of service contracts; procurement contracts; vouchers; loan guarantees; government-backed insurance	Contracted agent; grant recipient	Contracts and grants are tools that structure the relationships occurring between governments or private foundations and contracted agents. As legally binding agreements, grants or contracts bind two parties together in a principal–agent relationship. In essence, the government or private foundation, as the presumed "lead organization," is said to exercise some measure of control over the contracted agent. However, once a contract or grant is let, control of operational functions shifts over to the contracted agent – resulting in a more balanced form of administrative authority.
Partnership networks	Contracts; sometimes grants	Partner	Partnership networks, sometimes referred to as "public–private partnerships" (PPPs), are strategic alliances between public, private and/or nonprofit sector entities in which risk is shared and power between the partnering entities is relatively distributed in nature. PPPs are typically formed to "increase the scale and visibility of program efforts, to increase support for projects, and to leverage capital to enhance feasibility, speed, or effectiveness" (O'Toole, 1997, p. 46). The distribution of resources and power will likely vary across PPPs of differing functions and actor compositions (Linder and Rosenau, 2000).

continued

Table 5.1 Continued

Advocacy networks	Public information; grants from private foundations	Peer	Sometimes referred to as "interest group coalitions," advocacy networks are comprised of networks of organized interest groups, advocacy organizations and collective interest groups. These coalitions engage in coordinated action to influence the framing of public problems, the design and selection of policies, or the evaluation of policy implementation. Interest group coalitions "are arguably the central method for aggregating the viewpoints of organized interests in … politics. They serve as institutional mediators reconciling potentially disparate policy positions, in effect 'predigesting' policy proposals before they are served to the legislature" (Hula, 1999, p. 7).
Intergovernmental networks	Virtually all policy tools are prevalent	Outside of network, by definition	Modern democratic governments are organized around the separation of powers and levels of interlocking geographic jurisdiction that can be understood in terms of network configurations (see Wright's models of inter-governmental relations, 2000).
Regulatory networks	Economic, social, environmental regulations; permitting	Rare instances of being a third party regulator	The traditional outlook on regulation places government regulators as principals over regulated agents. These traditional ties are grounded in the state's capacity to render coercive power to control the behaviors of regulated agents.

Source: adapted from Koliba et al., 2010.

roles within grant and contract networks may be found within the extensive literature examining the utilization of nonprofit service providers in the US healthcare and social service sectors (Romzek and Johnston, 2005) in which nonprofit health clinics, social service organizations and mental health service providers are contracted through Medicare and Medicaid to offer patient services.

Increasingly, CSOs are partnering with public- and private-sector organizations to form "public–private partnerships" (PPPs) (Linder and Rosenau, 2000). Partnership networks are pursued when member organizations can only achieve their objectives through partnering with others. These PPPs are likely to entail the development and execution of capital improvement projects (for instance, in building a new community arts center) or some coordinated action to achieve specific policy implementation projects (for instance, executing a coordinated plan to reduce hunger and homelessness in a region). In many instances, PPPs will be enacted through the pooling of resources. All partners in a partnership network will have some "skin in the game." Very often, these PPPs are predicated on the forging of partnership ties and governed through some kind of shared governance or network administrative organization (NAO) or network backbone structures (Provan and Kenis, 2007; Kania and Kramer, 2011). In some instances, these NAOs or backbone organizations are nonprofit organizations that exist to coordinate network activities (Kania and Kramer, 2011). Tangible examples of nonprofit roles in PPPs may be found in the extensive literature on community economic development initiatives (Agronoff and McGuire, 2003), in which nonprofit community development corporations play a lead role in leveraging resources.

CSOs will very likely play an integral role in advocacy networks. Advocacy networks exist to heighten awareness of public problems, promote certain policy solutions, or pressure elected officials to take action. The role of nonprofits in serving as mediating institutions that sustain civil society is well documented (Couto and Guthrie, 1999, Enjolras and Steen-Johnsen, 2014; Siever, 2014). Some forms of CSOs exist to represent aggregated interests, bringing a level of technical and professional capacity and amplifying the voice of the interest group to the political arena. With the ability to frame an interests-based mission, CSOs are often the most active entities within inter-organizational networks focused on advocating for specific interests. Those who have studied such advocacy coalitions have acknowledged that these networks have become a common strategy to amplify the voice of interest groups (Hulu, 1999). The advocacy coalition concept has been most extensively studied through those applying advocacy coalition network theory (Sabatier and Jenkins-Smith, 1993). Such advocacy coalitions have been observed to persist in environmental, health and social service arenas, but can, arguably, extend across virtually all policy domains. The notion that nonprofits act on behalf of "special interests" has been defined in the now classical application of interest group liberalism (Lowi, 1969). In these contexts, nonprofit organizations act as true "civil society organizations," through which interests are aggregated and power is concentrated into a class of professional staff members (Couto and Guthrie, 1999; Crensen and Ginsberg, 2002). While in the advocacy networks themselves, CSOs will engage other CSOs as peers working to advance shared advocacy goals and objectives. Good examples of CSO-directed advocacy coalitions include the international non-governmental organization networks involved in climate change mitigation and adaptation responses (Zia and Koliba, 2011) and the countless public advocacy campaigns facilitated by CSOs to ban the use of landmines and sustain the gun ownership rights of US citizens.

Although CSOs are excluded, by definition, from intergovernmental networks, and the role of CSOs in most regulation of commerce, industry and markets is relatively marginal, we note the overlapping potential of network forms here. For instance, intergovernmental networks operating at the level of policy design and coordination may create or link up to grant and contract networks to implement policies. Certain advocacy networks may combine with intergovernmental networks to influence new policy formation, as in the case of the classical "iron triangle" in which lobbyists engage with legislative staffers and legislators to impact the final outcomes of policy deliberations (Adams, 1981). Some regulatory networks may use grants and contracts to execute technical assistance to support the achievement of certain regulatory aims. This technical assistance function may be taken on by nonprofit organizations. Also, CSOs may play a role in "third party" certification, a practice common in environmental and agricultural regulation. Examples include the regional- or state-level nonprofit organization's role in certifying organic foods in the United States and the Rainforest Alliance's role in the certification of sustainably grown and harvested wood products.

In summary, this assessment suggests that the roles that CSOs play within governance networks are differentiated according to the type of macro network form the network takes on. CSOs may be leaders, contracted agents, funders, partners or peers in governance networks. Therefore, the impacts of governance networks on CSOs and, likewise, the impacts of individual CSOs on governance networks are varied and contextually-driven. The type of governance network in which a CSO operates will determine the CSO's relationship (bureaucratic or collaborative) to other network members. As nonprofit entities, CSOs will bring a certain measure of democratic and market accountabilities to networks as well. When considering the role of CSOs in governance networks, the internal governance of CSOs matters a great deal. This is the topic we turn to next.

CSO governance and why it matters

Scholars who have studied the nonprofit sector have noted that the mission of nonprofit organizations may be "member-serving" or "public-serving" (Salamon, 2001), tailored to serving the needs and interests of narrowly or broadly constructed clientele, consumers or publics. The breadth and depth of public interest embodied within a CSO should be manifested in its mission. The contribution of the nonprofit sector essentially lies in its capacity to develop mission-driven actions that serve to meet a specific need, fulfill a specific function or undertake specific services in relation to its member-serving or public-serving purpose.

Regardless of the narrowness or expansiveness of its public- or member-serving interests, CSOs have been said to act as a bridge, providing the "public sector with a point of access into communities where they can begin to generate bonds of trust with citizenry" (Alexander and Nank, 2009, p. 365). As has been discussed in other chapters of this volume (Chapter 9 by Sievers; Chapter 11 by Enjolras and Steen-Johnsen), CSOs contribute to civil society and "are important to our concepts of community and citizen empowerment because they represent the efforts of people to take collective action outside the umbrella of government" (Smith and Lipsky, 1993, p. 72). This is why the civil society that is created through the nonprofit sector is said to be the intermediary between the public and private sectors (Janoski, 1998). Essentially, the nonprofit sector focuses on those social needs not taken on by the public and private sectors and for this reason requires its performance standards to be much more differentiated and rooted to specific aims and missions.

Nonprofits serve as civil society "mediating organizations" when they

> produce, directly or through advocacy of social and political provision, new forms and larger amounts of social capital, including the economic base of human community; when they provide their members representation and participation in the sociopolitical organizations of neighborhood, community, state, and nation; and when they expand their members' sense of common bonds with others and thus increase trust, cooperation, and collaboration.
>
> (Couto and Guthrie, 1999, p. 68)

Thus, CSOs must bring a measure of democratic accountability to a governance network through the social capital they provide.

In surveying the depth and breadth of the nonprofit governance literature, Stone and Ostrower observe that there is "a widely held belief that governance in nonprofit organizations is the province of their boards of directors" (Stone and Ostrower, 2007, p. 418), a finding later echoed by Cornforth (2012). In the United States, the 2002 Sarbanes–Oxley Act has impacted nonprofits by focusing federal attention on nonprofit governance issues, shedding particular light on the role of nonprofit boards in carrying out their critical fiduciary responsibilities (Stone and Ostrower, 2007, p. 430). It has been observed that the greater the stress placed on fiduciary accountability over other governing responsibilities, the more nonprofit boards tend to micro-manage (p. 429). Despite the attention given to boards to date, "very few studies ... have asked whether and how board composition affects measures of organizational performance" (Stone and Ostrower, 2007, pp. 419–420). Furthermore, "external factors, such as variations in funding environments, may significantly influence board composition and what a board does" (2007, p. 421). Because of the mission-driven nature of nonprofits (by comparison to for-profit organizations), nonprofit board functionality and accountability cannot be adequately explained by one theory (Callen *et al.*, 2009, p. 103).

CSOs may also be influenced by external funders who articulate their own funding priorities, indirectly impacting mission and/or operation on a day-to-day basis. Therefore, as conduits through which collective interests coalesce, CSO's goals are also shaped through a process of "negotiated meaning" among those identified within each organization's mission and practices. Because CSOs "mediate between the interests of their constituents and public policy or the political process" (Couto and Guthrie, 1999, pp. 46–47), many other stakeholders may be implicated in their accountability structures, "including executive directors, staff, volunteers, donors, and beneficiaries," all of whom "are likely to influence organizational mission, major policies, executive director performance, and external relationships" (Stone and Ostrower, 2007, p. 418).

In sum, CSO governance is tied to the mission-driven activities of boards of directors and the staff over whom they have oversight, funders, beneficiaries and other stakeholders. CSOs also serve as mediating institutions through which collective interests are conveyed, social capital is built and civil society is established. This heterogeneous picture of nonprofit accountability carries over into a governance network setting.

Hybridized accountability within governance networks

The social model of public, private and nonprofit sectors is a widely adapted framework that provides for some comparative capacity to analyze sector features (Janoski, 1998). Public-sector organizations are the formal institutions of the state, spanning the legislative, executive and judicial branches of government. As sovereign entities, these institutions have contractual obligations to serve the interests of their citizenry. Governmental institutions are guided by public interests and public policy goals, while private-sector organizations are driven by market forces and the pursuit of profit as the dominant performance measure. Property rights, ownership and corporate board governance play critical roles in defining corporate governing structures. As noted, nonprofit organizations are driven by a social mission designed to represent interests, advocate positions, inform the public or deliver social services. Therefore, it is difficult to pin down "the" performance standard of the nonprofit sector because the performance standards of nonprofits are shaped, in large part, by the mission of organizations and the interpretation of these missions by nonprofit managers and their boards of directors (Stone and Ostrower, 2007).

Within a networked context, the governance and accountabilities of nonprofit organizations combine, commingle and/or compete with a wider array of accountabilities adhered to in the public and private sectors. Accountability is defined here as "the obligation to give an account of one's actions to someone else, often balanced by a responsibility of that other to seek an account" (Scott, 2006, p. 175). These obligations are structured and/or enforced through the adoption of explicit standards and implicit norms (Kearns, 1996) and a recognition of and responsiveness to particular individuals, groups or organizations (Mashaw, 2006).

Accountability structures require that actors be responsive and responsible to particular constituencies. The eight different accountability types (Koliba *et al.*, 2010) found in Table 5.2 may be understood in terms of the set of actors *to whom* accountability must be rendered. These actors, be they elected representatives, citizens or courts; owners, consumers or workers; or supervisors, professionals or collaborators, are placed in the position of judging the performance of the agents that are being held accountable. Those *to whom* account is rendered (the "accounter") will inevitably prioritize different combinations of goals, performance measures and other desired procedures and outcomes, placing value on and rendering judgment of performance differently. It is also imperative that those to whom accounts are rendered are capable of or interested in fulfilling their roles.

The hybridized accountability framework for discerning how accountability is structured within governance networks includes democratic, market and administrative accountability frames, through which nine accountability types emerge (Koliba *et al.*, 2010). The private–public distinctions that dominate the three-sector (public–private–nonprofit) model plays out as accountability trade-offs between democracy, markets and administrative authorities. Market accountability includes the roles of owners/shareholders, consumers and labor. Democratic accountability encompasses the roles of elected officials, citizens and aggregated citizen interests, and the legal system. A third pillar of accountability is composed of administrative accountabilities that may be found in governance networks: hierarchically arranged accountability found in bureaucratic arrangements, horizontally arranged accountabilities found in collaborative or partnership arrangements, and accountability that coincides with professional practice. Table 5.2 displays the range of accountability frames, types, and explicit and implicit standards found in governance networks. This framework has been applied to study the emergency management networks responding to Hurricane Katrina (Koliba *et al.*, 2011), international climate change governance (Zia and Koliba, 2011), and the Deepwell Horizon Oil Spill (Mills and Koliba, 2014).

Of the three accountability frames to be considered, it is the democratic accountability frame that is most predicated on the mission and actions of civil society organizations due to the extent to which a CSO provides some measure of "democratic anchorage" to a governance network. The depth and breadth of the democratic anchorage of a governance network is said to depend on the roles of elected officials and public administrators and the extent to which the existence of the network expands the capacity for citizens to access networks and to benefit from the outputs and outcomes of network activity (Sorensen and Torfing, 2005). In democratic systems, democratic accountability is rendered when both citizens and the representatives they elect serve as the actors *to whom* accountability must be rendered. The standards and norms used by citizens and elected officials to hold public bureaucracies accountable may be understood in terms of the laws and regulations passed by elected officials, the rights of citizens to exercise their voice, and the kind of norms often ascribed to deliberations about public policy (Stone, 2002). Of the three sectors, government is the most directly democratically accountable. The private sector is likely the least,

Table 5.2 Governance network accountability framework

Accountability frame	Accountability type	To whom is account rendered?	Explicit standards	Implicit norms
Democratic	Elected representative	Elected officials	Laws; statutes; regulations created	Representation of collective interests; policy goals
	Citizen	Citizens	Voting; maximum feasible participation; sunshine laws; deliberative forums	Deliberation; consensus; majority rule
	Legal	Courts; juries	Laws; statutes; contracts enforced	Precedence; reasonableness; due process; substantive rights
Market	Owner	Owners; shareholders	Profit	Efficiency
	Consumer	Consumers	Consumer law; product performance	Affordability; quality; satisfaction
	Labor	Labor	Labor contracts; labor laws	Shared power arrangements; informal negotiation
Administrative	Bureaucratic	Principals; supervisors; bosses	Performance measures; administrative procedures; organizational charts	Deference to positional authority; unity of command; span of control
	Professional	Experts; professionals	Codes of ethics; licensure; performance standards	Professional norms; expertise; competence
	Collaborative	Collaborators; peers; partners	Written agreements; decision-making procedures; negotiation regimes	Trust; reciprocity; durability of relationships

Source: adapted from Koliba *et al.*, 2010.

although firms may be responsive to citizen outcry, elected official pressures and certainly the court system. CSOs sit somewhere in the middle. If the mission of the CSO is public-serving, then perhaps it can be said to carry the weight of citizens or at least a group of citizen interests into a governance network. It is also presumed that the democratic anchorage of a governance network also impacts the accountability structures of CSOs.

CSOs and network accountability dynamics

The extent to which CSOs are democratically accountable hinges on the type of mission that they carry. If a CSO's mission is public-serving, then there will be citizen interests that place pressure on a nonprofit to perform to certain implicit standards. A member-serving nonprofit will have a narrower band of interests or beneficiaries to be accountable to. The unique status of a nonprofit vis-à-vis a state's taxation policies carries with it certain legal accountabilities (Bies, 2010). We have noted how nonprofit boards function as a sort of shared ownership accountability structure. However, they may also be recognized as pillars of democratic accountability and as the conduits between a nonprofit and the collective or member-driven interests that it serves and/or represents. Citizens and elected officials may sit on the boards of directors of nonprofit organizations, bringing a very tangible signal of accountability to the nonprofit.

The market accountability frame encompasses the role of owners or shareholders (in a publicly traded firm), consumers and labor. Owners of a private firm have the ultimate control over the actions of the firm. The decisions to retract or expand production or services are ultimately made by the owner of a firm or through the fiat of a board of directors. Private firms are most often in the business of selling goods and services to consumers, who directly hold firms accountable through their purchasing decisions. With the institution of collective bargaining rights, labor accountabilities are evident through contracts, grievance procedures and work stoppages.

The sensitivities of nonprofits to market accountabilities may be found in certain "member-serving" cooperative ownership arrangements in which members have a say through a member-elected board of directors. Some nonprofits offer services or provide public goods tailored to specific kinds of consumers. Their success may hinge on the extent to which consumers use their services or purchase their goods. Although nonprofit organizations are less likely to enter into collective bargaining agreements with labor (Cohen, 2013), the implicit norms of being accountable to nonprofit labor is certainly evident, particularly in the case of smaller nonprofits that depend on their smaller workforce to do more with fewer resources, calling on their norms, expectations and actions to shape accountability. It should also be noted that labor unions are, unto themselves, a form of CSO.

The administrative frame of this model draws on the classical distinctions between vertical and horizontal administrative authorities. Bureaucratic accountabilities are denoted by classical command and control, principal-agent ties involving a supervisor and subordinate relationship, as well as the contractor–contractee or grantor–grantee relationship. Much has been written about the relationship between networks and collaborative ties. Administratively, the importance of collaborative management has become increasingly acknowledged (Agranoff and McGuire, 2003; O'Leary and Bingham, 2009). For collaboration to be sustained, trust and durable relations are needed (Axelrod and Cohen, 1999). The norms that support trust, reputation and durability are a form of accountability. Lastly, professional accountability has long been understood as a critical feature of public-sector governance (Romzek and Dubnick, 1987). This follows in line with Smith and Lipsky's early observations (1993) regarding the growing professionalization of the nonprofit workforce. The implicit standards that are transferred between members of a profession are a critically important means of ensuring accountability.

The importance of managerial oversight, collaborative management tools, and the professionalization of the nonprofit field have all been studied (Smith and Lipsky, 1993; Gou and Acar, 2005). Some boards of directors also take on management functions and exert some level of bureaucratic control over nonprofits (Stone and Ostrower, 2007). Other boards may support shared governance arrangements and may stress collaboration over control. Board members may also bring some measure of professional accountability to the nonprofit by bringing their professional lens to governance matters. These are, essentially, the accountabilities that CSOs bring to a governance network.

At the level of the whole network, CSOs are administratively tied to other members of the network. They may be embedded within a contracted, bureaucratically controlled arrangement with a government funder, or a private or community foundation funder. A CSO can also enter into a formal memorandum of understanding or informal understandings between partners, as in the case of partnership or advocacy networks.

Because any given nonprofit organization is a node within a network of other nodes tied together through policy tools, resource-sharing arrangements and information streams, little is known regarding how the accountability of an individual node influences the whole network. Space precludes an extended look into this issue. However, *we would propose to say that the level of influence of the accountability structures of any single organization within a governance network lies in direct proportion to the level of power it exudes or the level of trust it encumbers* (Kettl, 1993; Mintzberg, 1983).

Although we may not be in a position to consider how a CSO influences a whole governance network, we may explore how a phenomenon called "sector blurring" occurs. It has been demonstrated that public funding of nonprofit organizations "substantially increases the likelihood that nonprofits will engage in participatory governance practices" (LeRoux, 2009, p. 513). Writing about the implications of government's increasing influence over nonprofit organizations within grant and contract agreements, Smith and Lipsky (1993) have identified the impacts of government funding upon nonprofit organizations. They discuss how government funding changes the scale of the nonprofit organization and increases administrative demands to remain in compliance, an observation later echoed by Cooper (2003). The pursuit or maintenance of government grants and contracts leads to a deeper involvement of CSOs in "regulation-writing, the legislative process, and government budgeting cycles." Smith and Lipsky were early to recognize that such involvement has increasingly "professionalized" the management of nonprofit organizations (1993, p. 90). Couto and Guthrie have concluded that "this development implies a shift of norms from those of the local community to those of the government agency providing funds" (Couto and Guthrie, 1999, p. 63).

We may view the impacts of this particular form of sector blurring as a matter of commingled accountability types. The bureaucratic accountability structures of government funders are imported into the nonprofit agents. Cooper observes that "The same political abilities that allow [CSOs] to be supportive also allow them to resist change and to fend off accountability efforts" (Cooper, 2003, p. 66). As Smith and Lipsky (1993) note, the commingling of accountability regimes between governments and nonprofits has led to greater professionalization of the nonprofit sector.

As public and nonprofit sectors blur, the representative interests of CSOs attempt, sometimes with great success, to influence regulation writing, the legislative process and the government budgeting cycle. As CSOs interface with governments in this way, either through their development of grant and contract networks, their involvement within advocacy networks or active engagement in partnership networks, they impact the accountability regimes of the government actors in their governance networks. As civil society organizations, nonprofit organizations vie to have their interests integrated into the democratic accountability structures of governments and can do so through their involvement in governance networks.

Writing about the history of nonprofits in the United States, Boris observes that

> Historically, nonprofits pioneered public programs that became government responsibilities when the demand grew beyond nonprofits' capacity to respond. These programs include primary education, kindergarten, disease control, and many more. People also created nonprofits because existing business or government services were not considered sufficient because they were inaccessible, costly, barebones, culturally or religiously inappropriate, ineffective, or not innovative.
>
> (Boris, 1999, p. 22)

Addressing the role of interest group politics on the actions of nonprofits, Wise notes that interest groups form nonprofits to influence the structures, decisions and actions of governments. Some types of interest groups may become

> intensely focused and well informed on the issues of structuring government agencies that affect their interests ... [they] are in a position to pressure [elected officials] who have strong incentives to do what such groups want.

> Bureaucratic structure emerges from the battle of interests with features determined by the powers, priorities, and strategies of the various designers.
>
> (Wise, 1994, p. 85)

Although the coalescence of interest group pressures on governments may be generated from professional, profit-seeking lobbying firms, we are particularly interested here on the impacts of organized interest groups operating through CSOs. In the United States, nonprofit think tanks, public information firms and coalitions of interested parties are having increasing power over electoral politics in the country. They do so because of the accountabilities they engender through the sheer power to mobilize voters or purchase accountabilities by influencing campaign finance patterns.

Turning to the blurring of lines between nonprofits and private corporations, the very legitimacy of nonprofit organizations is said to be threatened when they partner with corporations. Corporate sponsorship or funding of nonprofit enterprises has been controversial for many decades. Corporate sponsorship of academic research highlights one of the clearest examples of the challenges associated with private–nonprofit sector-blurring, with widespread concerns regarding the levels of influence that corporate sponsors may have on the validity and rigor of scientific research.

Especially risky to the perceived legitimacy of nonprofit organizations is the decision to engage in brand licensing, e.g., corporate branding of organizational materials; likewise, a corporate partner's use of a nonprofit's brand is especially damaging to perceived legitimacy (Herlin, 2013, p. 24). Meanwhile, hybridized nonprofit for-profit organizations are beginning to be formed, including L3Cs (low-profit limited liability companies) and benefit corporations, that blend profit-making with social entrepreneurship. Much more remains to be understood about the influence of businesses over nonprofits.

Conclusion

In this chapter we explored how CSO organizations bring their own mission-driven accountabilities into governance networks by asking: how is accountability structured for nonprofit organizations? We concluded that nonprofit accountability is predominantly carried out through the mission-driven activities of boards of directors and nonprofit staff, as well as through the direct accountability to funders and the indirect accountability to citizens and member-driven interest groups. We noted the heterogeneity of CSO mission statements and recognized that the particularities of CSO governance are highly context-driven.

Because CSOs' influence within governance networks is context-driven, we must ask: under what conditions does CSO accountability influence a whole governance network or particular nodes in the network? In turn, we need to ask: under what conditions does a governance network or the properties of individual nodes influence the accountabilities and ultimately the behaviors of nonprofits?

In our attempts to begin to answer some of these questions, several practical considerations come to mind. By considering how accountabilities flow within CSOs, out of CSOs and into CSOs, managers, policy-makers and other contributors to CSOs have a clearer opportunity to consider the costs and benefits of participating within a governance network. This situational awareness may in turn lead to better-informed decisions. These decisions may be highly consequential – such as deciding whether to submit a proposal for funding, whether to invest in a public–private partnership, or whether to collaborate with other CSOs to get something done. By examining how CSOs function within network contexts, CSO managers, board members and others may consider how power flows through their networks and use this knowledge to make strategic, tactical and operational decisions.

From a public policy perspective, much more needs to be understood about the consequences of sector blurring for accountability structures and performance. As the conscious design and utilization of networks evolves, it will be critical to understand the role that mission-driven nonprofit organizations play within them. The role of nonprofits as political activists and as representatives of citizens and interest groups needs to be considered, as does the long-term sustainability of nonprofit organizations. As the "third leg" of the network governance stool, the nonprofit sector needs to capitalize on its function as both a "gap filler" (fulfilling functions that neither governments nor markets can render) and as a key actor in the democratic anchorage of governance networks. There is a need to identify clear and compelling roles for CSOs within partnership, grant and contract and advocacy networks and to safeguard against exploitation of CSOs. From the public policy perspective, nonprofit organizations are already seen as critical pieces of public service infrastructure, allowing Western democracies to devolve services away from direct government delivery. The draw of devolution and privatization has been the notion that markets provide more efficient service delivery. However, CSOs operate outside of the direct forces of markets and are much more reliant on funding regimes, board member directives and other environmentally sensitive forces. These factors are both a boon and a bane to CSOs. That which makes CSOs appealing (their flexibility, their generally smaller scale and leaner operations, their connectivity to interest groups) also makes them vulnerable and, to a certain extent, beholden to powers concentrated in sovereign governments and market-driven actors.

Because of the vital role that CSOs play within governance networks that fulfill public needs, it is essential that the nonprofit sector as it is currently comprised (of mission-driven, public- and member-serving organizations) be preserved. Prone to economic downturns that tend to dry up funding sources (states with fewer resources; funders with depleted endowments; donors with smaller bank accounts), CSOs are both threatened and buoyed by the promise of participating within governance networks. In turn, CSOs bring an important measure of democratic anchorage to governance networks.

Safeguarding the health and vibrancy of CSOs will likely be accomplished through these organizations' use of collaboration and the mobilization of network ties to achieve their mission and secure resources to ensure their continued performance and success. As responsive network members, governments and business, as partners, principals and agents, may seek to obtain mutual benefits in step with CSOs, achieving success together through shared accountabilities.

References

Adams, G. (1981). *The iron triangle: The politics of defense contracting.* New York: Council on Economic Priorities.

Agranoff, R. (2007). *Managing within networks: Adding value to public organizations.* Washington, DC: Georgetown University Press.

Agranoff, R., and McGuire, M. (2003). *Collaborative public management: New strategies for local governments.* Washington, DC: Georgetown University Press.

Alexander, J., and Nank, R. (2009). Public-nonprofit partnership: Realizing the new public service. *Administration and Society*, 41(3), 364–386.

Agranoff, R., Mandell, M., and Keast, R. (eds) (2014) Advances in network governance. New York: Routledge.

Axelrod, R., and Cohen, M. (1999). *Harnessing complexity: Organizational implications of a scientific frontier.* New York: Free Press.

Baumgartner, F. R., and Jones, B. D. (1993). *Agendas and instability in American politics.* Chicago and London: University of Chicago Press.

Bies, A. L. (2010). Evolution of nonprofit self-regulation in Europe. *Nonprofit and Voluntary Sector Quarterly*, 39(6), 1057–1086.

Boris, E. (1999). Nonprofit organizations in a democracy: Varied roles and responsibilities. In E. Boris and E. Steurle (eds), *Nonprofits and government: Collaboration and conflict.* Washington, DC: The Urban Institute Press, 2–29.

Bovaird, T. (2005). Public governance: Balancing stakeholder power in a network society. *International Review of Administrative Sciences*, 71(2), 217–228.

Callen, J. L., Klein, A., and Tinkelman, D. (2009). The contextual impact of nonprofit board composition and structure on organizational performance: Agency and resource dependence perspectives. *Voluntas*, 21, 101–125.

Cohen, R. (2013). Unions and the nonprofit workforce: A few considerations. *Nonprofit Quarterly*, 8(8). Accessed 15 March 2014: https://nonprofitquarterly.org/policysocial-context/22724-unions-and-the-nonprofit-workforce-a-few-considerations.html.

Cooper, P. (2003). *Governing by contract: Challenges and opportunities for public managers.* Washington, DC: CQ Press.

Cornforth, C. (2012). Nonprofit governance research: Limitations of the focus on boards and suggestions for new directions. *Nonprofit and Voluntary Sector Quarterly*, 41(6), 1116–1135.

Couto, R., and Guthrie, C. S. (1999). *Making democracy work better: Mediating structures, social capital, and the democratic prospect.* Chapel Hill, NC: University of North Carolina Press.

Crenson, M. A., and Ginsberg, B. (2002). *Downsizing democracy: How America sidelined its citizens and privatized its public.* Baltimore: Johns Hopkins University Press.

Gage, R. W., and Mandell, M. P. (eds) (1990). *Strategies for managing intergovernmental policies and networks.* New York: Praeger.

Goldsmith, S., and Eggers, W. (2004). *Governing by network.* Washington, DC: Brookings.

Guo, C., and Acar, M. (2005). Understanding collaboration among nonprofit organizations: Combining resource dependency, institutional, and network perspectives. *Nonprofit and Voluntary Sector Quarterly*, 34(3), 340–361.

Herlin, H. (2013). Better safe than sorry: Legitimacy and cross-sector partnerships. *Business and Society*, 1–37. Accessed 12 February 2014: http://bas.sagepub.com/content/early/2013/01/11/0007650312472609.

Hula, K. W. (1999). *Lobbying together: Interest group coalitions in legislative politics*. Washington, DC: Georgetown University Press.

Janoski, T. (1998). *Citizenship and civil society: A framework of rights and obligations in liberal, traditional, and social democratic regimes*. Cambridge: Cambridge University Press.

Kania, J., and Kramer, M. (2011). Collective impact. *Stanford Social Innovation Review*, Winter: 36–41.

Kearns, K. (1996). *Managing for accountability: Preserving the public trust in public and nonprofit organizations*. San Francisco: Jossey-Bass.

Kenis, P., and Provan, K. (2009). Toward an exogenous theory of public network performance. *Public Administration*, 87(3), 440–456.

Kettl, D. F. (1993). *Sharing power: Public governance and private markets*. Washington, DC: Brookings Institution Press.

Kickert, W. J. M., Klijn, E.-H., and Koppenjan, J. F. M. (eds) (1997). *Managing complex networks: Strategies for the public sector*. London: Sage.

Koliba, C. (2013). Governance network performance: A complex adaptive systems approach. In B. Agranoff, M. Mandell and R. Keast (eds), *Advances in network governance*. New York: Routledge, 84–102.

Koliba, C., Meek, J., and Zia, A. (2010). *Governance networks in public administration and public policy*. Boca Raton, FL: CRC Press/Taylor and Francis.

Koliba, C., Mills, R., and Zia, A. (2011). Accountability in governance networks: Implications drawn from studies of response and recovery efforts following Hurricane Katrina. *Public Administration Review*, 71(2), 210–220.

Koppenjan, J., and Klijn, E. H. (2004). *Managing Uncertainties in Networks*. London: Routledge.

LeRoux, K. (2009). Paternalistic or participatory governance? Examining opportunities for client participation in nonprofit social service organizations. *Public Administration Review*, May/June, 504–517.

Linder, S. H., and Rosenau, P. V. (2000). *Mapping the terrain of the public–private policy partnership*. Cambridge, MA: MIT Press.

Lowi, T. (1969). *The end of liberalism: Ideology, policy, ad the crisis of public authority*. New York: W.W. Norton and Company.

Mashaw, J. L. (2006). Accountability and institutional design: Some thoughts on the grammar of governance. In M. W. Dowdle (ed.), *Public accountability, designs, dilemmas and experiences*. Cambridge: Cambridge University Press.

Mills, R. and Koliba, C. (2014). The challenge of accountability in complex regulatory networks: The case of the deepwater horizon oil spill. Regulation & Governance. doi:10.1111/rego.12062.

Milward, H., and Provan, K. (2006). *A manager's guide to choosing and using collaborative networks*. IBM Center for the Business of Government.

Mintzberg, H. (1983). *Power in and around organizations*. Englewood Cliffs, NJ: Prentice-Hall.

O'Leary, R., and Bingham, L. (2009). *The collaborative public manager: New ideas for the twenty-first century*. Washington, DC: Georgetown University Press.

O'Toole, J. L. (1997). The implications for democracy in a networked bureaucratic world. *Journal of Public Administration Research and Theory*, 7(3), 443–459.

Provan, K. G., and Kenis, P. (2007). Modes of network governance: Structure, management, and effectiveness. *Journal of Public Administration Research and Theory*, 18, 229–252.

Rhodes, R. (1997). *Understanding governance: Policy networks, governance, reflexivity, and accountability*. Buckingham, UK: Open University Press.

Romzek, B., and Dubnick, M. (1987). *Accountability in the public sector: Lessons from the Challenger tragedy*. Boulder, CO: Westview Press.

Romzek, B., and Johnston, J. M. (2005). State social service contracting: Exploring determinants of effective contract accountability. *Public Administration Review*, 65(4), 436–449.

Sabatier, P. A., and Jenkins-Smith, H. C. (1993). *The advocacy coalition framework: An assessment*. Boulder, CO: Westview Press.

Salamon, L. A. (2001). Scope and structure: The anatomy of America's nonprofit sector. In J. S. Ott (ed.) *The nature of the nonprofit sector*. Boulder, CO: Westview Press, 23–39.

Scott, C. (2006). Spontaneous accountability. In M. W. Dowdle (ed.), *Public accountability, designs, dilemmas and experiences*. Cambridge: Cambridge University Press.

Smith, S. R., and Lipsky, M. (1993). *Nonprofits for hire: The welfare state in the age of contracting*. Cambridge, MA: Harvard University Press.

Sorensen, E., and Torfing, J. (2005). The democratic anchorage of governance networks. *Scandinavian Political Studies*, 28(3), 195–218.

Sorensen, E., and Torfing, J. (eds) (2008). *Theories of democratic network governance*. New York: Palgrave Macmillan.

Stone, D. (2002). *Policy paradox: The art of political decision making*. New York: Norton.

Stone, M. M., and Ostrower, F. (2007). Acting in the public interest? Another look at research on nonprofit governance. *Nonprofit and Voluntary Sector Quarterly*, 36(3), 416–438.

Turnbull, S. (1997). Corporate governance: Its scope, concerns and theories. *Corporate Governance: An International Review*, 5(4), 180–205.

Turrini, A., Cristofoli, D., Frosini, F., and Nasi, G. (2010). Networking literature about determinants of network effectiveness. *Public Administration*, 88(2), 528–550.

Wise, C. (1994). The public service configuration problem: Designing public organizations in a pluralistic public service. In A. Farazmand (ed.) *Modern Organizations*. Westport, CT: Praeger, 81–101.

Wright, D. S. (2000). *Models of national, state, and local relationships*. Washington, DC: CQ Press.

Zia, A., and Koliba, C. (2011). Climate change governance and accountability: Dilemmas of performance management in complex governance networks. *Journal of Comparative Policy Analysis*, 13(5), 479–497.

6 Multi-stakeholder governance in civil society organizations

Models and outcomes

Carlo Borzaga and Sara Depedri

Introduction

From the 1980s onwards in most European countries, problems with welfare service supply have opened a space for new actors to address emerging and unsatisfied needs. Many new civil society organizations (CSOs) have been created with the aim of providing welfare services not supplied by other actors. Due to the collective interest in welfare services and their social impact, CSOs by nature tend to actively involve people with diverse roles – such as users, financers, workers, and volunteers – in their strategic plans. Within these new CSOs, citizens with diverse needs, positions and roles in society contribute directly to the management of the organization and to the decision-making process. Since no particular interests must dominate, greater stakeholder participation is required in order to represent the diverse interests of the community.

As a consequence, the governance[1] of the most innovative of these organizations often diverges from the tradition of both for-profit and nonprofit firms. Unlike traditional nonprofits, in many CSOs – which often assume the legal form of social cooperatives or associations or other types of social enterprises – diverse member categories actively participate in the control of the organization. In other words, CSOs often assume a multi-stakeholder governance. The direct involvement in the decision-making process particularly occurs in organizations with a clear productive role[2] that are commonly defined as *social enterprises*.

This chapter devotes its attention to the governance models of these new CSOs since they provide an example of how citizens can coordinate and manage a common action in order to address social needs through providing welfare services. More specifically, this chapter focuses on the case of Italian social cooperatives.[3] These organizations emerged during the 1980s as bottom-up CSOs. Groups of citizens organized themselves for the production of welfare services (e.g., education, healthcare, social services, etc.) or for the work integration of disadvantaged people and chose the cooperative form, which in Italy is recognized by the constitution as having a social aim and being partially limited in profit distribution.[4] However, as opposed to traditional cooperatives, social cooperatives can autonomously decide how many and which types of stakeholder categories shall be involved in their governance. In other words, governance can be assigned to representatives of different classes of stakeholders (volunteers, users, workers, representatives of local institutions, financers, donors, etc.) or to a single class of stakeholders. Social cooperatives can therefore choose to assume the form of single- or multi-stakeholder organizations.

The emerging questions are the following: is multi-stakeholder governance really a new model of governance that can be sustainable in the long run, or is it simply a phase of an evolutionary process that will lead to a more traditional form of governance? And more specifically, do multi-stakeholder CSOs have real competitive advantages in the production of social services compared to single-stakeholder CSOs, or rather does multi-stakeholder governance increase the transaction costs of the decision-making process without providing any advantage?

After a brief description of the various ways of establishing multi-stakeholder governance processes and a theoretical analysis of the strengths and weaknesses of multi-stakeholder governances, this chapter presents an exploratory investigation of 320 Italian social cooperatives, about half of which are multi-stakeholder organizations. The empirical investigation aims to offer a better comprehension of the phenomenon of multi-stakeholder CSOs by comparing some of their characteristics with single-stakeholder CSOs. The analysis will specifically verify the hypothesis (introduced by Borzaga and Mittone, 1997) that CSOs incorporating a plurality of agents in their memberships and boards can serve as efficient devices for solving some of the problems that characterize the provision of welfare services. As those authors claim, multiple stakeholders' involvement could also be an efficient enforcement of the nonprofit distribution constraint, which can be bypassed in different ways.[5]

Defining multi-stakeholder organizations

All organizations are per se multi-stakeholder organizations in the sense that they involve many stakeholder categories: shareholders, users, workers, suppliers, and sometimes the local community – all with different needs. Organizations significantly diverge, however, in the level of involvement of their stakeholders in the decision-making process. In for-profit corporations the power lies typically in the hands of the shareholders, who aim at maximizing their individual benefits (i.e., the value of their shares and/or annual profit), while other stakeholders' interests do not easily infiltrate the organizational aims and the decisions undertaken by the owners of the organization. In cooperative firms the prevailing interests are those expressed by a unique stakeholder category other than shareholders; with few exceptions, cooperatives are not asked to take into account the interest of the other stakeholders. By contrast, the main aim of CSOs is to satisfy the interests of disadvantaged groups or the community in a broad sense; therefore they tend to maximize not the value granted to a single-stakeholder category but the value produced, inclusive of the part benefiting the most disadvantaged (Bacchiega and Borzaga, 2001) as well as positive externalities (Santos, 2012). A way that different interests can be taken into account is the involvement of diverse stakeholders in the governance and management of the organization.

As shown in recent literature (e.g., Vézina and Girard, 2014) the development of multi-stakeholder organizations is spreading in many countries. The idea likely began to take root as cooperative firms enlarged their missions from pursuing members' interests to devoting attention to the social impact of their activity and to the wellbeing of the community. Among the most noteworthy examples are Italian social cooperatives, the solidarity coops in Quebec and the Sociétés Coopératives d'Intérêt Collectif in France. These organizations have the common trait of being productive organizations whose membership involves different stakeholder categories. However, while the French and the Canadian laws stipulate that these organizations must involve multiple-stakeholder classes in their memberships (two categories in Quebec, three in France) the Italian law does not oblige social cooperatives to be multi-stakeholder organizations; it simply allows them to involve more than one category of members.

In general, in CSOs the level of involvement of diverse stakeholder categories can diverge from firm to firm, depending on two variables: (1) the categories of stakeholders that can be members and (2) the way and the level in which stakeholders – members and non-members – are involved. With respect to stakeholder categories, these organizations can have users, workers, producers, volunteers, etc. as members, but can also include financing members or other legal entities interested in supporting the organization. Depending on the law, CSOs can choose among different options for stakeholder involvement:

1   *multi-stakeholder ownership*, which provides for the involvement of various types of stakeholders as members of the CSO: in this case, representatives of different interests support the constitution of the organization and its activity and actively participate in the general assembly;
2   *multi-stakeholder governance*, which is implemented when various types of stakeholders are members of the board of directors; in this case, citizens with different roles effectively influence (and are part of) the decision-making process;
3   *other involvement strategies*, when CSOs consider the interest of some stakeholder categories by involving them not in the ownership or governance, but in some other decision-making processes; CSOs also implement other involvement strategies when they join networks with other organizations in order to find collaborative solutions to a common social problem.

Therefore, stakeholder involvement can transpire both in direct participation in the governance and management of the organization and in participation in networks that pursue community interests.

The relevance of participation and stakeholder involvement

Neither the efficiency nor effectiveness of multi-stakeholder governances has been tested yet. One of the main studies on involvement in CSOs is that by Ostrower and Stone (2006), who stress the effectiveness of governance structures characterized by democracy, high levels of stakeholder involvement, transparency in communication of organizational missions, and efficient management of relationships with the diverse stakeholders. Meanwhile, the authors observe that the existing empirical literature does not embrace a broader view of governance as a process engaging multiple actors and taking place at multiple levels (Stone and Ostrower, 2007).

One way to attempt to identify the various advantages and limits of multi-stakeholder governance in providing social and community services is to consider and integrate three different theoretical approaches: neo-institutional, behavioral and evolutionary economics.

The advantages of diverse governance structures in an integrated approach

From a neo-institutional perspective, the involvement of diverse stakeholders in the decision-making process can be justified if it helps to (1) minimize the sum of contractual and governance costs (Hansmann, 1980) and (2) reduce asymmetric information, which makes it difficult both for users to evaluate the quality of services provided and for the organization to collect complete information on the real demand for services. The inclusion of users as members therefore relaxes the contraposition of the two parties' interests and solves asymmetries by allowing users to directly monitor the service and to express their real preferences, needs and willingness to pay for service provision.

Although less considered by this literature, informational asymmetries also impact the relationships between employees and the organization. Since work in the social services sector is characterized by multi-tasking activities and the centrality of relationships with users, employee effort and performance are difficult to monitor since employees could behave opportunistically by exerting low effort and decreasing attention to users. Economic incentives (e.g., wages, bonuses and surpluses) rarely support employee performance and effort, while consistency between organizational mission and intrinsic motivations is a much stronger stimulus for employee performance. Hence the involvement of employees in the membership and decision-making process can enhance reciprocal control as well as their knowledge of organizational aims by decreasing inefficiency and transaction costs related to opportunistic behaviors (e.g., Borzaga and Depedri, 2009).

The behavioral approach helps to better understand the advantages of multi-stakeholder governance since it relates the participation in the decision-making process by different stakeholder categories to the emergence and the persistence of non-self-interested behaviors such as cooperation, involvement and value sharing. Multi-stakeholder governance enforces people's empowerment and helps to replace the logic of profit and value capture (which characterize for-profit or business firms) with the logic of value creation (Santos, 2012). In fact, these aims need to be supported by empowering citizens, beneficiaries and other stakeholders to become an integral part of the organization and its decision-making process. When members perceive themselves as part of the decision-making process, they develop a sense of self-esteem and self-activation, which means that they are more eager to engage in activities not explicitly required by contract (since this involvement provides a source of wellbeing and sense of morality). Due to this involvement, members self-coordinate to achieve common goals instead of pursuing individual aims; the result is a cooperative game that produces a higher level of social welfare.[6]

Furthermore, as the emergence of cooperation requires, multi-stakeholder governance can increase trust and reputation within society and among stakeholders. CSOs exchange with their stakeholders under the logic of trustworthy relationships and reciprocity instead of competition and market dynamics. Therefore, they rely on transparency of communication instead of informational asymmetry and empowerment instead of control. At the same time, trustworthiness and reputation developed among stakeholders and in the community as a whole ensure better outcomes. Since the nonprofit distribution constraint alone is often not enough to convince people to believe in the organizational aim (Borzaga and Mittone, 1997), the direct involvement of diverse stakeholder categories in the membership helps to increase trust. This enables the organization to gather more human and financial resources: citizens' trust that donations are spent to achieve social aims increases; volunteers devote more in terms of time and effort; other enterprises involved in the membership or in the network may offer financial support and may share knowledge and services. These additional resources may underwrite part of the production cost, thereby producing more or better services or reducing costs and thus enabling CSOs to offer some free or below-cost services.

From a different perspective, drawing on the evolutionary approach, it must also be considered that organizations evolve thanks to the development of knowledge and problem-solving abilities. The diffusion of information and knowledge among all or many stakeholders helps to develop new ideas and the sharing of values. Cooperation among groups with different abilities and knowledge helps to improve the performance of the enterprise and enhance problem solving. Since people have different needs, but also different perceptions of problems, innovation is therefore more frequent. CSOs especially tend to be more innovative than public bodies providing the same services, and this is often explained by the active participation of the diverse groups of people involved.

In order to completely understand the advantages theoretically generated by multi-stakeholder governance, two other aspects must also be considered: (1) the production of externalities, especially in terms of social capital, and (2) the ability to increase people's wellbeing, especially that of marginalized classes. With regard to social capital, it has been demonstrated that organizations that involve only one class of stakeholders tend to mainly develop "bonding social capital" by increasing the will of people to share a unique common goal (Putnam, 1993). Organizations which instead involve a heterogeneous group of stakeholders tend to develop "bridging social capital" by sharing the ideals and aims of people with diverse individual goals.

Some limits of multi-stakeholder governance

Notwithstanding the described advantages, multi-stakeholder governance may generate a number of costs. First, multi-stakeholder governance can create difficulties in the alignment of the interests of the firm with managerial policies (as seen in the approach to stakeholder societies examined by Tirole, 2001); additionally, the multiple interests of members cannot always be internalized in the firm's organizational policies and mission. Second, the decision-making process is more complex when different interests come into play. Time and resources are required to align the interests of heterogeneous stakeholders. Third, coordination of stakeholders with diverse interests involves a magnification of the costs of information transmission and communication. Since diverse stakeholder groups control and collect information, they may speak different languages and have varying needs and visions; specific costs can emerge in reaching a clear and unique goal. Fourth, due to organizational complexity, rigid norms must be imposed to coordinate the various actors; these norms increase the complexity of bureaucratic procedures and time spent in defining and adhering to norms. Finally, some of the involved categories of stakeholders may lose part of their autonomy and identity because of their adaptation to the general mission of the organization.

Comparing single- and multi-stakeholder CSOs: the case of Italian social cooperatives

Given this compound theoretical foundation, empirical analyses are needed in order to test the strengths and weaknesses of multi-stakeholder governance in CSOs. Unfortunately, few investigations on CSOs provide information on governance. The recent investigation on social cooperatives in Italy presented in this chapter can contribute to filling this gap. The survey collected information on a sample of social cooperatives, including both those with single- and those with multi-stakeholder governances, therefore allowing an exploratory comparative analysis of the main traits of each. The analysis presented in the following pages cannot provide a full understanding of the advantages and limits of multi-stakeholder governance, since a full comprehension would require more information on specific transaction costs. However, it helps to answer some of the questions highlighted in the introduction.

Italian social cooperatives can be considered prototypical of CSOs with a productive nature. They are distinguished by law as type A, which provides healthcare, education and social services, and type B, which produces other goods and services by employing disadvantaged people. As already stated, the Italian law allows social cooperatives to autonomously decide the composition of both membership and the board of directors without a minimum threshold in terms of numbers and types of stakeholders.[7] The analysis presented here utilizes the ICSI2007 database, which includes data from a representative sample of 320 Italian social cooperatives, their managers, and 4,134 paid workers employed by the same organizations.[8] Most social cooperatives operate in the social service sector (71.8 percent), while the rest are engaged in the integration of vulnerable people.[9] Social cooperatives are present in all Italian provinces and the sample represents the distribution by macro-region (with 56 percent located in the north, 20 percent in the center and the 24 percent in the south of Italy). About 40 percent of the Italian social cooperatives in the sample were founded before their institutionalization in 1991, while 23 percent were founded immediately after (between 1991 and 1995) and 8 percent between 2000 and 2006. Most social cooperatives were founded by groups of citizens with common ideals (51 percent of cases) reenforcing characterization of social cooperatives as CSOs.

Ownership and governance

The ownership of social cooperatives can be identified by the composition of the membership. Data show that the average number of members of social cooperatives is 65, but the median is 27, with a high standard deviation that indicates the ability of some social cooperatives to attract very high numbers of members. Most members are workers (77 percent of the membership on average), while 57.5 percent of social cooperatives have volunteers in their membership (while a small percentage of them have non-member volunteers). Most type B social cooperatives (82 percent) involve disadvantaged workers in their membership, while users of type A social cooperatives are only rarely involved in the membership (9.4 percent). Only a few cooperatives include other organizations in their memberships and the formal involvement of public organizations is also limited.

The governance of social cooperatives overlaps with the ownership structure: usually those stakeholder categories represented in the membership are also involved in the board of directors. By cross-tabulating data on membership and the board of directors, social cooperatives can be grouped (see Table 6.1) by

Table 6.1 Governance structures

	No. of coops	*%*
Single-stakeholder governances	55	21.2
Partial multi-stakeholder governances	53	29.2
Full multi-stakeholder governances	129	49.6

Source: authors' elaboration on ICSI2007 data.

distinguishing: (1) *single-stakeholder governances*, where social cooperatives have only workers in both their membership and board of directors; these represent 21.2 percent of the sample of social cooperatives interviewed; (2) *full multi-stakeholder governances*, where social cooperatives involve several types of stakeholders in both the membership and board of directors; this group represents 49.6 percent of social cooperatives interviewed, the majority of which include only workers and volunteers, with only a few including more than two stakeholder categories; and (3) *partial multi-stakeholder governances*, where social cooperatives have a single-stakeholder board of directors and multi-stakeholder membership; they represent 29.2 percent of the total. This last category will be not specifically analyzed.

Several differences characterize the two groups of social cooperatives. Single-stakeholder social cooperatives are more likely to produce social services (type A social cooperatives) and are more prevalent in the south of Italy, where unemployment problems are more widespread. The size of social cooperatives is quite varied, with the single-stakeholder social cooperatives being bigger on average than the multi-stakeholder social cooperatives (total average revenues amounting to €2.5 million in single-stakeholder social cooperatives versus €1.8 million in multi-stakeholders ones).

Other involvement strategies

As already highlighted, users are not well-represented in the membership and are also rarely asked to participate in meetings where relevant decisions concerning management are taken; furthermore, 39.4 percent of social cooperatives claim to not to involve users or their families at all when defining strategies. The formal involvement of users is very low both in multi- (3.8 percent) and in single-stakeholder social cooperatives (4.3 percent).

Notwithstanding these findings, social cooperatives follow other channels to ensure high-quality services for their users. They devote particular attention to communication and tend to build positive relationships with their users. Moreover, social cooperatives exhibit a high level of interest in the quality of services produced. For example, 83 percent of social cooperatives declare that the quality of their services has increased in the three years before the investigation thanks to innovations in both products and processes. When organizations evaluate their ability to achieve internal goals, the quality of services and the relationships established with users prove to be the most highly rated aspects (with an average score of 8.2 on a scale from 1 to 10 for both of these variables), followed by communication and transmission of information outside and inside the organization (score of 7.1). These behaviors positively impact the reputation that social cooperatives claim to have among their users: social cooperatives evaluate their reputation at a level of 6 on a scale from 1 to 7 – higher than their reputation level with other stakeholders, including the local community and public organizations. Consequently, social cooperatives' relationships with users seem not to be compromised by users' low involvement in membership and this statement is confirmed for both single- and multi-stakeholder organizations.

Among other involvement strategies, multi- and single-stakeholder social cooperatives diverge in the type of organizations with which they collaborate in networks (see Table 6.2). Multi-stakeholder organizations are more frequently involved in consortia and other networks with other social cooperatives (76.3 percent and 72 percent respectively), reflecting cooperative behaviors among similar organizations. Single-stakeholder social cooperatives are more frequently involved in networks with public institutions and with other non-social coopera-tives. This data shows that organizations involving only workers in the member-ship tend to find in networks with diverse organizational forms a strategy for them to increase their links to the community. In other words, networking is employed as an imperfect substitute for multi-stakeholder governance in order to relate with the representatives of local interests.

The impact of governance structures on organizational activities

The involvement of diverse stakeholder categories in the membership influences the organizational mission, especially in the start-up phase and in the identifica-tion of the organizational role. The foundation of multi-stakeholder social coop-eratives is motivated mainly by the will to address unsatisfied needs of the local community, in areas where no other organization was providing the same or similar services. By contrast, single-stakeholder social cooperatives have more frequently been founded in regions where public bodies or other organizations were providing the same or similar service and there was less need to identify the demand, define the type of services to provide, find resources to establish the supply, etc. Multi-stakeholder governance therefore seems to emerge especially when groups of citizens have unsatisfied needs and cooperation contributes to addressing them. The diversity in stakeholders' involvement also has different consequences for the organization's aims. Single-stakeholder organizations more frequently aim at becoming integrated in the local community (70.4 percent), and this result confirms the need for single-stakeholder social cooperatives to

Table 6.2 Involvement of social cooperatives in networks

Networks with ...	Single-stakeholder governances	Partial multi-stakeholder governances	Full multi-stakeholder governances
Consortia	70.0	65.6	76.3
Other social cooperatives	73.2	70.7	72.0
Non-social cooperatives	15.2	20.1	4.8
Public institutions	93.3	81.1	76.9
For-profit enterprises	0.0	26.4	25.8
Foundations	6.3	15.4	20.2

Source: authors' elaboration on ICSI2007 data.

better relate to citizens in order to balance the lack of formal involvement; multistakeholder governances seem to be less interested in becoming integrated in the community and more interested in better gauging local demand in order to respond to local needs (82.4 percent) and to acquiring human and financial resources (74.4 percent).

The relation between governance structures and human resources

When looking at the relation with workers, two possible dynamics have been stressed in the literature. On the one hand, multi-stakeholder organizations should tend to overshadow the workers' interests in favour of the other stakeholders' interests; therefore, their employees should be less motivated and satisfied with their jobs and thus should exert less effort. On the other hand, employees in multistakeholder cooperatives should relate more to other stakeholders and should thus develop altruistic behaviors and share the social mission of the organization.

The analysis of the ICSI2007 data shows that there are no large differences between the two types of governance structures: in both single- and multi-stakeholder social cooperatives employees express high intrinsic motivation towards their jobs, perceive their organizations as fair and communicative, and are uniformly satisfied both with their jobs in general and with most of the intrinsic and extrinsic aspects of the jobs. The most important motivations for employees are the opportunity to help disadvantaged people and to develop good relationships on the job; the satisfaction with these aspects is very high in both types of organizations. Furthermore, incentives provided to employees in both single and multi-stakeholder organizations are quite similar, as average wages do not differ. Consequently, the results do not support either the hypothesis of prevailing self-interest behaviors of employees in the single-stakeholder social cooperatives or the inability of the multi-stakeholder social cooperatives to satisfy their employees' needs and support their motivation.

No differences in the behavior of employees in single- and in multi-stakeholder social cooperatives emerge when employees were asked to evaluate their effort on the job or that of colleagues in their organization both in general and by considering the level of effort that the organization or users require. For all employees, effort perceived was "in line with the effort required." Furthermore, the level of productivity per worker does not prove a lower level of efficiency or performance in multi-stakeholder social cooperatives in comparison to single-stakeholder social cooperatives. Average revenues per worker are significantly higher in multi-stakeholder social cooperatives than in single-stakeholder ones, although the value can be explained at least partially by the high proportion of volunteers in the multi-stakeholder social cooperatives and by differences in the services provided.[10]

Looking at other human resources, multi-stakeholder social cooperatives demonstrate a higher ability to attract volunteers: almost 90 percent of multi-stakeholder social cooperatives have volunteers (both members and non-members) in their work forces versus 27 percent of single-stakeholder social cooperatives (where volunteers are non-members). Moreover, multi-stakeholder firms have a significantly higher number of volunteers (17 on average versus 3). This result is consistent with the hypothesis that a higher and more formalized involvement of a plurality of stakeholders enhances the possibility of gathering resources and that the involvement of citizens (as volunteers) in the membership helps to ensure a stable relationship with the community.

Conclusion

This chapter has offered a preliminary analysis of the incidence and outcomes of the involvement of diverse stakeholder categories in the governance of Italian social cooperatives as examples of service-providing CSOs. The analysis specifically allows a preliminary test of the hypothesis that multi-stakeholder governance is a source of efficiency and effectiveness since it helps to decrease some informational asymmetries among parties, reduce opportunism, increase innovation, and enhance reputation within the local community. Although the investigation must be considered an exploratory analysis and further research is suggested, it already provides some answers to the questions proposed.

First, the comparison between multi-stakeholder and single-stakeholder governance models reveals that the former are quite widely distributed and that diverse stakeholders can really be involved in founding and managing social cooperatives by actively participating in the board of directors. The most involved categories are workers and volunteers, whereas the engagement of users is seen to be much less frequent, except in social cooperatives engaged in work integration.

Second, it can be claimed that the strategy of involving stakeholders is not particularly influential on the organizational mission. The social aim seems to be much more important in balancing the interests of both workers and users. Indeed, the single-stakeholder governance model does not jeopardize users' interests nor does the multi-stakeholder governance model sacrifice employees' wellbeing. Furthermore, looking to other involvement strategies, where the membership does not include all of the diverse stakeholder categories, organizations tend to network with other organizations in order to share information and create ties with the community.

Finally, the findings support the hypothesis that multi-stakeholder governances are efficient from various perspectives. The multi-stakeholder governance model seems to be more successful in collecting additional resources, such as volunteers and members who contribute financial resources. Employee effort is also very high. In that way, multi-stakeholder social cooperatives seem to be able to achieve better results at least in terms of: (1) satisfaction of unsatisfied needs, since they more frequently operate in areas where no other similar service is supplied; (2) production of social capital, since they seem to operate in communities characterized by a lack of other social organizations and offer citizens the sole opportunity to become involved in activities of general interest; and (3) higher attention to the quality of services and probably better economic performance.

The findings presented here confirm the validity of the advantages that are associated with stakeholders involvement according to both neo-institutional and behavioral theories. Contrary to what is claimed by neo-institutional theory, though this research does not find that the costs generated by the management of multi-stakeholder organizations are particularly high. However, governance models are not the sole factor influencing the performance of organizations and employee effort. Also important are the intrinsic motivations of workers, their consistency with the mission of the organization, and the types of services supplied. As well, further study is needed on the advantages of user involvement in terms of efficiency, service quality and social wellbeing.

Notes

1 Governance (or corporate governance) can be typically defined as an organization's control system (Hart, 1995).
2 In comparison to nonprofit organizations that are only devoted to advocacy, protection of poorer social classes, etc., productive CSOs aim to provide social services (such as healthcare services, education, social services, on-the-job training for the disadvantaged, etc.).
3 In Italy, social cooperatives represent the main type of social enterprise. While social cooperatives developed first in Italy and Italy was the first country to recognize them as a legal form, the model has since diffused in other countries by taking the same name. All these organizations are frequently studied in the literature as social enterprises or civil society organizations, depending on whether attention is focused on their social aims or their emergence as bottom-up organizations promoted by a group of citizens.
4 Social cooperatives are recognized by Law 381/1991.
5 According to Hansmann, the nonprofit distribution constraint is only a "crude consumer protection device" (1996, pp. 234–235).
6 The outcome achieved in cooperative games differs from the Nash equilibrium that typically emerges in the Prisoners' Dilemma or in the investment game when people are selfish and do not cooperate or trust the other party.
7 The only restriction provided by law consists of the maximum threshold imposed on the percentage of volunteers involved in the membership: social cooperatives are not allowed to have more than 50 percent of their members as volunteers in the organization. Furthermore, the board of directors can also include non-members of the cooperative, although these directors must be elected by the general assembly.
8 The questionnaires administered to workers, managers and organizations had different sections. For workers, they collected information regarding levels of wellbeing and attitudes toward the job. For the organization, it covered both quantitative data (people employed and turnover, financial data and progress of budget items, etc.) and qualitative data on self-esteem concerning organizational aims, policies, social responsibility and social capital development.
9 75 percent of type A social cooperatives produce assistance and educational services; 50 percent of type B work integration social cooperatives operate in environmental maintenance.
10 When volunteer working hours are also included in the denominator, the average revenue per worker nonetheless continues to be higher in multi- than in single-stakeholder cooperatives. The result is obviously an impure index of worker effort and efficiency, but data cannot support the hypothesis of a reduced effort by employees in multi-stakeholder organizations.

References

Bacchiega, A. and Borzaga, C. (2001). Social Enterprises as Incentive Structures: An Economic Analysis, in Borzaga, C. and Defourny, J. (eds) *The Emergence of Social Enterprise*. London: Routledge, pp. 273–295.

Borzaga, C. and Depedri, S. (2009). Working for Social Enterprises: Does it Make a Difference?, in Amin, A. (ed.) *Social Economy: International Perspectives on Economic Solidarity*. London: Zed Press, pp. 82–114.

Borzaga, C. and Mittone, L. (1997). The Multi-stakeholder versus the Nonprofit Organization. Trento: Department of Economics discussion papers 7.

Hansmann, H. (1980). The Role of Nonprofit Enterprise. *The Yale Law Journal*, 89(5), pp. 835–901.

Hansmann, H. (1996). The Changing Roles of Public, Private, and Nonprofit Enterprise in Education, Health Care, and Other Human Services, in Fuchs, V. R. (ed.) *Individual and Social Responsibility: Child Care, Education, Medical Care, and Long-Term Care in America*. Chicago: University of Chicago Press, pp. 245–276.

Hart, O. (1995). *Firms, Contracts and Financial Structure*. Oxford: Oxford University Press.

Ostrower, F. and Stone, M. M. (2006). Governance, Research Trends, Gaps and Future Prospects, in Powell, W. W. and Steinberg, R. (eds) *The Nonprofit Sector: A Research Handbook 2*. New Haven, CT: Yale University Press.

Putnam, R. (1993). *Making Democracy Work: Civic Traditions in Modern Italy*. Princeton: Princeton University Press.

Santos, F. M. (2012). A Positive Theory Of Social Entrepreneurship. *Journal of Business Ethics*, 111, pp. 335–351.

Stone, M. M. and Ostrower, F. (2007). Acting in the Public Interest? Another Look at Research on Nonprofit Governance. *Nonprofit and Voluntary Sector Quarterly*, 38(3), pp. 416–438.

Tirole, J. (2001). Corporate Governance. *Econometrica*, 69, pp. 1–35.

Vézina, M. and Girard, J. P. (2014). Multistakeholder Co-operatives as an Inspiration for the Co-operative Movement: A Comparative Perspective, in Gijselinckx, C. and Zhao, L. (eds) *Cooperative Innovations in China and in the West*. New York: Palgrave Macmillan, pp. 64–78.

7 Two sides of the governance coin

The missing civil society link

Filip Wijkström and Marta Reuter

Introduction

Civil society and its organizations are rapidly becoming more integrated into and relevant to our understanding of how society is being reorganized, in terms of both how society operates and how it is governed. At the same time, many of these organizations are becoming more complex and increasingly interwoven with other types of actors, in new and different ways. New or altered governance principles, practices, institutions and actors in society contribute to substantially re-negotiated social contracts in many countries and contexts, laying the foundations for new social architectures in fields where blurred institutional borders seem to be the rule rather than the exception. As a response to this development, the wealth of relevant, cutting-edge and interdisciplinary governance studies, research and literature where civil society organizations are included into the analysis is growing by the year (for salient examples see Djelic and Sahlin-Andersson, 2006; Graz and Nölke, 2008; Jönsson and Tallberg, 2010; Osborne, 2010; Hale and Held, 2011). Many of the new governance ideas and practices tend to move – invite, push, force, welcome, lure – civil society organizations further into the limelight.

The increased questioning of both state and market solutions as the dominant blueprints for governance in society "has stimulated a growing interest in the regulatory capacities of civil society" (Torfing, 2007, p. 1). Many earlier governance solutions or models – institutions and procedures – seem inadequate to solving or even addressing many contemporary and future challenges. In the words of Anheier (2013, p. 7):

> There are more and more issues of national, international and even global concern that seem difficult to address and resolve with the institutions, rules and players we know – or used to know. For even these familiar institutions, rules and players seem to change rapidly, and new ones multiply so fast it is hard to keep track of all the changes.

Civil society is increasingly being included in many of the new solutions brought forward. Civil society organizations have, in a variety of forms and in differing terminology, already become important in the analytical toolbox of governance scholars. As a consequence, we argue that the matter of governance will increasingly become a more urgent topic also for scholars of civil society (Stone and Ostrower, 2007; Steen-Johnson *et al.*, 2011; Maier and Meyer, 2011; Cornforth 2013; Renz and Andersson, 2013).

This situation calls for a clearer analytical conceptualization of the role and position of civil society organizations in basically all forms of governance, no matter in which policy field or part of the world. The situation further calls for a better understanding of how these organizations themselves are organized internally, i.e., how they are operated and governed (see, for example, Ostrower and Stone, 2006; Kumar and Roberts, 2010; Cornforth and Brown, 2013). Apart from those two different scholarly tasks we also need to bring these two analytical endeavors together to chisel out in which ways the huge variety of internal governance principles and practices existing in civil society affect the role, position and impact of these organizations in the wider – external – governance context.

The aim of the chapter

The aim of this chapter is twofold. First we seek to disentangle and conceptualize the analytical relationship between "civil society" and "governance." This is a tricky endeavour, not only because civil society itself is an elusive concept understood differently by different actors and in different contexts (Cornforth 2013), but also because governance has hitherto been theorized in at least two distinct ways within different social science disciplines. While for organization theorists or management scholars "governance" primarily means the internal management of an organization (usually a firm), for political scientists and international relations scholars it rather implies the regulation, organization and "management" of the wider society at the local, national or global level. As a consequence, the topic of civil society governance has primarily been studied either in terms of how civil society organizations are governed and managed internally, or in terms of when, how and why they contribute to the governance of society.

Here we propose an analytical model that links these two dimensions, thus stressing the interdependence between internal organizational governance and the governance of society. In particular, we seek to stress the importance of including the internal governance principles and practices found in civil society organizations – such as political parties and churches – in the analysis of the impact of civil society organizations in the wider, external governance of society.

Our second contribution concerns that very impact and its nature. Unlike those scholars who see the role of civil society organizations in societal governance as consisting primarily of their involvement in, or influence over, different kinds of policy-making processes, we highlight that on a more fundamental level, it is the organizations in civil society that – in a continuous normative struggle among themselves – shape and define the constitutive norms and rules of governance as such. These organizations thus not only take part in governance in their various fields, they are also the primary actors in society who provide the ideas and models that fundamentally define and redefine the very principles of governance – as for example in our understanding of democracy, the definition of a just society, or what constitutes a proper citizenship, all important in the general governance of society.

The importance of civil society organizations in governance thus lies not primarily in their roles as the champions of "good" or "noble" causes, which often seems to be the more common understanding; they are instead important in shaping our understanding of which values and causes are to be seen as "good," important and worthy of our support (Reuter *et al.*, 2014). While the role of these organizations as "norm entrepreneurs" has already been noted and elaborated elsewhere (e.g., Finnemore and Sikkink, 1998), we argue here that the extent to which they function as the primary sources of governance norms – as the ones setting the rules and redrawing the borders of how good governance is supposed to be exercised in society – is regularly underestimated.

Our definition of civil society is straightforward and grounded in a model of the organization of society inspired by new institutionalist organization theory, with the four main societal spheres – the state, the business sphere, the family sphere and civil society – seen as constituting the institutional habitats of actors who share a common institutional and organizational logic (Thornton *et al.* 2012; Wijkström, 2011). The sphere of civil society is conceptualized as including not only nonprofit or voluntary service providers but also organizations (as well as less formal networks) of private citizens who get together to further their own goals, cultivate (and defend) their interests or promote their visions of society (see Heinrich, 2002; Salamon *et al.*, 2003). Such a definition of civil society is intentionally both broad and normatively neutral (see also Reuter, 2007) and includes not only traditional nonprofits, voluntary organizations, associations and interest groups but also political parties, trade unions, and religious groups and churches.

This chapter is conceptual and exploratory rather than empirical. As noted by Collier and Mahon (1993), stable analytical concepts and a shared understanding of primary categories constitute an important foundation of any research community. It is our intent to offer such a foundation here. The concept of civil society being as wide, ambiguous and contested as it is carries the risk of civil society scholarship being less cumulative and comprehensive than it could be given the advantages of its broad multidisciplinary composition and outlook. When the idea of governance is added to the civil society concept, complexity is not reduced but greater conceptual unity is achieved.

The remainder of this chapter is organized as follows. We start by identifying the two strands of research concerned with governance: research on organizational or corporate ("internal") governance developed primarily in the fields of finance and business administration, and research on the governance of wider society (here labeled "external") developed in fields such as international relations and public administration. Next, we argue for analytically linking these two dimensions in order to further our understanding both of how civil society organizations are operated and governed and of their role and importance in governing wider society. We particularly focus here on the necessity of unpacking the "black box" of internal governance in civil society organizations. Finally, we take the discussion on the latter a step further by pointing to a role often overlooked: the provision by civil society organizations of the constitutive ideas and values that underpin society's governance arrangements.

On internal and external governance

In the existing literature, there are two major but so far mostly unrelated ways to deal with civil society and the matter of governance: "internal" versus "external" governance, exercised respectively in and by civil society organizations. Here we connect these two dimensions of governance and treat them as different steps, parts or links in what we tentatively describe as the "civil society governance chain." In this approach, the first step of internal governance in civil society organizations is understood as being linked in a second step in the chain to societal (external) governance, where it affects the way societal governance is exercised (the third step). A fourth step in the chain then links back into the internal governance procedures and processes of civil society organizations (as well as other organizations such as for-profit corporations or public-sector entities) as these organizations are exposed to the consequences of the chain reactions in terms of "outside impulses" or other types of impacts emerging from the many and diverse environments they are part of (Aguilera *et al.*, 2008).

The literature relevant to the "internal" governance of civil society organizations includes the very strong classical (internal) corporate governance approach so often applied in the for-profit world (Berle and Means, 2009). A vast majority of the studies in the corporate governance field focus on "internal problems associated with managerial opportunism, misalignment of objectives of managers and stakeholders, and distortions of managerial incentives" (Filatotchev and Nakajima, 2010, p. 593). Most proponents (at least the more influential ones) of this approach depart, in one way or another, from a fairly simple understanding of governance that could be described as "a manifestation of a classical and rather uncomplicated view of the principal-agent relationship" where "the shareholders (principals) simply define the goals, and the executives (agents) attempt to realize them" (Kallifatides *et al.*, 2010, p. 17).

Interesting alternatives exist that might be better suited for understanding how the internal governance of civil society organizations functions, such as the stewardship theory approach where the assumed distrust between principal and agent built into the principal–agent model is understood to be offset through a shared interest or common value frame between principal and agent (Caers *et al.*, 2006; Kreutzer and Jacobs, 2011). Most civil society governance approaches in this genre focus on internal governance only, which often develops along the same lines as corporate governance, as expressed by Hughes (2010, p. 87): "Governance is about running the organizations, about setting up structures to enable the organizations to be run."

In the second major strand of governance research, where the importance of civil society organizations as actors in the wider societal governance is highlighted, we often find a more systems-oriented approach. In an early definition suggested by Rosenau (1992, p. 4), governance is described as a "system of rules that is as dependent on intersubjective meanings as on formally sanctioned constitutions and charters." The capacity to act collectively is not just a matter of sharing interests and values, according to such a definition; such capacity also requires a prior and shared understanding of the constituent elements of both problems and possible solutions (Gauri *et al.*, 2011). Therefore, to be able to ascribe a common intersubjective meaning to various situations and processes is as important as the formal governance arrangements. And this is where civil society organizations also have a unique role in providing the initial input and impulses for changing or upholding – governing – the shared understanding of what are to be understood as problems as well as solutions in society and in this way being part of the external or societal governance. Later contributions by Rosenau are more straightforward: the governance system is approached "as the purposive activities of any collectivity that sustain mechanisms designed to ensure its safety, prosperity, coherence, stability, and continuance" (Rosenau, 2000, p. 171).

Although Rosenau primarily writes in the international relations tradition, his understanding of governance relates closely to the way this concept has developed also in the field of public administration studies recently. Authors such as Nielsen and Pedersen (1990), Kooiman (1993), Rhodes (1996), Peters and Pierre (1998) and Jessop (2002) have laid a solid foundation for a debate on emerging new governance modes at the level of society where different (nation-) state or government actors are no longer viewed as the only possible policy-making actors, and where various civil society organizations in different ways play increasingly visible roles. "Governance" has thus been replacing the earlier "government" view with its limited capacity to include in the analysis the role and importance of civil society organizations – as well as private corporations.[1]

This is a partly new viewpoint where "state actors indeed must share legislative power and authority with international organizations on the one hand, and with multinational companies and representatives of civil society, on the other," as summarized by one political scientist (Mörth, 2006, p. 119). One result of this development is the blurring of institutional borders on a societal level that civil society scholars by now are so used to including in their analysis, including the recent surge in "hybridity" studies (see Billis, 2010; Brandsen *et al.*, 2005; Skelcher and Smith, 2014; Smith, 2014).

As one of the early leading theorists in this strand of governance research, Stoker (1998, p. 17) points to a kind of "baseline agreement that governance refers to the development of governing styles in which boundaries between and within public and private sectors have become blurred." Civil society organizations have since then often been understood to be important and a special type of actor in this link in the governance chain. Hale and Held (2011, p. xxiii) recently summarized this thinking well:

Private actors like non-governmental organizations and companies are engaging in rule-making, implementation, monitoring, enforcement and service provision – that is, in governance – at all levels, either as the partners of states or intergovernmental organizations, or as private authorities in their own right. New modes of accountability and enforcement based on capacity building, transparency, market incentives or moral suasion are joining formal rules and key features of the governance architecture.

Linking the two worlds of governance

The two strands of governance literature are seldom connected in the social sciences. In particular, in most attempts to conceptualize societal governance as something wider and richer than "government" only, the internal governance principles and practices of civil society organizations are absent from the discussion. The internal level is treated as a kind of "black-box" phenomenon, with no distinction made between different types or systems of civil society internal organizational governance. The internal governance solutions are assumed, at least implicitly, to be either similar among different organizations in civil society (which of course is not the case) or of no important consequence for the behavior or impact of these organizations in the way they take part in societal governance, and thus for the outcomes and impacts resulting from those processes.

Challenging this state of affairs, we argue that a better understanding of the link between these two levels of governance – the internal (organizational) and the external (societal) – is crucial if we are to enhance our capacity to analyze the internal workings of these organizations further as well as improve future studies of the role of civil society and its organizations in wider society. Indeed, the necessity to do so is also expected by some observers to increase in the future: "This distinction is particularly relevant given that nonprofits are assuming increasing responsibility for what historically have been public services" (Renz and Andersson, 2013, p. 18).

The notion of such a link has also been identified by some writers in the wider corporate governance tradition (e.g., Aguilera *et al.*, 2008; Filatotchev and Nakajima, 2010), and recently the link has been argued to be of importance more specifically also in civil society governance research (Renz and Andersson, 2013; Stone and Ostrower, 2007). These two different "dimensions of governance are closely intertwined: internal governance shapes the conditions for the organization's positions and actions in the external governance environment, and vice versa" (Steen-Johnson *et al.*, 2011, p. 556).

We further develop these ideas by sketching an analytical model that consists of three propositions about the nature of the complex relationship between civil society and governance. These propositions can be understood as three consecutive steps in a chain-like or loop-like relationship, but they can also be visualized as three different and separate reasons why internal organizational governance and societal governance are relevant for the understanding of one another.

The first proposition relates to the internal organization and management of civil society organizations themselves. These organizations have other primary purposes or roles in society and follow other institutional logics than commercial organizations or public-sector entities. They are therefore also often organized and governed according to other principles, which we argue should be understood as an important part of their distinctiveness in society. Therefore, many of the more standardized models for understanding or explaining internal organizational governance and management developed in academia today (read: corporate governance or new public management) are relatively ill-suited for the study of civil society organizations. We would in fact like to underscore that one of the most distinctive organizational characteristics of civil society as an institutional sphere in society is the impressive diversity and heterogeneity of more or less intricate and complex organizational governance models, principles, practices and solutions found there. Each of the two spheres of business and the state or public sector present a considerable internal convergence when it comes to their major organizational governance principles – most of the world's major for-profit corporations and states follow more or less the same two or three major models. Meanwhile, the huge diversity of civil society organizations are goverened according to a multitude of principles or models derived from the unique aims, purposes and missions of these organizations.

This latter relationship is crucial; the diversity of organizational governance models found in civil society should in our view be understood – and analyzed – as a result or consequence of the diversity of purposes found in the organizations of civil society. While organizations found in the public or state sector or in the corporate sphere pursue relatively simple and straightforward aims, the aims and purposes of civil society organizations seem to vary almost infinitely. So consequently should the governance models and arrangements by which these organizations run in order to fulfill their particular missions and reach their particular goals. Civil society and its many organizations could thus be considered a sort of a hotbed or greenhouse of governance models and practices in society, enriching considerably our understanding of how different forms of human endeavours can be organized and managed.

Our second proposition concerns the consequences for the governance of wider society, i.e., the link in the chain between "internal" organizational governance and "external" or societal governance. Arguably, this link works both ways; for example, scholars like Filatotchev and Nakajima (2010) stress the importance of external governance activities of an organization for the (internal) governance of the organization itself. We would however like to highlight the importance of the internal governance of an organization (analytically viewed as a sub-system) as being of consequence also for the governance of the wider societal system. We argue, in other words, that the internal governance of civil society organizations is *not* only about running the organizations – as is in the earlier quote by Hughes (2010) – but also at least partly about running society, and that the societal role of these organizations cannot be understood without insight into the internal workings and arrangements of civil society.

Let us briefly illustrate the importance of this particular angle on the "civil society governance chain" through examples from two, admittedly atypical but nevertheless key, types of civil society organizations: a political party and a church. The (internal) process that resulted in Barack Obama standing as the presidential candidate for the Democratic Party in the United States in 2008 has had consequences not only for the members of the party itself but for people all over the globe, through the American president's position as head of state in one of the superpowers of the world. Similarly, the internal governance procedures in a religious organization can have political and policy-related impact far outside of the church as an organization. The election and pontification of Karol Wojtyla as Pope John Paul II and the head of the Catholic Church in 1978 has had far-reaching worldwide consequences, as the church's work under Wojtyla's leadership is said to have been instrumental in the crumbling of the Soviet empire and the symbolic fall of the Berlin Wall a decade later.

Even if not always as dramatic, the different internal governance procedures and principles – and their results – of civil society organizations must be understood to have consequences and effects that well surpass and outpace the limited organizational borders and consequences of the organizations themselves, be they religious, cultural or political organizations; trade unions, environmental or sports associations; or any other of the many shades of civil society. Societal governance, in the words of Börzel and Risse (2010, p. 115), "includes hierarchical steering by state actors, but also includes the involvement of non-governmental actors (companies, civil society) in the provision of collective goods through non-hierarchical coordination."

CSOs as seedbeds for governance

The third and final proposition closely follows on the first, focusing more narrowly on one of the most important ways in which civil society actors participate in "running the world." We suggest that civil society and its many organizations not only take part in the governance game or policy-making processes but, more fundamentally (and often in conflict and competition with each other), also create and shape these very games and processes; they are setting the agendas, framing the discussions and defining the relevant matters to be addressed. We even dare to stretch the argument so far as to say that it is and has always been various civil society organizations (sometimes behind the scenes) that are the powerhouses and seedbeds where new, alternative or challenging ideas and visions about what "legitimate" governance is supposed to look like are developed and provided. We can safely bet that future "legitimate" governance processes and principles – no matter which ones (and not only new policy issues, as argued above) – will have been nurtured, kept alive and made relevant in a civil society context before being brought to the table by these organizations as viable and relevant governance solutions in our societies.

Salient – and contemporary – examples of this are the idea of representative democracy introduced and implemented in many countries of the world during earlier periods, or the more market-based or business-like governance models we are experimenting with lately in many fields of society almost worldwide (Donahue and Nye, 2002). Be they political parties or religious communities, social movement organizations or corporate think-tanks, these are the organizations where the next round of procedures and principles for governance – how power matters are to be regulated – are developed and defended, shaped and sharpened, translated and diffused.

The battle over the content and extension of citizenship

To further illustrate our argument, we examine the development of the institution of citizenship, which arguably is a cornerstone in modern societal governance. Today, the concept of citizenship is increasingly under scrutiny, with social scientists and public intellectuals asking what this notion may entail in our late-modern, globalized and electronically connected societies. In this context the question of the relationship between civil society and citizenship is often raised, with calls for the examination of the ways in which civil society actors may or should contribute to re-inventing, modernizing and invigorating the institution of citizenship (see for example Chapter 11 by Enjolras and Steen-Johnson in this volume). Empowerment of underprivileged groups in society, inclusion of previously excluded groups, voices and perspectives through different civil society initiatives, and innovations aimed at increasing political participation and engagement are often emphasized in this context.

Since World War II, in the Western public mind as well as in academia, the set of rules and practices connected to the broadly understood ideal of liberal democracy has become more or less synonymous with the best way of governing our complex societies. One important dimension of this ideal is the question of who is to enjoy democratic rights (see, e.g., Barbalet, 1988) as a citizen; put differently, who is, in the eyes of society and the law, a "real individual" or Marshall's "full and equal member of society" (Marshall, 1950). The expansion of political citizenship – that is, the evolution of the idea of who is worthy of being included in the democratic community – is historically one of the most important elements of the process of democratization.

This evolution of citizenship is illustrated in North America, where the concept evolved from including white property-owning Protestant men only, to gradual extension to "women, the working class, Jews and Catholics, blacks and other previously excluded groups" (Kymlicka and Norman, 1994). In Western Europe, similarly, several countries had by the second half of the nineteenth century parliamentary governments and some form of competitive party systems; however, their electorates were severely limited by property and/or income qualifications, which meant that only a minority of wealthy males counted as citizens. And yet, by 1918, suffrage in most Western European countries had been extended to all males irrespective of property and income status, and in the decades that followed also to women (see, e.g., Huber and Stephens, 1997; Finnemore and Sikkink, 1998). Even more importantly, since then the norm of universal suffrage itself has become just as entrenched in the public mind as the norm of only wealthy men being capable of running state affairs had been just a few generations ago.

What happened from a civil society perspective in that relatively brief period of time to bring about this kind of institutional and normative change? In short: the step-wise entry of labor and women's movements. These movements and their organizations in civil society were the most important agents in the process of shaping the contemporary understanding of who is worthy of being a full citizen – as in "not only wealthy men" and "not only men." Importantly, however, this process is far from being settled. On the contrary, the norms that regulate our understanding of citizenship – as well as our understanding of who is considered to be an "individual" from which the notion of "citizen" subsequently is derived – are constantly being challenged and reshaped by movements similar to, and/or derived from, the two mentioned above.[2] What we today understand as "an individual," "a citizen" or finally "the democracy" in which these individuals and citizens are supposed to act and have a say – to govern – are thus just snapshots or stills of what in reality is a constantly changing worldview. It is further not only possible but also highly probable that in another 50 or 100 years from now, our understanding of these concepts will have evolved maybe even beyond recognition.

And, we would argue, we will find civil society organizations, in one way or another, at the core of these transformations: as the contributors or providers of the new ideas and components changing the governance landscape.

Children and animals: next in line for voting rights?

We may in fact get a glimpse of this development if we take a closer look at contemporary examples of the normative struggles in this field. The standards of citizenship and of individual personhood are being continuously renegotiated in terms of new subjects conceptualized as "persons" or as "citizens." The children's rights movement (e.g., Howes, 1991) and the animal rights movement (see Regan, 2004; Singer, 2006) are perhaps the most salient and interesting examples, where we can follow in real time how civil society actors constantly seek to expand the boundaries of one of our at present most prominent governance systems, liberal representative democracy, through efforts to expand and redefine the core idea of where the borders of individual personhood and citizenship are to be drawn.

This normative power – the strength of civil society organizations as "norm entrepreneurs" (Finnemore and Sikkink, 1998) – does not necessary come about through the introduction of these principles or practices in the internal governance of these organizations themselves but rather through the promotion of the idea that these categories should be understood as new types of citizen. In more concrete terms, the improved position for children as well as animals in various governance arrangements has for example been promoted through the inclusion of various ombudsman solutions in society, often with the explicit aim to provide these new categories of "citizens" a voice in politics (CASJ, 2013; Save the Children Norway, 2005).

These examples illustrate the crucial role of civil society organizations as the primary actors and drivers of change, which shape our understanding of the principles that should underlie legitimate governance structures in our societies. Who should be included as legitimate stakeholders or carriers of political power and influence? Which are the processes and institutions that in the future will be considered the proper ones for governing our societies? Civil society organizations are thus of particular interest not because they are the champions of "good" causes but rather because among them are the actors who are shaping our understanding of which values and norms in the field of governance are to be seen and defined as "good," "just" and "fair." In this process they will define which governance principles are legitimate and acceptable in society. Through a continuous normative struggle within and between civil society actors, the components of governance architectures – such as a redefined or expanded concept of citizenship – develop and emerge.

The values and principles affiliated today with "good," "just" or "fair" governance appeal to us because certain (and not other alternative) civil society actors were remarkably successful in developing and disseminating their particular visions of what kinds of elements or components the governance system of a just society should contain. Only after certain civil society actors have planted, nourished and catapulted into the political agenda the idea of equal citizenship rights does it become possible for us to ask what civil society actors can do to invigorate the institution of citizenship or how civil society can contribute to democracy in this respect. This is how strong the "real power" of civil society is in governance terms, as we also have argued elsewhere (Reuter *et al.*, 2014).[3]

The above points also to the essential meaninglessness – at least from an analytical point of view – of dividing civil society organizations into progressive and reactionary actors or forces, as these two qualities are related not to some objective moral indicators but to the extent to which an organization or movement is successful in its promotion of certain values, worldviews or governance principles.

This point is illustrated by the fate of the concepts and practices of philanthropy and charity in Sweden, understood in the nineteenth century to be one of the staunchest examples of a modern welfare state. During most of the twentieth century, such concepts as charity, philanthropy, volunteering and the organizations practicing it were pushed out or marginalized by a politically more successful social-democratic vision of a state-provided and tax-funded general welfare system. These practices and organizations were, together with the idea and usage of foundations, seen during the post-World War II period as morally reprehensible or at least suspicious (Lundström and Wijkström, 1997; Wijkström and Einarsson, 2004). In the last decade or two, however, charity and philanthropy practices have enjoyed a revival in Swedish civil society, riding on a wave of liberal as well as more conservative sediments of civil society aimed at reducing both the extent of the welfare state and the general level of taxation

(Vamstad and von Essen, 2013; Wijkström, 2011), thus appearing both respectable and progressive in Swedish society today. The opposite can be said to have happened to the earlier social-democratic vision of statist-provided welfare (Hort, 2014; Trägårdh, 2012), as it has lost much of its political and normative hold over people's minds and hearts, at least partly through an increased privatization and outsourcing of regular welfare services such as healthcare, social services and education to corporations as well as to civil society actors (Hartman, 2011; Lundström and Wijkström, 2012). The idea of a return to a welfare system delivered by the state alone is today not feasible but rather perceived as backwards and reactionary.

The main argument here is that the moral components of these different civil society struggles today have become part of a value package that functions as a strong proxy for good governance more or less worldwide in our societies. These values have today been adopted by many national governments as well as organizations at the global or transnational level such as the United Nations, the World Bank and the International Monetary Fund. They are often respected and referred to as well by national and multinational corporations striving to gain legitimacy and acceptance in their ways of doing business. Today, the new "ownership" over these values and adoption by many governments across the world is obvious. This is how influential and successful the civil society actors behind these ideas have been.

It is the agency of civil society actors that continuously shapes and reshapes the normative content of what "good governance" is, and many nation-states are now the new guardians of agendas previously held and nurtured in civil society. Transparency International is just one of the latest and most obvious organizations in this respect, with its clear – and seemingly successful – intent to affect the way our societies are governed by combating corruption through increased transparency using, for example, the Corruption Perception Index (Norad, 2011). Similarly, an older and more established organization, the International Committee of the Red Cross, has also had a significant impact on the rules for how wars should be fought through and governed what later would be known as the Geneva Convention, as Finnemore (1999, p. 164) reminds us: "The codification of Red Cross principles into international law is best understood as the result of competing world-cultural principles, not competing interests."

Conclusion

In this chapter we argued that civil society governance matters should be understood within a holistic systems approach through the idea of a "civil society governance chain," and that the link between "internal" and "external" governance is crucial to understanding civil society actors from a governance point of view. In this approach, individual civil society organizations are understood as subsystems of a much wider system in which society is governed. By connecting the literature on "internal" and "external" governance through this chain, the two types of governance systems thus become integrated and part of each other.

Previously, this link has been identified and used to expand corporate governance analysis by highlighting the importance for governance of the organization of the external governance context to which it belongs. What we have done in this chapter is to turn the link in the chain the other way around and to make the point that internal (organizational) governance also matters in wider societal governance. To summarize, the internal governance of civil society organizations is not only about running the organizations but also – at least partly and sometimes – about running society.

Moreover, the prevailing view of civil society's place in the governance of wider society is challenged even further. Much research exists already on the role of civil society organizations in the various stages of policy-making processes. The normative influence of these actors on the content in the policy processes has also been noted, not the least in the international or transnational context. However, the power of civil society organizations in governance terms has been underestimated in the current scholarly debate on civil society and governance. Using the example of the development of the institution of citizenship in the Western hemisphere, we showed that the importance of civil society organizations in governance matters is related not only to their participation in the existing governance arrangements per se, but also to their function as the main source of the ideas and values that shape the governance arrangements themselves – altering the boundaries and the rules of the game. We argue that developing, defining and defending the ideational and normative principles for governance – i.e., ultimately how society should be run – is a central role for civil society. This role as producer or shaper of the normative and ideological content of the current liberal democratic value package has to a large extent been missing in civil society research on governance. This is problematic since this value package is also an important part of the overarching normative framework in which we all, as scholars, are heavily embedded and where many social scientists often take an active but not always explicit part.

Notes

1 Note, however, that the wording "replacing" in no way implies "excluding," as different forms of state or government actors still are among the most influential actors in the way different policy fields, regions or other matters are being governed and regulated. Some scholars even argue that states "tend to be more popular than ever" (Jacobsson, 2006: 205).
2 For example, the particular family of social movements that have struggled against racial and ethnic exclusion from the political realm and from society in general in different parts of the world – such as, e.g., the American civil rights movement in the 1960s or the global movement against apartheid in South Africa.
3 See Mansell (2013) for an interesting parallel analysis of the successful negotiation where even the idea of the private for-profit corporation increasingly seems to be reframed as a "socially responsible citizen" in society today.

References

Aguilera, R., Filatotchev, I., Gospel, H. and Jackson, G. 2008. An Organizational Approach to Comparative Corporate Governance: Costs, Contingencies, and Complementarities. *Organization Science*, 19(3), pp. 475–492.

Anheier, H. K. 2013. Governance: What Are the Issues? in Hertie School of Governance (ed.) *The Governance Report 2013*. Oxford: Oxford University Press.

Barbalet, J. M. 1988. *Citizenship: Rights, Struggle and Class Inequality*. London: Open University Press.

Berle, A. A. and Means, G. C. 2009. From the Modern Corporation and Private Property, in L. S. Kroszner and L. Putterman (eds) *The Economic Nature of the Firm: A Reader*, 3rd edition. Cambridge: Cambridge University Press.

Billis, D. (ed.) 2010. *Hybrid Organizations and the Third Sector: Challenges for Practice, Theory and Policy*. London: Palgrave Macmillan.

Börzel, T. A. and Risse, T. 2010. Governance Without a State: Can it Work? *Regulation and Governance*, 4, pp. 113–134.

Brandsen, T., van de Donk, W. and Putters, K. 2005. Griffins or Chameleons? Hybridity as a Permanent and Inevitable Characteristic of the Third Sector. *International Journal of Public Administration*, 28(9–10), pp. 749–765.

Caers, R., Bois, C. D., Jegers, M., Gieter, S. D., Schepers, C. and Pepermans, R. 2006. Principle–Agent Relationships on the Stewardship-Agency Axis. *Nonprofit Management and Leadership*, 17(1), pp. 25–47.

CASJ 2013. *Towards Joined-up Animal Welfare Policy*. Centre for Animals and Social Justice.

Collier, D. and Mahon, J. T. 1993. Conceptual Stretching Revisited: Adapting Categories in Comparative Analysis. *American Political Science Review*, 87(4), pp. 845–855.

Cornforth, C. 2013. Nonprofit governance research: The need for innovative perspectives and approaches, in C. Cornforth and W.A. Brown (eds) Nonprofit Governance. Innovative perspectives and approaches. *Nonprofit Governance: Innovative Perspectives and Approaches*. London: Routledge.

Cornforth, C. and Brown, W. A. (eds) 2013. *Nonprofit Governance: Innovative Perspectives and Approaches*. London: Routledge.

Djelic, M. -L. and Sahlin-Andersson, K. (eds) 2006. *Transnational Governance: Institutional Dynamics of Regulation*. Cambridge: Cambridge University Press.

Donahue, J. D. and Nye, J. S. Jr. (eds) 2002. *Market Based Governance: Supply Side, Demand Side, Upside and Downside*. Cambridge: Visions of Governance in the twenty-first Century, and Washington, DC: Brookings Institution Press.

Filatotchev, I. and Nakajima, C. 2010. Internal and External Corporate Governance: An Interface between an Organization and its Environment. *British Journal of Management*, 21, pp. 591–606.

Finnemore, M. 1999. The International Red Cross and Rules of War, in J. Boli and G. M. Thomas (eds) *Constructing World Culture: International Non-governmental Organizations Since 1875*. Stanford, CA: Stanford University Press.

Finnemore, M. and Sikkink, K. 1998. International Norm Dynamics and Political Change. *International Organization*, 52(4), pp. 887–917.

Gauri, V., Woolcook, M. and Desai, D. 2011. Intersubjective Meaning and Collective Action in "Fragile" Societies: Theory, Evidence and Policy Implications. Policy Research Working Paper 5707, Washington: The World Bank.

Graz, J. -C. and Nölke, A. (eds) 2008. *Transnational Private Governance and its Limits*. London: Routledge.

Hale, T. and Held, D. (eds) 2011. *Handbook of Transnational Governance: Institutions and Innovations*. Cambridge: Polity Press.

Hartman, L. 2011. *Konkurrensens konsekvenser: Vad händer med svensk välfärd?* Stockholm: SNS.

Heinrich, V. F. 2002. Managing Trade-offs: Challenges Faced in Designing the Implementation Approach of the CIVICUS Civil Society Index. Paper presented at the ISTR 5th International Conference, Cape Town, 6–10 July.

Hort, S. E. O. 2014. *Social Policy, Welfare State, and Civil Society in Sweden, Vol. II The Lost World of Social Democracy 1988–2015*, 3rd enlarged edition, Lund: Arkiv förlag.

Howes, J. 1991. *The Children's Rights Movement: A History of Advocacy and Protection*. Boston: Twayne Publishers.

Huber, E. and Stephens, J. D. 1997. The Bourgeoisie and Democracy: Historical and Contemporary Perspectives from Europe and Latin America. Paper delivered at the 1997 meeting of the Latin American Studies Association, Guadalajara, Mexico, 17–19 April.

Hughes, O. 2010. Does Governance Exist? in S. P. Osborne (ed.) *The New Public Governance? Emerging Perspectives on the Theory and Practice of Public governance*. London: Routledge.

Jacobsson, B. 2006. Regulated Regulators: Global Trends of State Transformation, in M.-L. Djelic and K. Sahlin-Andersson (eds) *Transnational Governance: Institutional Dynamics of Regulation*. Cambridge: Cambridge University Press.

Jessop, B. 2002. *The Future of the Capitalist State*. London: Polity.

Jönsson, C. and Tallberg, J. 2010. *Transnational Actors in Global Governance: Patterns, Explanations and Expectations*. New York: Palgrave Macmillan.

Kallifatides, M., Nachemsson-Ekwall, S. and Sjöstrand, S. -E. 2010. *Corporate Governance in Modern Financial Capitalism: Old Mutual's Hostile Takeover of Skandia*. Cheltenham: Edward Elgar.

Kooiman, J. (ed.) 1993. *Modern Governance: Government-Society Interactions*. London: Sage.

Kreutzer, K. and Jacobs, C. 2011. Balancing Control and Coaching in CSO Governance: A Paradox Perspective on Board Behavior. *Voluntas* 22(44), pp. 613–638.

Kumar, S. and Roberts, J. 2010. Governance, Organizational, in H. K. Anheier and S. Toepler (eds) *International Encyclopedia of Civil Society*. New York: Springer.

Kymlicka, W. and Norman, W. 1994. Return of the Citizen: Overview of the Recent Work on Citizenship Theory. *Ethics* 104(2), pp. 352–381.

Lundström, T. and Wijkström F. 1997. *The Nonprofit Sector in Sweden*. Manchester: Manchester University Press.

Lundström, T. and Wijkström, F. 2012. Från röst till service: Vad hände sen? in F. Wijkström (ed.) *Civilsamhället i samhällskontraktet*. Stockholm: European Civil Society Press.

Maier, F. and Meyer, M. 2011. Managerialism and Beyond: Discourses of Civil Society Organizations and their Governance Implications. *Voluntas* 22(44), pp. 731–756.

Mansell, S. F. 2013. *Capitalism, Corporations and the Social Contract: A Critique of Stakeholder Theory*. Cambridge: Cambridge University Press.

Marshall, T. H. 1950. *Citizenship and Social Class and Other Essays*. Cambridge: Cambridge University Press.

Mörth, U. 2006. Soft Regulation and Global Democracy, in M. -L. Djelic and K. Sahlin-Andersson (eds) *Transnational Governance: Institutional Dynamics of Regulation*. Cambridge: Cambridge University Press.

Nielsen, K. and Pedersen, O. K. 1990. *Forhandlingsokonomi i Norden*. Copenhagen: Jurist- og Okonomforbundets Forlag.

Norad 2011. *Evaluation of Transparency International, Report 8/2010, Evaluation Department*, Oslo: Norwegian Agency for Development Cooperation (Norad).

Osborne, S. P. 2010. *The New Public Governance? Emerging Perspectives on the Theory and Practice of Public Governance*. London: Routledge.

Ostrower, F. and Stone, M. M. 2006. Boards of Nonprofit Organizations: Research Trends, Findings and Prospects for Future Research, in W. Powell and R. Steinberg (eds) *The Nonprofit Sector: A Research Handbook*, 2nd edition. New Haven, CT: Yale University Press.

Peters, B. G. and Pierre, J. 1998. Governance Without Government? Rethinking Public Administration. *Journal of Public Administration Research and Theory*, 8(2), pp. 223–243.

Regan, T. 2004. *Empty Cages: Facing the Challenge of Animal Rights*. Lanham, MD: Rowman and Littlefield Publishers.

Renz, D. O. and Andersson, F. O. 2014. Nonprofit Governance: A Review of the Field, in C. Cornforth and W. A. Brown (eds) *Nonprofit Governance: Innovative Perspectives and Approaches*. London: Routledge.

Reuter, M. 2007. *Networking a Region into Existence? Dynamics of Civil Society Region-alization in the Baltic Sea Area*. Berlin: Berliner Wissenschafts-Verlag.

Reuter, M., Wijkström, F. and Meyer, M. 2014. Who Calls the Shots? The Real Normative Power of Civil Society, in M. Freise and T. Hallmann (eds) *Modernizing Democracy? Associations and Associating in the twenty-first Century*. New York: Springer.

Rhodes, R. A. W. 1996. The New Governance: Governing without Government. *Political Studies* xliv: pp. 652–667.

Rosenau, J. N. 2000. Change, Complexity, and Governance in a Globalizing Space, in J. Pierre (ed.) *Debating Governance: Authority, Steering, and Democracy*. Oxford: Oxford University Press.

Rosenau, J. N. and Czempiel, E. -O. 1992. *Governance without Government: Order and Change in World Politics*. Cambridge: Cambridge University Press.

Salamon, M. L., Sokolowski, W. and List, R. 2003. *Global Civil Society: An Overview*. Baltimore: The Johns Hopkins University Institute for Policy Studies, Center for Civil Society Studies.

Save The Children Norway 2005. *Children's Ombudsman: Save the Children Norway's Experiences with Supporting and Cooperating with Independent Institutions Protecting Children's Rights*, vol. 1, Report 05/2005, April. Oslo: Save The Children Norway.

Singer, P. 2006. *In Defense of Animals: The Second Wave*. Oxford: Blackwell Publishing.

Skelcher, C. and Smith, S. R. 2014. Theorising Hybridity: Institutional Logics, Complex Organizations, and Actor Identities – The Case of Nonprofits. *Public Administration*, DOI: 10.1111/padm.12105.

Smith, S. R. 2014. Hybridity and Nonprofit Organizations: The Research Agenda. *American Behavioral Scientist*, 21 May.

Steen-Johnsen, K., Eynaud, P. and Wijkström, F. 2011. On Civil Society Governance: An Emergent Research Field. *Voluntas*, 22(4), pp. 555–565.

Stoker, G. 1998. Governance as Theory: Five Propositions. *International Social Science Journal*, 50(155), pp. 17–28.

Stone, M. M. and Ostrower, F. 2007. Acting In The Public Interest? Another Look at Research on Nonprofit Governance. *Nonprofit And Voluntary Sector Quarterly*, 36(3), pp. 416–438.

Thornton, P. H., Ocasio, W. and Lounsbury, M. 2012. *The Institutional Logics Perspective. A new approach to culture, structure and process.* Oxford: Oxford University Press.

Torfing, J. 2007. Introduction: Democratic Network Governance, in M. Marcussen and J. Torfing (eds) *Democratic Network Governance in Europe.* Houndmills: Palgrave Macmillan.

Trägårdh, L. 2012. Det borgerliga samhällets återkomst, in F. Wijkström (ed.) *Civilsamhället i samhällskontraktet.* Stockholm: European Civil Society Press.

Vamstad, J. and von Essen, J. 2013. Charitable Giving in a Universal Welfare State: Charity and Social Rights in Sweden. *Nonprofit and Voluntary Sector Quarterly*, 42(2), pp. 285–301.

Wijkström, F. 2011. "Charity Speak and Business Talk": The Ongoing (Re)hybridization of Civil Society, in F. Wijkström and A. Zimmer (eds) *Nordic Civil Society at a Cross-Roads: Transforming the Popular Movement Tradition.* Baden-Baden: Nomos.

Wijkström, F. and Einarsson, S. 2004. *Foundations in Sweden.* Stockholm: European Civil Society Press/Stockholm School of Economics.

Part II

Introduction to Part II

Jean-Louis Laville, Dennis R. Young and Philippe Eynaud

The analysis in Part I suggests that we need to enlarge our vision of CSO governance and not focus exclusively on governing boards. Institutional and neo-institutional theory helps us to address these challenges, especially to understand how social enterprises deal with the involvement of stakeholders. However this conceptual framework does not tell us precisely how democracy engages with CSO governance. In particular, one major concern is the capacity of CSOs to govern themselves democratically while maintaining the collective identity necessary to contribute to the solution of social problems. An intent in the second part of this book is to explore new and fruitful approaches to CSO governance that address this question. Three avenues are specifically analyzed.

The first avenue follows from the work of Ostrom. New forms of institutional and organizational arrangements emerge when a large number of stakeholders interact around the governance of collective goods. This proposition is relevant to CSOs because it posits the need to supersede the dualism of state and market. For Ostrom, there is a third way, based on the concept of the commons, to analyze how people can self-organize, define their own rules and act collectively in specific situations. This idea is very powerful because it can be applied broadly to the analysis of new frontiers of the contemporary economy including the informational commons, the phenomenon of planned obsolescence, and the shortening of supply chains based on local production. Chapters 9 and 10 explore this first perspective.

The second avenue is about the pluralism of democracy, reflecting the work of Habermas. In contrast to representative democracy, Habermas argues for what he calls deliberative democracy. He reasons that the concept of the public sphere helps us to understand how a diverse community of equal individuals can deliberate rationally. This idea is very useful for understanding how CSOs can strengthen their legitimacy and bolster their democratic ethos by sharing their own issues with the public at large. Chapters 11 and 12 address this theoretical perspective.

The third avenue, rooted in the works of major theorists including Polanyi and Ramos, suggests the importance of employing more comprehensive frames of reference. These include the para-economy, social management, and a pluralistic approach to the economy that accounts not only for markets but also for redistribution and reciprocity. This perspective, explored in Chapters 13 and 14, is intercultural and based on experiences in different continents.

Given these three ways of thinking about societal governance and the role and governance of civil society, Part II of the book unfolds as follows. Chapter 8 by Laville and Salmon serves as an overall introduction for Part II. The authors first examine the conceptual framework of Friedrich Hayek, characterizing it as the economization of the political sphere. They argue that this notion promotes a limited functional approach to understanding third-sector organizations. Next, the authors explore the concept of the solidarity economy, which they define – in opposition to Hayek's proposition – as the democratization of the economy. Here, the concept of governance has a completely different meaning. It opens questions about the goal of CSOs, the pluralism of democracy and the pluralism of the economy. To demonstrate their points, Laville and Salmon reference the works of Ostrom, Habermas, Guerreiro, Ramos and Polanyi. They conclude by calling for interdisciplinary critical studies of CSO governance, so that CSO governance research can benefit from a broader vision of the economy not limited to the market. They argue that this is a necessary condition for allowing the economy to potentially strengthen democracy.

Chapter 9 by Sievers highlights the deep ambiguity that characterizes the relationship of civil society to governance in the modern democratic polity. The failures of states to provide important collective goods, such as protection of the global environment, have drawn civil society ever closer towards filling government's role. The assumption of this new role, however, has raised issues traditionally associated with the responsibilities of government, particularly questions of legitimacy and accountability. Sievers notes that Ostrom and others have demonstrated that civil society can address collective action problems through the cultivation of norms of trust and openness of communication. Growing awareness by civil society organizations of the need to cooperate, increase transparency, develop mechanisms of self-accountability, and increase public access offer the promise that civil society can indeed address some of the challenges of governance. In particular, Sievers shows in this chapter that network theory and design thinking can offer new paths for creating collaborative and constructive relationships among civil society organizations.

Chapter 10 by Nyssens and Petrella explores the responsibilities of public and private actors in the provision of local collective goods. These authors note that contracting out processes, tenders and public–private partnerships are increasingly common. With this background, the chapter analyzes a specific manifestation of CSO ownership – multi-stakeholder CSO ownership in the provision of quasi-collective goods. Quasi-collective goods differ from classical collective goods in the nature of their benefits for the community. They can be considered as multilateral externalities. The involvement of a diverse collection of stakeholders in a CSO's ownership structure can therefore be a valuable asset. In particular, it can bring key resources to the organization including skills, networks, political influence and financial resources. The participation of stakeholders, especially users, in the ownership structure is also seen as a way to build trust by reducing the risk of opportunistic behavior in the provision of services in the presence of imperfect information. Through the conceptual framework of Ostrom, this chapter recognizes the multiplicity of governance forms that transcend the state-market dichotomy.

Chapter 11 by Enjolras and Steen-Johnsen investigates the potential for strengthening citizenship through newly emerging forms of governance. The authors point out two paradoxes. First, CSOs may have an impact on governance even when their internal governance is not democratic. Second, the role of CSOs in democratic governance is conditioned on the prevailing institutional governance regime. Drawing on these two paradoxes the authors assess the capability of different institutional governance models – in particular "corporative governance," "network governance" and "deliberative corporative governance" – to enhance citizenship and active participation, via three "models of democracy": participatory, deliberative and competitive democracy. The essential contribution of this chapter is to show how different governance regimes presuppose different types of democracy and citizenship.

Chapter 12 by Hulgård explores three ways of conceptualizing the relationship between the state and civil society. The first approach emphasizes the role of volunteerism and the building of society one (civic) unit at a time from the bottom up. Within this "tradition," civil society reflects family and community values as well as volunteerism. The second approach applies the concepts of social networks and social capital to examine the impact of micro-level interaction on individual mobility, urban cohesion and democratic performance. This approach is marked by a communitarian concern about the condition of civic engagement. The third approach stresses the historic relation between civil society organizations and government. Here, the author posits that CSOs should be equally recognized for their political dimension in matters of decision-making, and for their capacity for service provision delivered by volunteers and social entrepreneurs. As such, the author highlights the potential of an institutional–reciprocal model of the welfare state.

Chapter 13 by França Filho and Boullosa notes the originality of Ramos's work in reframing conventional organization theory. The authors explain how the idea of the para-economy is designed to implement the foundations of a political theory favoring a reallocation of resources and the establishment of relations among all social strata. In contrast to a market-oriented approach, this paradigm suggests a society that allows its members to take care of themselves according to their own criteria. Based on the phenomenon of social management in Brazil, the authors posit that governments and civil society actors can participate in the construction of public policies necessary to promote isonomy (equal rights) and fenonomie (environment conducive to creativity and autonomy, where the individual has a chance to act and not just behave passively), in order to promote a more sustainable world.

Chapter 14 is not a conventional book chapter. Rather, it is a collective and intercultural vision statement signed by researchers from Africa, Asia, Europe and Latin America (Eynaud, Ferrarini, França Filho, Gaiger, Hillenkamp, Kitajima,

Laville, Lemaître, Sadik, Veronese, Wanderley). Its purpose is to help point the way for future research that better accounts for cultural diversity worldwide. The authors note the difference between North American and European approaches to this issue. The latter, based largely on the work of EMES (the European Association for Social Enterprise Research), emphasizes the importance of participative governance. The authors claim a need to deepen the political dimension beyond participative governance. Going in such a direction, they argue about the need to examine carefully the realities (including the informal ones) of different continents. Then with this new impulse, the authors propose an ideal type of social enterprise from a solidarity economy perspective. They based it on three dimensions – economic, social and political (already present in the previous work of EMES). On the economic side, the authors suggest hybridization of economic principles and consistency of economic, social and environmental commitments. On the social side, they focus on indicators of transformation, social repair, democratic solidarity, and organizational autonomy. On the political side, they argue for publicness of mission service to support their role as intermediaries in public spaces, institutional entrepreneurship and political embeddeness. The authors suggest that this comprehensive framework can accommodate diverse cultural perspectives. This last chapter is just an exploratory example of how intercultural research can lead to new theoretical proposals.

Rather than present particular propositions about civil society and societal governance, we offer this last chapter as a demonstration of the possibilities for intercultural exchange in research on the social economy. In particular, the chapter illustrates how researchers with different cultural perspectives and from different national contexts can draw on each other's thinking to address some of the common issues of social enterprise. By extension, we argue in this book that such an approach can also enrich future research on governance and civil society. Until now, the debates have been largely confined to the US and Europe. An expansion of such exchange through the integration of ideas of scholars from the rest of the world can only enhance the prospects for improving the governance of CSOs and the societies in which they are embedded – worldwide and over the long term.

8 Rethinking the relationship between governance and democracy

The theoretical framework of the solidarity economy

Jean-Louis Laville and Anne Salmon

Introduction

In Part I of this volume, governance has been addressed at the organizational and inter-organizational levels, but it is also necessary to consider the context in which this concept has spread. Use of the term "governance" is linked to the questions raised for democracy by the recurrence of crises at the end of the twentieth century and the beginning of the twenty-first.

The three decades of post-war growth were marked by the establishment of a socio-economic compromise symbolized by the 1945 Declaration of Philadelphia, which affirmed that economic development was only worthwhile if it served social development. In other words, the role of government was accepted in the form of Keynesian interventionism and the welfare state, both intended to prevent the return of the disorders that had led to World War II. A first cultural crisis which started in the late 1960s manifested the exhaustion of this compromise, with new social movements such as ecology or feminism challenging the assimilation between economic growth and improvement of living conditions as the modes of action of the traditional social state impregnated with patriarchal norms. The protests that resulted were seen by the established powers as factors of social troubles which could render society uncontrollable.

This fear of a destabilization of the social order, combined with the eruption of the economic crisis triggered in the 1970s by the rise in oil prices, created the opportunity for the recognition of a current of thought, monetarism, more often known from the 1980s as neoliberalism. In reaction against the Declaration of Philadelphia, the Washington Consensus in 1989 advocated remedies to the crisis such as fiscal equilibrium (tax reform, reduction of public expenditure and subsidies, liberalization of external exchanges of goods and capital, privatization, deregulation, transparency of decision-making bodies, counter-inflation measures). It was at that historical moment that the term "governance" became widely used in the international literature, with "good governance" being understood by the World Bank in the 1990s as the introduction of structural adjustment policies applying the remedies recommended by the Washington consensus. Their massive adoption testifies to the attention paid to them by the governments open to the influence of the major international organizations.

So the invocation of the third sector to justify the withdrawal of the state coincides with the introduction of the concept of good governance advocated within the International Monetary Fund and the World Bank in a shift towards a minimal state (Smouts 1988). In a context in which political decision-makers were being called upon to strengthen the role of the private sector, civil society, through the international associations and the non-governmental organizations, which were treated as its representatives, became a tool in the service of the financial institutions: in 1988 they were intervening in 5 percent of World Bank projects, by 1997 in 47 percent (Azoulay 2002: 300–308).

The argument put forward in this chapter presenting the second part of this book is that this neoliberal project within which the abovementioned understanding of "governance" and the third sector took their place is of great importance, because it aims at a limitation of democracy, as Hayek makes clear in the work whose original content is presented in the first part.

It is by being aware of the scope of these questions raised by Hayek that it is conceivable to answer them from the opposite standpoint, that of a deepening of democracy. The theory of the solidarity economy envisages the third sector in this light, which the second part of this chapter explains. From this standpoint, it largely converges with the approaches of the key authors invoked below, namely Ostrom, Habermas, Guerreiro Ramos and Polanyi.

The central hypothesis that follows is that these theorists of reference can consolidate the theoretical framework of the solidarity economy and strengthen it as an alternative approach to the third sector to that proposed by Hayek, an alternative centred on its contribution to democracy. The emergence of the commons presented in the third part of this chapter, together with the plurality in democracy and in the economy detailed in the fourth and fifth parts respectively, provide the bases for another conception of governance. This alternative conception can be described as institutionalist in the sense that, in an interdisciplinary perspective, it looks for the processes, norms and values favorable to democracy through a valorization of institutional diversity as the condition for a renewal of public action that presupposes recognition of the role of the state but is not limited to this. The modes of governance of the third sector are then envisaged as belonging to the sphere of public action, which includes "the activity of the public authorities" but also "any activity articulated on a public space and entailing reference to a common good" (Laborier and Trom 2003: 11).

Neoliberalism and economization of the political sphere

Hayek (1981) endeavours to identify the means capable of protecting society from the danger of what he calls unlimited democracy. He situates himself in a tradition that advocates a system based on the homogenization of behaviors around the principle of personal interest.

But he adds a new clause: the need to dissociate democratic institutions from the formation of the popular will, whose unlimited sovereignty he contests in the framework of majority voting. What is more specifically at stake is the idea that the legitimacy of power stems from the popular will and that it manifests itself through purposive public action oriented towards the general interest and the common good. The teleological perspective contained in public action is regarded as an "anthropomorphic error" entailed by saying that society acts or wants something. According to Hayek, this interpretation imposes a factitious intentionality on the result of spontaneous processes. He evacuates all teleological dimensions from state action in favor of a "self-generated" order, but he also eliminates all teleological dimensions from collective and individual action. A society purged of human will needs to be constructed in which the spontaneous order of the market will stimulate the creation of organizations that are themselves self-generated. On the one hand a "sovereign law" has to be instituted, based on an agreement on general rules, or general principles derived from universally applicable rules of behavior, and on the other hand a spontaneous network has to be developed through the relations among individuals and among the various organizations created by them which he calls societies.

So it would be wrong to suppose that only the action of the state is in question. In fact all voluntary human actions and especially those stemming from the deliberately promoted organization of units of collective action, i.e., first and foremost groupings, associations, trade unions in all sectors, are suspected of paralyzing the play of the spontaneous forces of the market. The weakening of sovereignty comes, for Hayek, both from the challenging of public authority, which is regarded as unlimited in modern democracies, and also from the collective action of organized groups, which has gained an artificial preponderance over the forces of the market. Hayek understands very well that public action feeds on the collective actions of organized groups whose moral influence has powerful effects in terms of demands for social justice. Workers' associations are the first targets. Hayek seeks therefore to confine associations to a functional role as a depoliticized "independent third sector" between the private and the public which is capable of providing many services more effectively than the state.

Hayek talks about institutions but seeks to reduce them to organizations. In fact, he eliminates the institutional dimension, that of legitimacy and meaning. He judges private, public and third sector entities only in terms of their effectiveness and efficiency.

Solidarity economy and democratization of the economic sphere

This homogenization advocated by Hayek was echoed by governments in the 1980s, when the strength of social movements led some elites to fear an "excess of democracy" (Crozier *et al.* 1975). The spectre of an ungovernable society incited the authorities to endorse Hayek's suggestions. But it may be wondered, on a world scale, whether the period is not characterized by the loss of credibility of neoliberalism, the pursuit of spontaneous order having led to generalized disorder.

The social movements of the 1960s have fragmented, but the questions they raised remain open and other democratic dynamics have reasserted themselves. As Ogien and Laugier say in their survey on the new forms of politics, an effervescence has broken out:

> demonstrations and occupations, protest movements against the authorities, civil insurrections, transnational mobilizations, cyberactivism, creation of new parties, calls to disobedience.... This global wave of political protest started to roll in January 2011 in Tunisia, then swept through Cairo, moving on to Madrid, Athens, New York, London, Moscow, Quebec, San'aa, Tel Aviv, Dakar, Paris, Istanbul, Rio de Janeiro, Kiev, Caracas, Bangkok and Phnom Penh.
>
> (Ogien and Laugier 2014: 7)

So there is an opposition in the interpretation of the role of CSOs. Hayek's economistic and homogenizing vision can be contrasted with the approach of solidarity economy theory, constructed, mainly in Europe and South America, on the basis of observation of citizens' initiatives since the 1960s, which makes clear their contribution to institutional diversity. It is then not so much their efficiency that would be evaluated but their capacity to generate inventions, to widen the spectrum of solutions available to solve the problems of society.

Relative to the usual visions of the third sector, the solidarity economy introduces three main characteristics to account for the innovations in these initiatives.

- This access to the institutional reality presupposes the acknowledgement that the finalities of action cannot be solely determined by any interest; they involve reference to a common good that touches on a model of society. To put it in the terms of Lipietz (2001: 56), "in what name it is done" takes priority over "how, with what status and under what norms of organization it is done." For example, in organic farming and renewable energies, environmental costs are internalized that other enterprises externalize; the finalities chosen by the actors lead them to take charge of functions that are otherwise neglected, such as maintenance of the local heritage or defence of the environment. In fair trade, solidarity finance or "proximity services" (Laville and Nyssens 2000), respect for the criteria of social justice and accessibility of services are also constant.

The adequate means to achieve the finalities that are sought lie in the grouping of the stakeholders concerned, so as to specify the co-construction of a supply and a demand that were hitherto only latent or vaguely evoked. Thus, in proximity services, they are not only asymmetries of information, which according to Hayek would be signals orienting behaviors, but there is also an uncertainty about the very co-construction of the services. The promoters brought together around the project handle this informational uncertainty in the framework of an explicit pursuit of social justice, for example in equitable access to services or a "decent" job (Laville and Nyssens 2001: 9–21) or the social construction of what are called "positives externalities" in the orthodox economic approach (Fraisse *et al*. 2000: 192–207). As soon as these benefits are no longer a phenomenon induced by the economic activity but a dimension demanded by the promoters, it is logical that the latter be recruited from among the users and the professionals in the activity, joined by voluntary partners who believe in its rightness. For the pursuit of collective benefits hardly attracts private investors, and the dynamic of creation lies elsewhere, in the mobilization of a social capital or more precisely a civic capital (Borzaga and Defourny 2001) since it is constituted around collective benefits activating democratic social bonds.

* For all the reasons that have been mentioned, the second characteristic of the theoretical framework of the solidarity economy lies in pluralism in democracy. Contrary to Hayek, it is not a matter of being alarmed at the prospect of unlimited democracy but of favoring experiments in deepening democracy by drawing on the participatory and deliberative registers.

If contemporary initiatives have a twofold dimension, the traditional separation between advocacy and service CSOs is no longer valid. As has just been noted, the services provided are characterized not only by informational asymmetries but more fundamentally by informational uncertainty. What are in question are the nomenclature hypothesis and the probabilistic hypothesis which, according to Orléan, characterize the traditional approach in economics. The first consists in postulating the existence of goods of homogeneous quality among which it is possible to choose. The second assumes states of the world that are supposed to describe everything that can happen in the future. Since this information is not known to the persons for whom the question of engaging in relational services arises, their capacity to exchange depends on the construction of common guidelines (Orléan 2002). Given the radically incomplete character of the information available, it becomes necessary to step outside the aggregative paradigm according to which an economic fact can be explained by the aggregation of individual preferences.

The theory of the solidarity economy contests this aggregative paradigm on the basis of deliberative conceptions of democracy. As Elster (1986) puts it, aggregative conceptions consider that preferences are exogenous to political processes: in so doing they confuse behaviors appropriate to the "market" and to the "forum," the former being dedicated to the pursuit of efficiency and the latter to the pursuit of the just definition; they do not consider that expressed preferences do not necessarily reflect real preferences, since actors may have reasons to conceal the latter or to adapt to the context. Above all, as Sunstein (2000) also points out, because it ignores the specificity of the forum the aggregative paradigm is unable to give any meaning to the idea of the public space. Ultimately what is denied by Hayek is the involvement of third sector entities in the self-government of the people, in which discussion is not indexed on individual preferences but "is the result of general deliberation of all" (Manin 1985: 83).

In the deliberative perspective which is that of the solidarity economy, CSOs are inseparable from what Fraser (1992) calls the discovery of the dimension of public space present in civil society. They are not only within deliberative democracy but at the interface of deliberative and representative democracies, undergoing the constraints of the institutional framework but also able to take part in changing it.

* Their resistance to normalization is moreover linked to their capacity to mobilize pluralism in the economy. On the basis of the principles identified by Polanyi in a substantive economy (market, redistribution, reciprocity, householding), a variety of combinations have developed historically. They can also be used to define not three sectors but a tripolar economy in today's world.

The market economy is one in which the production of goods and services is based on the motivation of material interest and their distribution is entrusted to the market, which sets the price that brings supply and demand together for the exchange of goods and services. The relationship between supply and demand is established contractually, based on a calculation of interest that allows for increasing autonomy in terms of other non-market social relations. However, the market economy is certainly not the product of the market principle alone. Market economies are not only organized around the market; they include many non-market contributions, such as collective infrastructures and grants for businesses. Nevertheless, the distinctive feature of the market economy is the priority given to the market and the subordination of the non-market and non-monetary contributions to it.

The non-market economy is an economy in which the production and distribution of goods and services are entrusted to redistribution organized by either private bodies, such as foundations, or public bodies, when it is under the tutelage of the welfare state. Public redistribution is mobilized to provide citizens with individual rights, thanks to which they are entitled to social security benefits or last-resort assistance if they are part of the most disadvantaged groups. Public service is defined by a delivery of goods and services involving a redistributive dimension, and the rules governing this dimension are laid down by a public authority subject to democratic control. Redistribution in a broad sense covers all forms of levy and resource allocation, whether the purpose is financing social transfer or playing the role of a macroeconomic stabilizing force.

The non-monetary economy is the one in which the distribution of goods and services is based primarily on reciprocity and householding. Clearly, a number of reciprocity-based relationships take a monetary form but it is definitely within the non-monetary economy that the main reciprocity-based contributions are generated, whether by self-production or by the private household economy. The reciprocity or householding cycle is the opposite of a market exchange because it is inseparable from human relationships that bring into play the desires for recognition and power. It must be distinguished from redistributive exchange because it is not imposed by a central authority.

Each division of the economy is therefore organized around the predominance of one principle, and the main examples of the present-day economy reflect a hierarchy of these divisions, with the market economy considered as primary, the non-market economy as supplementary, and the non-monetary economy as residual. Within such a framework of understanding, the specificity of the third sector can therefore be interpreted as a hybridization between the three poles of the economy, existing in a state of tension with their hierarchical structure. In other words, the third sector is not defined as a clear-cut sector and is approached more as a hybridization of different economic principles.

It is clear that this concept overlaps with the "welfare pluralism" of Evers (1990) and the "welfare mix" of Pestoff (1991). In all cases it is emphasized that third sector organizations are influenced simultaneously by different spheres that make up their social and historical context, and that their survival as something "different," instead of adapting to the core values of state and market or regressing to informal settings and networks, cannot be taken for granted. Despite their differences, all the approaches of "welfare mix and welfare pluralism" argue for a "mixed "or "plural" economy.

The emergence of the commons

The thinking of Ostrom, as formulated in 1990 in *Governing the Commons*, is close to that evoked in the introduction to this book with regard to the third sector. Ostrom identifies types of goods from the point of view of the rivalry and non-exclusivity that correspond to the space of common goods.

The contributions of such an approach are indisputable. The concepts of the commons and the third sector precisely signal the move out of a mode of thought clouded by the opposition and complementarity between the market and the state. The debates of the twentieth century were centered on market–state dualism. This is seen clearly in the opposition between liberalism and state socialism that structured the political space of the twentieth century. But this binary reasoning is becoming worn out. It is in this context of crisis of the synergy between market and state, private and public, that the ideas of the commons and the third sector are emerging. Ostrom has assembled the empirical evidence and given currency to the idea that throughout the world there is a specific space for commons, precisely in the gaps left by the market and the state. She shows that systems of production, fisheries, pastures, forests or irrigation systems are "commons" because their management must be governed by collective rules to prevent exhaustion of the resources by predatory individual exploitation. So neither the market nor the state is best suited to satisfy a certain number of needs. This is a first displacement which has made it possible to start to go beyond the ideological confrontation of neoliberalism and statism. It is not negligible to observe that the standard economy, far from being reduced to the discourse of total marketization, is examining the conditions in which it proves legitimate to find solutions by recourse to commons or the third sector. The limits derive from the fact that orthodox postulates remain in force, namely:

the market is not a universal response in economic matters, the state is only sub-sidiary, and commons or the third sector are only residual. Above all individual maximizing rationality is not contested. While the choices of organizations are diverse, they are all explained by the pursuit of personal interest and competitive pressure. The logic remains aggregative in the sense used above; the interde-pendencies among actors are manifested in comparisons between the preferences established by each of them, without communication or collective deliberation. Finally, institutions stem from cost-benefit calculations and are only maintained if they demonstrate effectiveness in adapting to changing environments.

The ambiguity lies in the partial recognition of a diversity that remains hierar-chized. In the course of her works, however, Ostrom enlarges the breach she has opened by enriching our understanding of institutional diversity (Ostrom 2005) and underscoring the importance of the instituted collective rules that character-ize the governance of commons. She moves away from the neo-institutionalism of Williamson and closer to the historical institutionalism of Commons and Veblen on the basis of three criteria: "the idea that institutions affect what people think and what they value"; the fact that action is not oriented solely by interest but "also depends on habits of doing and thinking, as well as particular circum-stances and contexts"; and the rejection of "static theories" and the conviction that a genealogical approach is pertinent because economics is an evolutionary science (Chanteau and Labrousse 2013: 90–91). In Chapter 9 of this volume, Sievers adds the trust that the institutional structures have managed to create and that networked governances authorize. Moreover, the advent of new fields for commons, in information technology for example, with open-source software, favors reflections on the cross-cutting characteristics that make it possible to break out of the economic naturalism that confines the commons to certain domains. The commons principle can be extended to a number of collective action. This can only be done by articulating the finality of the activity, which must be guided by the predominance of the right to use the goods over owner-ship and accumulation, and the norms of their governance, whether natural resources, knowledge or other types of activities. Extended in two directions, to take account of the question of power and that of overall institutional architec-tures (Weinstein 2013: 67–68), Ostrom's investigations enable us to set out in detail the relationship with public authorities, as Nyssens and Petrella note in Chapter 10 of this book.

The additional requirement implied by the move from common goods to a political principle of commons is analogous to the move from economic ana-lysis of the third sector to a pluridisciplinary analysis such as that of the solid-arity economy. Conventional economics both in theoretical and practical terms distinguishes carefully between democracy and economic production and even sets them against each other. The first is regarded as alien to the economy, and even anti-economic. This is one of the characteristics of liberal democracies, which set up two universes, the political domain and the economic one, that are completely separate. This radical separation is challenged by the principle of the commons and the solidarity economy. They converge on what might be termed associationism, i.e., a politics that proposes democratizing society through practices belonging to associative life, in the sense of França Filho's and Boullosa's chapter, which are marked by an establishment and modification of the rules that self-organized collectives make for themselves. In other words, CSOs maintain their associationist specificity if they develop the deliberative aspect within themselves and also through the wider debates to which they contribute.

The plurality in democracy

As Enjolras and Steen-Johnsen show in their chapter, democracy is pluralistic. It may be representative, but it is also participatory and deliberative. As regards the participatory and deliberative dimension, the work of Habermas is an essential additional resource. In his conception of politics he "thematizes the structural tension in democratic constitutional states between administrative and communicative power" (Ladrière 2001: 408). Administrative power corresponds to politics as understood by Weber, meaning the domination exercised by public powers which impose their authority through the monopoly of legitimate violence. Against this vision of power, Arendt invokes another tradition, that of the power that Habermas calls communicative, the "being together" that is expressed in a public space where appearance within a plurality of equals authorizes the exchange of opinions, deliberation and decision.

The genesis of this public forum in its modern version was retraced by Habermas as early as 1962 in his work *Strukturwandel der Offentlichkeit* translated into English in 1989 under the title *The Structural Transformation of the Public Sphere*. This book focuses, as Calhoun says, "upon the bourgeois political life of the seventeenth through mid-twentieth centuries" and its subsequent "partial degeneration" (Calhoun 1992: 1–2). "The ideal of the public sphere calls for social integration to be based on rational–critical discourse. Integration, in other words, is to be based on communication rather than domination," as Calhoun adds (1992: 29), but it is prone to colonization and social pathologies when the isomorphic pressure from economic and administrative systemic rationality replaces real life actions and structures. This first position of Habermas provides a sharp criticism of voluntary associations: "The public sphere has become more an arena for advertising than a setting for rational–critical debate" (Calhoun 1992: 26) and CSOs, like political parties, "move people to offer their acclamation without providing political education or remedies for the 'political immaturity' of voters" (1992: 27). Plebiscites and bargaining between special-interest groups serve as a substitute for public rational–critical debate.

But in the new foreword written in 1990, influenced by the conference organized in September 1989 on the occasion of the publication of *The Structural Transformation*, Habermas takes a second position, reformulating the main question of the book as "the rediscovery of civil society" (Habermas 1990). He acknowledges the necessary pluralization of the public space. In this new theoretical framework, civil society can influence representative democracy because it is open to public spaces. As Hulgård shows in Chapter 12 of this volume, Habermas has the merit of clarity: he is opposed to a vision of civil society centered on its moral and voluntary potentials; he maintains that they are public spaces within civil society and it is necessary to take them in account. Otherwise, "civil society talk will remain hopelessly one-sided and analytically useless" if "it cannot articulate the complex relation between social and political institutions" (Cohen 1998: 14).

Communicative activity oriented towards justice and sincerity (Habermas 1984) cannot be reduced to the exchange of rational arguments; it involves acts which presuppose the conviction and commitment of those who perform them, as well as efforts to persuade or even seduce. The concept of the public space can be "sociologized" if one is more interested in the concrete process through which the citizens, whose relations are governed by the principles of equality and freedom, question the gap between the affirmation of democracy and the reality. If the approach is inflected in this way, it is the refusals of recognition violating democratic principles that are one of the mainsprings of collective action. The public space in the generic sense symbolically constitutes the matrix of the political community, but, as Eley (1992) says, it is also in the concrete forms of expression through which an arena of contested meanings manifests itself. Different publics strive to make themselves heard there and are opposed in controversies. The public space undergoes continual redefinition. Part of it is constrained by the pressure of the systems, while new spaces for the formation of opinion and the political are generated by many forms of grouping among citizens. This permanent reconfiguration leads one to speak, as Habermas himself recognized (1990: 32), of a "polycentric public space" rather than a single public space.

One can then move from the identification of a plurality of public spaces to the study of the oppositions within them. A number of public spaces have been progressively dominated by the mass media and taken over by functional imperatives. The quality of democratic life is therefore dependent on the constitution of other, autonomous public spaces; hence the link with the associationism made up of collective actions implemented by free and equal citizens making reference to a common good. To break free from the rational action paradigm, it is necessary to mobilize this concept of voluntary association, which allows one to think of spontaneously emergent, domination-free relationships in non contractualist terms (Habermas 1997: 53). Habermas then converges with other authors such as Offe in emphasizing associative relationships and the prominent position in civil society of CSOs around which autonomous public spaces can crystallize, which justifies paying attention to voluntary association and associative life as a principal medium for the definition of public commitments (Habermas 1992: 186). Why then does he hardly study these associative relationships which he considers essential for the future of democracy?

First, Habermas's valorization of associative relationships is somewhat lacking in precision. He privileges associations oriented towards demands, aiming to defend forms of solidarity and culture, such as regionalist, feminist or ecological movements. In the book edited by Calhoun, his "neglect of social movements" is indeed discussed especially by Eley, Baker, Garnham and Fraser, who argue for a notion of multiple, sometimes overlapping or contending public spheres (Calhoun 1992: 37). For Fraser (2014), the too-sharp distinction that Habermas makes between associations in which opinions are formed and the public authorities who make decisions diverts him from an investigation of the complex relationship between civil society and public authorities. This compartmentalization prevents analysis of the interdependencies that would presuppose a broader conception of public action, not limited to the activity of the public authorities but including each activity articulated within a public space and requiring reference to a common good. From this standpoint Ostrom's works provide material proving that CSOs are not limited to the formation of opinions and include decision-making in the framework of a situated action.

Moreover, Habermas focuses only on associations that are neither economic nor linked to the state. The exclusion of others stems from the fact that the spheres of the economy and the state are related to the systems, and those of the public space and the family to lifeworlds. Given the unsustainability of such a separation, it is preferable to accept that the oppositions between systems and lifeworlds run through each sphere with varying intensity. The corollary is that there are not different categories of associations, some of which escape reification; rather, each association is torn between attempts at autonomization and a tendency to isomorphic normalization. The resulting unstable equilibria can only be untangled if one rejects the confluence of public action and administration and also that between market and the economy.

Plurality in the economy

Political plurality is matched by the economic plurality that is conceivable on the basis of a substantive definition that recognizes the principles of the market and redistribution but also those of reciprocity and household administration (Polanyi 1977). This is why it is relevant to complement Habermas with Guerreiro Ramos and Polanyi. Guerreiro Ramos points out that Weber distinguishes between two rationalities. Formal rationality (*Zweckrationalität*) refers to "conventional maximization of utility, under conditions of scarcity and expressed in quantitative terms." Substantive rationality (*Wertrationalität*) "refers to allocation within the guidelines of other principles, such as communal loyalties" (Smelser and Swedberg 1994: 5). He observes that Weber was studying a world in which formal rationality was spreading and impregnating the science of organizations. As an antidote to the ethnocentrism with which it is therefore charged, Guerreiro Ramos proposes to explore a substantive theory of associative human life, bearing in mind that substantive rationality can be found in thinkers of different periods and societies. This anthropological orientation leads him to distinguish substantive and formal economies, converging with Polanyi. The substantive meaning of "economic" derives from man's dependence for his livelihood upon nature and his fellow man. It refers to the "institutionalized interaction between himself and his natural surroundings ... which supplies him with the means of satisfying his material wants." The formal meaning of "economic" stems from the logical character of the means–ends relationships, as apparent in such words as "economical" or "economizing." It refers to a definite situation of choice, namely, that between the different uses of means induced by their scarcity (Polanyi 1977: 20).

Polanyi remarks that even Menger identified the distinction between these two meanings in the posthumous edition of his *Grundsätze del Volkwirtschaftlehere (Principles of Economies)* in 1923. The first is the economizing direction, dependent on scarcity; the second is the "techno-economic" direction, independent and linked to the physical conditions of production. But when the English translation was published, the previous edition, written in 1871, was selected, the posthumous text being described by Hayek in his preface as "fragmentary and disordered." "Hayek concluded: 'The results of the work of Menger's later years must be regarded as lost.'" (Polanyi 1977: 23). For Polanyi this omission is serious because the basis of the substantive concepts is the empirical economy itself. It can be briefly (if not engagingly) defined as an institutionalized process of interaction between man and his environment, which secures the satisfaction of his material wants. The classification of empirical economies, then, might best take its start from the manner in which economies are integrated. Integration is one of the effects of the instituting of the economic process. We find the main forms of integration to be reciprocity, redistribution and exchange. Reciprocity denotes movements between correlative points of symmetrical groupings in society; redistribution designates movements towards an allocating center and out of it again; exchange refers to vice-versa movements taking place as between "hands" under a market system (Polanyi 1977: 31). Keeping in mind that Polanyi in other texts includes a fourth principle of householding, if one adopts this wide view of the economy embracing these diverse principles, which are not separate sectors but can be combined in various ways, it becomes easier to envision the scope of what is possible in the economic activity of CSOs: they articulate these principles both in their project and in response to the constraints of the institutional frameworks.

Thus every association potentially draws its resources from the three poles of the economy: a market economy, through the sale of goods and services that produces competition; a non-market economy, in which it receives contributions in the form of transfer revenues and also private donations; and a non-monetary economy based on the active support it receives through various forms of voluntary engagement, including mutual help networks and the involvement of users.

Economic activities are not apprehended solely by reference to the market. Associations are not limited to market services; nor do they belong to a sector organized solely around reciprocity (Eme *et al.* 1996). For, while their founding impulse may be that of reciprocity, their evolution can lead to a strengthening within them of other principles, in particular those of the market and redistribution. Some associations even follow a trajectory that leads them to resemble quasi-administrations when their resources come almost entirely from redistribution or quasi-enterprises when they turn towards the market.

In each CSO, it becomes possible to examine the various elements of their general accounts and break them down so as to bring out more clearly the types of resources: market, non-market and non-monetary. One also needs to re-integrate resources lying outside the accounts (exemption from charges, provision of personnel or premises, etc.) and make explicit the different components of budget lines that may be conflated in the general accounts (provision of services that may include an element of subsidy from the public authorities to reduce the cost paid by all consumers or some of them on the basis of their income, etc.). Market resources come essentially from the sale to consumers and the fulfillment of private orders. But the payment of services may also be made by redistribution agencies, in various forms: subsidies to consumers, subsidies to producers, invitations to tender with or without particular clauses. When there is a public call for tenders, the competitive conditions do not mean leaving the framework of redistribution. The allocation of public finances to the consumers in order to cover part of the costs of service provision and the use of calls for tender make clear the recourse to quasi-market mechanisms, i.e., ones close to market mechanisms, even if social environmental criteria may influence the choice of service provider. Operating subsidies are generally of public or semi-public origin, but they may also come from private organizations such as foundations. The provision of means in kind, whether human or material, belongs to the same register. Other aids may be granted, not for the activity carried on but in the framework of employment policies, whether general or selective, i.e., targeted at particular groups. Subscriptions and membership fees may be preconditions for market exchanges, and should then be classified as market resources. But they may also be voluntary, and are then to be considered as reciprocity, as are the individual donations of people wishing to support the work of the CSO. Though reciprocity may therefore be expressed in monetary form, it generally takes non-monetary forms through the time devoted by volunteers and through partnerships. These non-monetary contributions may recompensed through calculation of a monetary equivalent, but it is important to remember its reductive character, since this equivalent is far from fully covering the meaning of a voluntary commitment.

The economic equilibrium of every CSO thus results from a hybridization of the three poles of the economy, each requiring a specific study. This hybridizing manifests a twofold movement. The institutionalist process of the economy in modern democracies has been characterized by the priority given to market exchange, even to the point of the economistic fallacy of identifying the market with the economy (Polanyi 1977: 5–17). But another, contradictory movement has been made possible by the secularization of society: the invention of modern solidarity. By reviewing the forms this takes, it is possible to specify what Habermas refers to as the socially integrating force of solidarity to counter the power of money and administrative power.

Democratic solidarity takes two forms. The first is that of self-organization in the mode of the commons, which can be related to the principle of egalitarian reciprocity; the second is that of the social state guaranteeing rights and incomes through public redistribution. This democratic solidarity contrasts with a philanthropic solidarity that substitutes for the vocabulary of equality and rights that of private benevolence. The split between democratic and philanthropic solidarity, which has been present since the nineteenth century, has reappeared on the scene in this twenty-first century debate, with an expansion of the new "big philanthropy," which "undermines democracy" (Barkan 2013), combined with "social business" or "corporate social responsibility" models and "bottom of the pyramid" or "social impact bonds" tools.

Conclusion

The conceptualization of the solidarity economy is inseparable from an interdisciplinarity enabling one to understand the economy beyond the market and the political beyond the state (Laville 2011).

In this regard, the solidarity economy converges with the new economic sociology inspired by Granovetter (1985), bringing to light the institutional construction of markets in rules, which leads one to speak of pluralistic markets. But the solidarity economy aims to go much further in the critique. If markets in their concrete multiplicity do not correspond to the abstract representation of the self-regulating market, the latter still has a performative character. For this reason, the framing of markets does not in itself protect against the political shaping of a market society (Polanyi 1957). To counter this, beyond the distinction between markets, a further distinction must be added: that between the economy and the market. An economy that sustains democracy rather than threatening it cannot dispense with markets, but cannot be limited to them. The re-embedding of the economy as a means to serve human goals presupposes an institutional framework that leaves room for several logics of economic action. It is not only markets that are plural, but also economic motives and, ultimately, the economy itself. The preservation of markets and their decentralized arbitrages must be accompanied by protection against their hegemony.

Respect for markets has to be balanced by recourse to the principles of redistribution and reciprocity. Redistribution needs to be revalued as a resource allocation system for everything that involves the public good. Reciprocity for its part should be regarded as a taking account of the commons: in a largely immaterial and relational economy, trust based on mutual understanding can allow a co-elaboration for creative and productive purposes. It is important in this regard to rehabilitate fully the collective power flowing from reciprocity, which is learned and experienced in collective mobilizations (Cefaï 2007) but which also has an economic potentiality. The affirmation of a reciprocity that combines the "spirit of the gift" (Godbout 2000) with the concern for equality is moreover an antidote to philanthropy enrolled as the conscience of liberalism, offering the idea of the "gift without reciprocity" (Ranci 1990).

But if the economy cannot be reduced to the market alone, nor can social solidarity be confined to the state. The CSO, in its generic sense, is far from having every virtue; it is liable to many commercial or bureaucratic flaws, but it gives shape to social practices that cannot happen in other places. For this reason, associationism can make it possible to restore to politics a place that economism denies it, without thereby focusing on the state. To move beyond small-scale experiments, plural economy and plural democracy reinforce each other. To put it another way, representative democracy can be strengthened by forms of direct democracy that are not only granted but also won through collective actions. This linkage between deliberative and representative democracy is, however, only conceivable if fears of a destabilization of existing powers give way to the conviction of the urgency for a more active citizenship. The problem is not that of choosing between civil society and the state, but rather of envisioning a reciprocal democratization of civil society and public authorities. The social state has promoted a conception of solidarity based on individual rights and redistribution. The reconquest of its legitimacy can only succeed if it integrates within itself opportunities for increased participation for employees and users and is extended by an associationism impregnated with democratic solidarity.

The theoretical framework of the solidarity economy, revisited with the aid of the contributions of the authors cited, is characterized by the reintegration of three salient features (see Figure 8.1) which Hayek undertook to eliminate.

*   Ostrom reintroduces a teleological perspective and connects the common good with co-activity to convert it into a problematic of the commons that links the goals sought with the means used to attain them. This perspective is backed by recourse to public spaces in Habermas and various economic principles in Polanyi and Guerreiro Ramos.

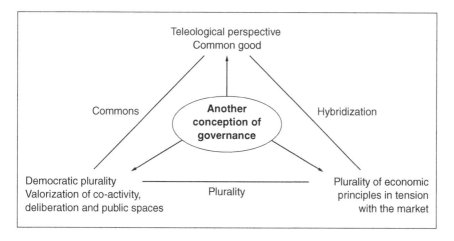

Figure 8.1 The solidarity economy framework revisited.

- Habermas, for his part, contests the pertinence of the aggregative paradigm of individual preferences and shows the importance of deliberation. Ostrom demonstrates that it is not simply a matter of the formation of opinions but that deliberation can be mobilized as a means of decision in the framework of the activity of a collective. Polanyi and Guerreiro Ramos urge a move away from the reduction of the economy to the market, from which Habermas has not broken free.
- Finally, Polanyi and Guerreiro Ramos reject the conceptual anachronism of catallaxy, i.e., the spontaneous order of the market as understood by Hayek, by referring to a plurality of economic principles. They can be complemented with recourse to Habermas as regards the springs of democratic action and to Ostrom for a resistance to marketization that does not turn towards statism.

There is thus a complementarity among all these contributions, through which another conception of governance takes shape. This is explored in this second part of the book, suggesting an outline of what could become a program for research.

References

Azoulay, G. (2002) *Les Théories du développement: Du rattrapage des retards à l'exclusion des inégalités*, Rennes: Presses Universitaires de Rennes.

Barkan, J. (2013) "Plutocrats at Work: How Big Philanthropy Undermines Democracy," *Social Research*, 80, pp. 635–652.

Borzaga, C. (2004) "From Suffocation to Re-emergence: The Evolution of the Italian Third Sector," in A. Evers and J.-L. Laville (eds) *The Third Sector in Europe*, Cheltenham: Edward Elgar, pp. 139–153.

Borzaga, C. and Defourny, J. (2001) *The Emergence of Social Enterprise*, New York: Routledge.

Calhoun, C. (ed.) (1992) *Habermas and the Public Sphere*, Cambridge, MA: MIT Press.

Cefaï, D. (2007) *Pourquoi se mobilise-t-on? Les théories de l'action collective*, Paris: La Découverte.

Chanteau, J. -P. and Labrousse, A. (2013) "L'institutionnalisme méthodologique d'Elinor Ostrom: Quelques enjeux et controverses," *Revue de la regulation* [online], 14, published 12 December 2013, accessed 11 October 2014, http://regulation.revues.org/10555.

Cohen, J. -L. (1998) "American Civil Society Talk," *Philosophy and Public Policy Quarterly*, 18(3), pp. 14–19.

Crozier, M., Huntington, S. and Watanuki, J. (1975) *The Crisis of Democracy: Report on the Governability of Democracies to the Trilateral Commission*, New York: New York University Press.

Eley, G. (1992) "Nations, Publics, and Political Cultures: Placing Habermas in the Nineteenth Century," in C. Calhoun (ed.) *Habermas and the Public Sphere*, Cambridge, MA: MIT Press, pp. 289–339.

Elster, J. (1986) "The Market and the Forum; Three Varieties of Political Theory," in J. Elster and A. Hylland (eds) *Foundations of Social Choice Theory*, Cambridge: Cambridge University Press, pp. 103–132.

Eme, B., Laville, J.-L., Favereau, L. and Vaillancourt, Y. (1996) *Société civile, Etat et économie plurielle*, Paris: Crida-Lsci, and Montreal: Crises.

Evers, A. (1990) "Im intermediären Bereich: Soziale Träger und Projekte zwischen Haushalt, Staat und Markt," *Journal für Sozialforschung*, 30(2), pp. 189–210.

Favereau, O. (1989) "Marchés internes, marchés externes," *Revue économique*, 40 (2), pp. 273–328.

Fraisse, L., Gardin, L. and Laville, J. -L. (2000) *Le Fonctionnement socio-économique du troisième système*, Recherche européenne pour la Direction de l'emploi et des affaires sociales de la Commission des communautés européennes.

Fraser, N. (1992) "Rethinking the Public Sphere: A Contribution to the Critique of Actually Existing Democracy," in C. Calhoun (ed.) *Habermas and the Public Sphere*, Cambridge, MA: MIT Press, pp. 109–142.

Fraser, N. (2014) interview with J. -L. Laville, M. Hersent and M. Saussey, working paper, Paris, Cnam.

Granovetter, M. (1985). "Economic Action and Social Structure: The Problem of Embeddedness". *American Journal of Sociology* 91 (3): 481–510.

Guerreiro Ramos, A. (1989) *A nova ciência das organisações – uma reconceituação da riqueza das nações*, Rio de Janeiro: Editore de Fundaçao Getulis Vargas.

Godbout, J.-T. (2000) *Le Don, la dette et l'intérêt*, Paris: La Découverte.

Habermas, J. (1962) *Strukturwandel der Offentlichkeit*, Frankfurt: Hermann Luchterhand.

Habermas, J. (1984) *Theory of Communicative Action*, Boston, MA: Beacon Press.

Habermas, J. (1986) "The New Obscurity: The Crisis of the Welfare State and the Exhaustion of Utopian Energies," *Philosophy and Social Criticism*, 11, pp. 1–18.

Habermas, J. (1989) *The Structural Transformation of the Public Sphere*, Cambridge, MA: MIT Press.

Habermas, J. (1990) "Vorwort zur Neuaflage 1990," in *Strukturwandel der Öffentlichkeit*, Frankfurt: Surhkamp, pp. 11–50.

Habermas, J. (1997) "Popular Sovereignty as Procedure," in J. Bohman and W. Rehg (eds), *Essays on Deliberative Democracy*, Cambridge, MA: MIT Press, pp. 35–66.

Hayek, F. A. (1981) *Law, Legislation and Liberty*, Volume 3: The Political Order of a Free People.

Laborier, P. and Trom, D. (2003) *Historicités de l'action publique*, Paris: Presses Universitaires de France.

Ladrière, P. (2001) *Pour une sociologie de l'éthique*, Paris: Presses Universitaires de France.

Laville, J. -L. (2011) *Politique de l'association*, Paris: Le Seuil.

Laville, J. -L. and Nyssens, M. (eds) (2000) "Solidarity-based Third-sector organizations in the Proximity Sciences Field: A European Francophone Perspective," *Voluntas*, 11(1), pp. 67–84.

Laville, J.- L. and Nyssens, M. (eds) (2001) *Les Services sociaux entre associations, état et marché: L'aide aux personnes âgées*, Paris: La Découverte.

Lipietz, A. (2001) *Pour le tiers secteur*, Paris: La Découverte/La Documentation française.

Manin, B. (1985) "Volonté générale ou délibération? Esquisse d'une théorie de la délibération publique," *Le Débat*, 33, pp. 72–93.

Menger, C. (1923) *Grundsätze del Volkwirtschaftslehere*, Vienna: Carl Menger.

Menger, C. (1950) *Principles of Economics*, Glencoe: The Free Press.

Nyssens, M. (2000) "Les approches économiques du tiers secteur: Apports et limites des analyses anglo-saxonnes d'inspiration néoclassique," *Sociologie du travail*, 42 (4), pp. 551–565.

Ogien, R. and Laugier, S. (2014) *Le Principe démocratique*, Paris: La Découverte.

Orléan, A. (2002) "Pour une nouvelle approche des interactions financières: L'Économie des conventions face à la sociologie économique," in I. Huault (ed.) *La Construction sociale de l'entreprise: Autour des travaux de Mark Granovetter*, Paris: Editions EMS, pp. 207–229.

Ostrom, E. (1990) *Governing the Commons: The Evolution of Institutions for Collective Action*, New York: Cambridge University Press.

Ostrom, E. (2005) *Understanding Institutional Diversity*, Princeton: Princeton University Press.

Pestoff, V. (1991) *Between the Market and Politics: Cooperatives in Sweden*, Frankfurt am Main and Boulder, CO: Campus Verlag and Westview Press.

Pestoff, V. (1998) *Beyond the Market and the State: Social Enterprises and Civil Democracy in a Welfare Society*, Aldershot: Ashgate.

Polanyi, K. (1957) *The Great Transformation: The Political and Economic Vision of our Time*, Boston: Beacon Press, Beacon Hill.

Polanyi, K. (1977) *The Livelihood of Man*, New York: Academic Press.

Ranci, C. (1990) "Doni senza reciprocità: La persistenza dell'altruismo sociale nei sistemi complessi," *Rassegna italiana di sociologia*, 31(3), pp. 363–387.

Smelser, N. J. and Swedberg, R. (eds) (1994) *The Handbook of Economic Sociology*, Princeton: Princeton University Press.

Smouts, M. -C. (1988) *Les Nouvelles relations internationales*, Paris: Presses de Sciences Po.

Sunstein, C. (2000) "Deliberative Trouble? Why Groups Go to Extremes," *The Yale Law Journal*, 48, pp. 947–969.

Weinstein, O. (2013) "Comment comprendre les 'communs': Elinor Ostrom, la propriété et la nouvelle économie institutionnelle," *Revue de la régulation* [online], 14, Autumn, published 12 December 2013, accessed 11 October 2014, http://regulation.revues.org/10452.

9 Civil society and governance

Contemporary challenges

Bruce R. Sievers

Introduction

In the Western tradition, civil society has long been demarcated as a separate sphere from government – as an arena in which private associations shape public opinion and champion social causes but do not seek to participate in formal governing activity. This complementary relationship between civil society and government has indeed become the defining model of liberal democracy. In recent decades, however, civil society has been increasingly called upon to fill gaps in policy and social service provision where government is inadequate or nonexistent. As civil society has expanded ever more widely into the governmental sphere, the boundaries between the two have become blurred, with important consequences for each. This transformation raises a fundamental question about civil society's relationship to governance: how are we to understand the changed role of CSOs when they act in a quasi-governmental capacity in the modern liberal democratic state? Lacking the traditional legitimacy of the state, CSOs find themselves in a dilemma: they must seek to respond to particularistic interests of their members while at the same time serving the wider interests of the public. Although part of the solution to this dilemma can be found in the current emphasis on improved internal governance structures – greater transparency and representation – important new possibilities are contained in two contemporary arenas of social interaction: networks and design. Both offer novel prospects for bridging the civil society–government gap by supplying new forms of legitimacy and accountability to CSOs.

Civil society's historical relationship to government

A distinctive characteristic of the modern democratic state has been the evolution of a dynamic balance between government and civil society. In what has become the widely accepted model of this relationship, citizens mandate the provision of public goods through the state's legitimate governing authority while, at the same time, they act voluntarily through civil society to provide public goods not supplied by the state or to influence the state's provision of public goods. The democratic state thus has enjoyed the power of public authority, while civil society has enjoyed the freedom of private action.

This model of the democratic state has been foundational to the idea of liberal democracy. A central strand of this tradition in the United States has been the Tocquevillian notion that private associational life is an essential precondition of American democracy and that certain values fostered by civic interaction in voluntary bodies – tolerance, public-spiritedness, social trust and "generalized reciprocity" – create the platform of behaviors and attitudes necessary for successful democratic governance.[1]

In this tradition, civil society's relationship to government ranges from complementary to oppositional, but in all cases the two spheres have been seen as distinct. Civil society enables the free formation of public opinion and the expression of competing views of policy positions on behalf of diverse segments of society, reflecting the fundamental rights of voluntary association and free expression. Government, for its part, generates universally accepted rules and electoral procedures for deciding among proposed policies and adopting mandatory laws and regulations applied equitably throughout society. In this relationship, civil society *proposes* alternative solutions to policy dilemmas and urges their public adoption, while government *disposes* by acting to mandate and enforce the chosen policies. Citizens take on a dual role in which they act at times as advocates and volunteers, and at times as legislators and law-abiding members of the public.

In Posts and Rosenblum's description of this standard model the boundary between civil society and government is portrayed as an ever-shifting line of demarcation between voluntary and mandated action:

> The boundary functions to set civil society and government in productive tension. It defines the pluralism and particularism of civil society in opposition to the inclusive and overarching norms of government. Push the boundary too far in the direction of government, and civil society can wither away. Push the boundary too far in the direction of civil society, and government can collapse into anarchic disorder. Wherever the distinction between civil society and government is marked, however, there must always exist a boundary between them, because each is defined in opposition to the other.
>
> (Post and Rosenblum, 2002, 10–11)

In the modern world, however, the line between civil society and government has become increasingly blurred. In the traditional model, government served as the authoritative, universal, equitable and accountable allocator of public goods, while civil society acted as the freely acting proponent of alternative solutions and a voluntary provider of such goods. But in the contemporary world government has receded from, or in some cases abdicated entirely, its role in the provision of many public goods, leaving civil society to fill the gap. This trend poses serious new challenges to civil society's relationship to governance in the liberal democratic polity.

Liberal democratic theory, as it has developed since the seventeenth century, has conceptualized civil society as an autonomous sphere.[2] In practice, the line between the state's and civil society's responsibilities for the provision of public services has evolved over time, but the distinction between that which is properly mandated by government and that which is voluntarily provided by donors and volunteers has remained clear. In the United States, as Dobkin Hall has noted, "government and private voluntary associations ... coexisted uneasily – and often turbulently – through the first century of the republic's existence"[3] (Hall, 1992: 3). The growth of the modern welfare state since the mid-eighteenth century, with its expanded provision of such public goods as education, healthcare, shelter, public safety, environmental protection and care for the aged, has led to an even stronger delineation between the mandated services of the state and the voluntary services of civil society.

The end of the twentieth century and the beginning of the twenty-first, however, have witnessed a reversal of this trend in favor of greater limits on the state's role. This has been especially evident in the United States, corresponding to successive phases of fiscal crises in government and leading to growing expectations of civil society as a substitute provider of public goods.

The state's retreat has thus drawn civil society increasingly into governmental space: for example, for protection of the environment or as provider of basic services such as healthcare, education, food and shelter. Civil society must therefore newly contend with problems that have traditionally confronted government – those that presume state legitimacy, norms of equity and universal enforcement – which civil society has been ill suited to address. As a result, gradually, and without any formal recognition of the fact, both civil society and the state find themselves in unfamiliar roles of power and responsibility. Civil society then confronts a dilemma: how to reconcile its identity as the sphere of voluntary, free and pluralistic social activity, unfettered by what James Douglas calls government's "categorical constraint" (Douglas, 1987: 46), with the responsibilities of a governing body, especially the requirements of administering rules equitably and universally?

It is useful here to note the distinctive characteristics of the democratic state's governance authority. Primary to the state's functions is the generation of solutions to four key public problems: (1) *resource generation* – the development of sufficient resources, typically through taxation, to provide public goods demanded by the society; (2) *collective voice* – creating a vehicle for resolving differences and establishing positions on public issues for the entire society; (3) *equity* – providing fair and equitable allocation of public goods; (4) *accountability* – insuring democratic oversight and control of the public process.

In recent centuries, democratic states have worked out solutions to these four problems, albeit always provisionally due to the complex and ever changing nature of public goods. To generate resources, the state exerts legitimate governing authority, enabling it to mandate the provision of goods for the entire public. This is consistent with the state's solution to the broader problem of collective action – the problem in which the pursuit of individual interests works against the achievement of collective goals, classically described as the problem of the "free rider." The state prevents free riders and enforces participation in the provision of public goods primarily through taxation, using its legitimate exercise of governmental power.[4]

In achieving collective voice, the democratic state resolves disputes among groups holding conflicting values through an accepted decision-making process involving elections, legislation, the exercise of office and judicial decisions. It thereby addresses the problem of value pluralism – the challenge of reconciling inherently conflicting definitions of the good life in a society that protects the pursuit of pluralistic values.[5] This process generates policy decisions that represent (at least in principle) majority views of the public.

The third responsibility of the democratic state is the equitable allocation of public goods. Because of its legitimate exercise of authority and centralized power, the state has the ability to distribute goods according to rules agreed to by society as a whole. These rules, determined in the political process, serve as a counterbalance to the influence of private wealth and power.

Finally, the most fundamental tenet of the democratic state, governance by the people, presumes accountability by those in power. Typically accomplished through elections, accountability may also be achieved through legal or administrative means. Designed to keep power structures responsive to the popular will, formal accountability can also have downside effects in limiting innovation and deterring policy experimentation beyond majoritarian preferences.

Civil society's response

When civil society enters into the sphere of governance, it must engage the four problems traditionally solved by the state. To the degree that it seeks to act on behalf of society as a whole, civil society confronts the issues of legitimacy and enforcement. Lacking state authority, it must employ other mechanisms to solve the problems of collective action, value pluralism, equity and accountability.

(1) To fulfill the task of resource generation, civil society faces the fundamental challenge of gaining *voluntary* compliance with the norms and commitments required to produce public goods. A large body of literature has addressed this challenge through exploration of the generation of public goods by non-governmental means. Ostrom and many others have demonstrated that associations in civil society can, under certain conditions, successfully solve collective action problems, ranging from preserving watersheds to protecting the information commons (Ostrom, 1990).

In Ostrom's analysis, producing public goods and preventing free riders in voluntary associations requires first and foremost the cultivation of norms of trust and open communication. In societies in which these norms and practices have been established, public goods can be voluntarily produced and protected over long periods of time. For example, voluntary giving rather than taxation can provide a sustainable source for CSOs' work in the public arena. Societies lacking norms of trust and open communication have great difficulty providing public goods on a voluntary basis.[6]

(2) Historically, civil society has reflected diversity in all its forms – cultural, ideological, ethical – expressing the competition and conflict among private groups in the pursuit of particular visions of the good.[7] Thus it has avoided an obligation to be accountable to the general public. Yet when assuming the responsibilities of government, civil society must move beyond advocating for particular private visions and take on a role of decision-making for the public at large. This creates ambiguities in internal goal-setting, decision-making, the role of stakeholders, and other questions of organizational identity.

(3) Although many CSOs pursue equity and social justice goals, civil society as a field prioritizes norms of individual and associational freedom above norms of distributional equity. This stance is rooted in the field's inherent pluralism – a history of defending private belief and associational rights against the state. Pursuit of distributional equity norms presumes centralization of power and adjudication inherent in the state but alien to civil society. While modern civil society is founded on a commitment to equal rights of speech and association, these are rights of *procedural equality* rather than *distributional equity*. The tension between equal rights and distributional equity has in fact characterized the evolution of liberal democracy as expressed by Post and Rosenblum above. Yet when CSOs enter into the role of governance, this tension moves from a give-and-take *between* government and civil society to an internal tension *within* CSOs themselves. The role of private associations, including the private wealth and power they represent, becomes problematic in setting public agendas.[8]

(4) Historically, strict accountability has not been a defining feature of civil society. Indeed, one of the virtues of civil society is that it is able to operate in an unaccountable fashion, freely championing unpopular causes, pursuing innovative ideas, and acting as a sometimes critical, sometimes visionary voice in society. In the United States, the First Amendment provided religious institutions with an additional layer of insulation from public oversight. The result has been an ongoing struggle between the free exercise of private associational activity and efforts by government to define and regulate that activity. The fundamental lines in this arena in the US were initially drawn by the Dartmouth College case in 1819 but have been continually redrawn throughout American history, illustrated in periodic congressional efforts to exercise oversight over private philanthropic foundations. The advent of significant indirect public support of nonprofit organizations through the tax code since the mid-twentieth century has given further impetus to stronger government oversight of CSOs.

In the post-World War II era America civil society organizations became even more heavily immersed in state activity through the massive infusion of funding by government into the nonprofit sector. In what Salamon has dubbed "third party government" (Salamon, 1995: 3), such nonprofits in fact take on many of the responsibilities of governmental organizations. However, this funding relationship still prioritizes ultimate accountability to the state through such vehicles as contracts and grants, through which civil society organizations serve as extensions of government and are essentially controlled by government agencies.

By contrast, when CSOs act *in place of* government, they fill an entirely different function. They seek to provide services, protect natural areas, regulate behavior, and affect public life in ways that would otherwise be carried out by governmental agencies. In doing so, they are governed by their own internal procedures rather than elections or other democratic accountability processes. This trend has led to significantly increased attention to accountability issues.[9] But then questions immediately arise about the nature of accountability. To whom – clients? Donors? The public at large? For what – finances? Performance? Tax revenue saved? By what means – client surveys? Outside evaluators? Public input?

Governance dilemmas in practice

The organizational conflicts that emerge when civil society assumes governmental responsibilities become tangible in the operational life of many contemporary CSOs. In education, healthcare, the environment, international development and many other fields in which CSOs are active, private organizations are moving beyond advocacy and the provision of supplemental services into the arenas of public agenda-setting and essential service delivery. Here they confront the dilemmas of governance in concrete form.

Charter schools provide an example. Although charters take on many different forms and structures, their common purpose is to serve as an alternative to the public school administrative and structural model. Unlike standard public schools, charters are free to design their own curricula, organize schedules and teaching practices, select students, and hire and fire staff as they see fit. Most are supported by significant sources of private funding to enable them to engage in educational innovation. Although they are nominally under the control of the public systems, they are intended to act with the freedom and non-bureaucratic character of private CSOs. In doing so, they generate resources from the private sector (although benefiting from tax support as well), reflect pluralism in diversity of approaches toward education, prioritize freedom of choice over strict equity in the allocation of resources, and adhere to broad accountability requirements for results rather than narrower operational accountability.[10]

In sum, charter schools straddle the divide between private associational freedom and the public responsibilities of governance. Critics of charters, such as Ravitch, argue that they over-emphasize private control and discretionary wealth at the expense of public responsibilities and equitable access to resources (Ravitch, 2013). Charter schools thus reflect an inner tension between the freedom of private action and the obligations of public provision of services.

A second example is that of nonprofit free clinics. Such clinics, like charter schools, occupy an important public space by providing essential health services to the public. Primarily targeted toward low-income populations who are unable to qualify for or afford health insurance, their primary mission is to fill a critical need for healthcare where government services are unavailable. Although the future role of such clinics is subject to the implementation of provisions of the

Affordable Healthcare Act, they will continue to fill a vital need for a portion of the population who remain without coverage due to undocumented status or other circumstances.

Most free clinics, even those that accept Medicaid reimbursement, generate a significant portion of their resources from private sources and thus are heavily dependent on philanthropy. Because of their diverse organizational structures, constituencies served, and staffing patterns, they do not seek to serve more general public healthcare needs. Although their focus on low-income communities reflects a strong commitment to social equity norms, due to their limited resources, geographic focus and other limitations, they cannot make their services available on a strictly equal basis to the public at large – hence the freedom to be selective takes precedence over the norm of universal social equity. Similarly, since they are privately organized and financed, their primary accountability is to their boards, donors and clients, rather than to the public at large. Free clinics play an important role in shaping the delivery of healthcare but remain intrinsically controlled by and primarily accountable to private associational bodies rather than the general public.

A third type of organization exemplifying the conflict between the goals of civil society and government is the large international environmental organization. Here the complex role of CSOs acting in lieu of government comes into even sharper relief than in domestic fields. For example, in the absence of a global governmental body that can impose taxes and regulatory rules to counter global climate change, CSOs seek to promulgate standards and promote worldwide actions to reduce energy consumption and CO_2 emissions. But lacking governmental authority to mandate actions, CSOs encounter fundamental challenges. By what process are the standards developed? Who pays for their implementation? Do they favor one constituency (for example, the developed nations) over others? How can free riders be prevented? How is accountability assured? Thus, in the international arena where no supervening governmental entity exists (the United Nations Environmental Program acts essentially in an advisory role), CSOs must continually grapple with the issues of governance: resource generation, collective voice, equity and accountability.

The Brundtland Report, *Our Common Future*, issued in 1987 by the World Commission on Environment and Development, clearly articulates the governance problem: "most of the institutions facing [environmental challenges] tend to be independent, fragmented, working to relatively narrow mandates with closed decision processes" (World Commission on Environment and Development, 1987). Since the issuance of that report, some progress has been made toward addressing climate change from a worldwide perspective, yet the fundamental challenges facing independent CSOs working in a space absent government authority remain. The authors of a book on global gridlock state the case starkly:

> Global problems like climate change and the systemic links that increasingly define most environmental issues reveal a tragic irony. Environmental

problems are increasingly unified, but the institutions we have designed to govern them are increasingly fragmented.

(Hale *et al.*, 2013: 269–270)

They join others in calling for a massive change in scale of formal global governance to address these issues. At the same time, they point to the positive potential for a networked system of decentralized CSOs, local governments and businesses to provide an alternative path toward addressing climate change. We now turn to an examination of two avenues toward such an approach.

New possibilities for civil society and governance

CSOs that find themselves in the position of exercising the powers of governance confront a fundamental dilemma. They must solve the problems of public agenda setting and the exercise of authority in society without the benefit of traditional governmental legitimacy. In so doing, they must simultaneously serve two masters: (1) the will of the voluntary associations on which they are based, with their inherent freedom to set goals and take action; and (2) the will of the general public on behalf of which they are acting, with its presumptive requirements of open input, equity and accountability.

Two paths of recent organizational development show promise for new approaches to bridging the divide between independence and governance. They offer novel ways to overcome the structural problem of blending private control with public obligation. Rather than understanding social agenda setting as purely within the purview of either government or civil society, these approaches understand the process as *interactive* and *iterative*, bridging the gap between the two spheres.

Networks

In recent decades networks have become recognized as an increasingly powerful force in all aspects of economic and social life. The traditional notion of the autonomous rational actor is rapidly being supplemented by an understanding of the dominant influence of interactions that occur among people through networks of political, social and economic behavior. The explosive expansion of the Internet has greatly magnified the importance of this phenomenon.

Networks not only shape social behavior but also behave quite differently from traditional social relationships. Rather than top-down or bottom-up linear flows of social change, networks highlight horizontal peer-to-peer interaction, with participants mutually influencing and being influenced by others in the network. Information and values are constantly shared in the process, which leads to a continuously evolving status of the network as a whole, because in a network "each individual's actions have implicit consequences for the outcomes of everyone in the system"[11] (Easley and Kleinberg, 2010: 4).

The phenomenon of *reflexivity*, described by Soros and others, is a defining characteristic of such networks (Soros, 2000). Reflexivity functions in networks in three ways that bear importantly on the relationship between civil society and governance. Reflexivity presupposes (1) a precondition of free and open communication; (2) an iterative process in which ideas and agendas are mutually formed and re-formed in a continual interaction among network participants; and (3) decentralization – a modern version of the older tradition of subsidiarity – in which decision-making occurs at the lowest possible level. All three are necessary for the successful functioning of civil society as well as networks, and all open new possibilities of connecting civil society to governance.

When citizens connect interactively through a network, they participate in an iterative process that typically begins with a common topic of concern but may evolve into a larger discussion and proposals for action. This interactive process begins to bridge the gap between civil society and the realm of governance by opening access to all, rather than being limited to membership in a particular private association, and developing a collective voice that emerges from the "crowd wisdom" of the process. While network interactions do not typically aim to produce specific government mandates, they can create legitimacy for a cause through open access and transparency that can become a significant influence in the political process.[12]

Such networks have a hybrid character, containing the characteristics of both civil society – voluntary, independently resourced, emphasizing free expression – and governance structures – openly accessible, accountable through transparency, developing a collective voice. They can therefore provide a bridge between civil society and government that moves toward resolution of the issues of legitimacy, fragmentation and accountability faced by civil society entities working in the public arena.

The capability of networks working at the local level to take on difficult large-scale social problems – through collaboration between CSOs, governments and businesses – is gaining increased recognition. For example, in the case of international environmental organizations, a report from the international Rio+20 conference on climate change documented that, despite the inability of governments to reach significant results, 209 partnerships emerged from the conference representing "action-oriented initiatives that bring national governments, cities, non-governmental organizations companies, and other kinds of actors together around specific projects" (Hale *et al.*, 2013: 271). The growing legitimacy of environmental organizations such as Worldwatch Institute, World Wildlife Fund and National Resource Defense Council, due to their reliance on interactive networks of information and accountability through transparency, allows them to shape local, national and international environmental policy.

Of course, there are limits to networks' ability to solve large-scale social problems. The challenges of establishing the communication and trust required for self-imposed enforcement are significant. Trust is much easier to generate in local communities than in national or international settings, where networks can be unstable. Moreover, at some point a formal decision-making body must be invoked to resolve disputes, posing the traditional challenges of the exercise of legitimate authority.

Nevertheless, network-based activity can satisfy Ostrom's requirements for the creation of enduring solutions to public problems by non-governmental entities. In her analysis of communities throughout the world that self-organize to preserve precious local resources over the long term – forests in Switzerland and Japan, irrigation programs in the Philippines and Spain, a fishery in Turkey, and groundwater basins in California – she lists as key criteria for the success of these groups *open sharing of information* and *mutual trust*. Functioning networks at all levels with these characteristics have the potential to solve many of the problems of CSOs working in public space. In her Nobel Prize lecture, Ostrom called for just such a polycentric approach to environmental governance (Ostrom, 2009).

Design

A second approach to social problem-solving that holds promise for bridging the civil society–governance gap is *design thinking*. Particularly as conceived in its social constructivist version by Schön and Rein, design thinking presumes an analytical framework that moves beyond simple technical–rational problem-solving toward a sequenced dialectic in which "policy-makers function as designers and exhibit, at their best, a particular kind of reflective practice" (Schön and Rein, 1994: xi).[13] Policy-makers begin this process with an initial understanding of a problem (the problem frame), but, as it is introduced into practice, this frame undergoes continual revision through interaction with clients, other professionals and the public at large and may, in the end, differ significantly from the original, even in the most fundamental understanding of the basic goal of the effort. This process, like that of network interactions, is rooted in the fundamental concept of reflexivity.

Design thinking has begun to be applied more widely to social problem-solving in recent years as an effective means of addressing seemingly intractable ("wicked") policy controversies as well as to solve basic challenges of such difficult undertakings as cross-cultural assistance programs. These policy controversies typically involve

> two or more parties [who] contend with one another over the definition of a problematic policy situation and vie for control of the policy-making process. Their struggles over the naming and framing of a policy situation are symbolic contests over the social meaning of an issue domain, where meaning implies not only what is at issue but what is to be done.
>
> (Schön and Rein, 1994: 28–29)[14]

When policy-makers begin to think as designers, their approach becomes iterative rather than instrumental. In the most productive cases, policy controversies are no longer battlegrounds for supremacy among fixed ideological positions but evolve into transformative interchanges in which mutual learning takes place among participants. In Tim Brown's phrase, design thinking is "open-minded, open-ended, and iterative" (Brown, 2009: 17). The intentions and agendas of all players evolve in this process so that policy-makers, interest group representatives and the public alike feel ownership of the process, and all who take part accept the resulting policies as fair, legitimate and responsive to their needs. Schön describes this process as "reflection-in-action":

> In this reflective conversation, the practitioner's effort to solve the reframed problem yields new discoveries which call for new reflection-in-action. The process spirals through stages of appreciation, action, and re-appreciation. The unique and uncertain situation comes to be understood through the attempt to change it, and changed through the attempt to understand it.
>
> (Schön and Rein, 1994: 132)

Schön and Rein examine this process as it has played out in several policy arenas – among them, public policy on early retirement in Germany and homelessness in Massachusetts. In both cases they conclude that the formal policies initially proposed by policy-makers (the designers) became transformed through the discourse with other players, which led to reframing in ways that resulted in fundamentally new understandings of the problems by the original designers. This led to creative and broadly accepted policy solutions that synthesized the values and policy intentions of both civil society and governmental actors.[15]

A third case, the attempt to implement an educational computing initiative at MIT, demonstrates the limits of design thinking in social problem solving. If differing frames of policy reference are held too deeply by stakeholders, as was the case with opposing factions at MIT, they may be unable to reach a reflexive consensus. This intransigence may be exacerbated in the cases where there is severe power imbalance, such as between office holders and constituents or between philanthropic donors and grant recipients.

Yet design thinking has already demonstrated promise in the fields of education and health, suggesting that it could be applied beneficially to the examples of charter schools and free clinics cited above. The process of interactive inquiry and design, involving administrators, teachers, students, parents, medical practitioners, clients, funders and the general public (or any combination of these), could contribute significantly to securing resources, achieving collective voice, advancing equity and increasing the accountability of these institutions.

If multiple participants from both civil society and government participate in both framing a policy problem and implementing a solution, the outcome can be seen as legitimized by both. Especially in blurred boundary arenas in which CSOs act in lieu of government, design thinking could provide an innovative approach to integrating the freedom and creativity of civil society with the universality and accountability of government.

Conclusion

As states increasingly limit the provision of collective goods, civil society becomes ever more drawn into the fundamental normative and pragmatic challenges faced by government. Although civil society's commitment to the freedom and pluralism of private action resists assumption of the tasks of governance, when CSOs are thrust into the role of public actors in arenas such as education, health and the environment they are compelled to find new ways to solve the problems of resource generation, collective voice, equity and accountability. Network theory and design thinking offer new paths for creating an iterative relationship among organizations, the constituencies they serve and the general public in order to address these problems. The new relationships are characterized by a reflexivity that confers broad public legitimacy while allowing CSOs to continue to serve pluralistic interests. As civil society's role in governance continues to grow, further empirical research by scholars of civil society, network theory and design thinking is called for to explore how civil society can best address the complexities of operating in its increasingly hybridized social space.

Notes

1 A substantial body of literature on liberal democracy emphasizes the reciprocal relationship between civil society and the democratic state. See, for example, Almond and Verba, 1965; Clemens and Guthrie, 2011; Galston, 2005; and Putnam, Leonardi and Nanetti, 1994.

2 The historical origins of the civil society idea as an integral part of liberal democratic theory has clear expression in the classic formulations of Spinoza, Hobbes, Locke, Ferguson, Hegel, and other seventeenth- and eighteenth-century theorists. See contemporary accounts of this theoretical development in Becker, 1994; Colas, 1997; Gellner, 1994; Habermas, 1991; Keane, 1988; Kocka, 2000; Seligman, 1992; and Sievers, 2010.

3 Hall describes the complex evolution of private and governmental responsibilities in public life in American history in Hall, 1994 and Hall, 1982.

4 The problems of collective action and free riders are typically analyzed in terms of game theory and the literature of the "tragedy of the commons." See, for example, Hardin, 1968; Olsen, 1965; Sandler, 1992.

5 A classic articulation of this challenge is Isaiah Berlin's observation that "human goals are many, not all of them commensurable, and in perpetual rivalry with one another." Berlin, 1969, p. 171. Kenneth Arrow's "impossibility theorem" demonstrates the difficulty of combining pluralistic social preferences in economic terms.

6 See, for example, the contrast between northern and southern Italy in Putnam, Leonardi and Nanetti, 1994.

7 Although the classic Tocquevillian vision of civil society presumes a broadly shared civic ethos, this shared civic spirit has been traditionally understood as the product of the combined associational activity of diverse groups pursuing highly differentiated interests.

8 The critique of the role of private power steering public agendas is particularly relevant to the activity of private donors. A recent version of this critique is found in Barkan, 2013.

9 One prominent example was a national Advisory Committee on Self-Regulation to the Panel on the Nonprofit Sector convened by Independent Sector in 2007, of which

the author was a member. The panel issued a report, "Principles for Good Governance and Ethical Practice: A Guide for Charities and Foundations" with 33 recommended standards on transparency, accountability and governance for nonprofit organizations in the United States (Independent Sector, 2013).

10 The issue of accountability is in fact an ongoing conundrum for charter schools due to their dual public/private constituencies. A 2013 report by the National Association of Charter School Authorizers (NACSA), for example, calls for recognition of accountability standards adapted to the assessment of "alternative" charter schools: see NACSA, 2013.

11 They argue that it follows that "not only will [participants] appreciate that their outcomes depend on how others behave, but they will take this into account in planning their own actions" (Easley and Kleinberg, 2010, p. 5). See also Ormerod, 2012.

12 This is a worldwide phenomenon. Describing the emergence of civil society in China, Zixue Tai observes,

> the quick rise of the Internet as a popular tool of public communication in China has essentially turned Chinese cyberspace into an Habermasian public sphere of the twenty-first century, imperfect as it is – important issues are debated and public opinion gets formed.
>
> (Tai, 2006, p. 206)

13 Schön develops his general theory on design in practice in Schön, 1983.

14 Another example of applying this approach to intractable problems is the work of a leading organization in the field, IDEO.org, which has undertaken a number of initiatives that draw upon design thinking to shape international aid programs.

15 Schön and Rein attribute this transformation to their insight that "Designing is also a process of discovery and learning. In the course of seeing/moving/seeing, the designer discovers unanticipated patterns, relationships, and possibilities, which may inform further designing" (Schön and Rein, 1994, p. 85).

References

Almond, G. and Verba, G. (1965). *The Civic Culture: Political Attitudes and Democracy in Five Nations.* Princeton: Princeton University Press.

Barkan, J. (2013). Plutocrats at Work: How Big Philanthropy Undermines Democracy. *Dissent* 60(4), pp. 47–54.

Becker, M. (1994). *The Emergence of Civil Society in the Eighteenth Century: A Privileged Moment in the History of England, Scotland, and France.* Bloomington: Indiana University Press.

Berlin, I. (1969). *Two Concepts of Liberty: A lecture delivered to Oxford University in 1958; Four Essays on Liberty.* Oxford: Oxford University Press.

Brown, T. (2009). *Change by Design: How Design Thinking Transforms Organizations and Inspires Innovation.* New York: Harper Business.

Clemens, E. and Guthrie, D. (eds) (2011). *Politics and Partnerships: The Role of Voluntary Associations in America's Political Past and Present.* Chicago: University of Chicago Press.

Colas, D. (1997). *Civil Society and Fanaticism: Conjoined Histories.* Translated by Amy Jacobs. Stanford: Stanford University Press.

Douglas, J. (1989). Political Theories of Nonprofit Organizations. In Powell, W. (ed.) *The Nonprofit Sector: A Research Handbook.* New Haven: Yale University Press, pp. 43–54.

Easley, D. and Kleinberg, J. (2010). *Networks, Crowds, and Markets: Reasoning About a Highly Connected World.* Cambridge: Cambridge University Press.

Galston, W. (2005). *The Practice of Liberal Pluralism.* Cambridge: Cambridge University Press.

Gellner, E. (1994). *Conditions of Liberty: Civil Society and its Rivals.* London: Hamish Hamilton.

Habermas, J. (1991/1962). *The Structural Transformation of the Public Sphere: An Inquiry into a Category of Bourgeois Society.* Translated by Thomas Burger. Cambridge, MA: MIT University Press.

Hale, T., Held, D. and Young, K. (2013). *Gridlock: Why Global Cooperation is Failing When We Need it Most.* New York: Polity.

Hall, P. (1982). *The Organization of American Culture, 1700–1900: Institutions, Elites, and the Origins of American Nationality.* New York: New York University Press.

Hall, P. (1994). Historical Perspectives on Nonprofit Organizations in the United States. In Herman, R. (ed.) J*ossey-Bass Handbook of Nonprofit Leadership and Management.* San Francisco: Jossey-Bass, pp. 3–43.

Hardin, G. (1968). The Tragedy of the Commons. *Science* 162, pp. 1243–1248.

Independent Sector (2007). *Principles for Good Governance and Ethical Practice: A Guide for Charities and Foundations.* October. Available at http://independentsector. org/uploads/Accountability_Documents/Principles_for_Good_Governance_and_ Ethical_Practice.pdf (accessed 6 August 2014).

Keane, J. (ed.) (1988). *Civil Society and the State.* New York: Verso.

Kocka, J. (2000). Zivilgesellschaft als historisches Problem und Versprechen. In Hildermeier, M., Kocka, J. and Conrad, C. (eds) *Europäische Zivilgesellschaft in Ost und West: Begriff, Geschichte, Chancen.* Frankfurt: Campus Verlag.

NACSA (National Association of Charter School Authorizers) (2013). *Anecdotes Aren't Enough: An Evidence-Based Approach to Accountability for Alternative Charter Schools.* Available at www.pageturnpro.com/National-Association-of-Charter-School-Authorizers/53998-Anecdotes-Arent-Enough/index.html#1 (accessed 6 August 2014).

Olsen, M. (1965). *The Logic of Collective Action: Public Goods and the Theory of Groups.* New York: Schocken.

Ormerod, P. (2012). *Positive Linking: How Networks Can Revolutionise the World.* London: Faber and Faber.

Ostrom, E. (1990). *Governing the Commons: The Evolution of Institutions for Collective Action.* Cambridge: Cambridge University Press.

Ostrom, E. (2009) *Beyond Markets and States: Polycentric Governance of Complex Economic Systems.* Available at www.nobelprize.org/nobel_prizes/economic-sciences/laureates/2009/ostrom_lecture.pdf (accessed 4 August 2014).

Post, R. and Rosenblum, N. (eds) (2002). *Civil Society and Government.* Princeton: Princeton University Press.

Putnam, R., Leonardi, R. and Nanetti, R. (1994). *Making Democracy Work: Civic Traditions in Modern Italy.* Princeton: Princeton University Press.

Ravitch, D. (2013). *Reign of Error: The Hoax of the Privatization Movement and the Danger to America's Public Schools.* New York: Knopf.

Salamon, L. (1995). *Partners in Public Service: Government-Nonprofit Relations in the Modern Welfare State.* Baltimore: Johns Hopkins University Press.

Sandler, T. (1992). *Collective Action: Theory and Applications.* Ann Arbor: University of Michigan Press.

Schön, D. (1983). *The Reflective Practitioner: How Professionals Think in Action.* New York: Basic Books.

Schön, D. and Rein, M. (1994). *Frame Reflection: Toward the Resolution of Intractable Policy Controversies*. New York: Basic Books.

Seligman, A. (1992). *The Idea of Civil Society*. Princeton: Princeton University Press.

Sievers, B. (2010). *Civil Society, Philanthropy, and the Fate of the Commons*. Lebanon, NH: Tufts University Press.

Soros, G. (2000). *Open Society: Reforming Global Capitalism*. New York: Public Affairs.

Tai, Z. (2006). *The Internet in China: Cyberspace and Civil Society*. Oxford: Routledge.

World Commission on Environment and Development (1987). *Our Common Future (The Brundtland Report)*. Oxford: Oxford University Press.

10 The social and solidarity economy and Ostrom's approach to common pool resources

Towards a better understanding of institutional diversity[1]

Marthe Nyssens and Francesca Petrella

Introduction

Since the mid-1970s there has been a strong emergence of concepts that underline the existence of organizations distinct from the private capitalist sector and the public sector: social economy, solidarity-based economy, social enterprise, nonprofit, third sector, etc. These observations invite us to move beyond a conception of the economy based on a state–market dichotomy and recognize its plurality and complexity. The works of Ostrom share this perspective and contribute to the recognition and understanding of an "eco-diversity" seen as a necessary plurality of institutional forms.

That is why in this chapter we propose to set up a dialogue between the analyses of the quasi-collective production of goods and services by social and solidarity economy (SSE) organizations and Ostrom's works on common resources, from three angles: the analysis of property regimes, the characteristics of the goods and services provided, and the production of norms. We shall identify the convergences and divergences between these approaches to see how Ostrom's works can raise questions for the SSE. The analysis will be centered on an Ostromian reading of common resources and not on the abundant literature on the new "commons" which expands this idea, thus moving away from the common resources studied by Ostrom. The chapter is structured by this aim of dialogue.

In the first part of the chapter, we underscore the importance of studying complex institutional forms which go beyond the state–market dichotomy to solve the problems related to the management both of common resources and of quasi-collective goods and services. Starting out from this observation, we shall show how analysis of the property regimes of SSE organizations and of Ostrom's common resources question, each in their own way, the classic definition of property and the supposed supremacy of capitalist ownership.

In the second part, we start out from the need to widen the analysis to other types of goods than purely public and purely private goods (Ostrom 1990). Common resources, like the quasi-collective goods and services produced by the SSE, are neither pure public goods nor classic private goods but also have a collective dimension, which is not adequately taken into account in actors' individual decisions. However, the nature of the collective interest at stake can be seen to be different in the two situations.

In the third part, we analyze the role of the collective production of norms to create an environment of trust in a context of imperfect information and agents' limited rationality. Trust is a central issue, both in the management of common resources and in the production of many quasi-collective goods and services. Ostrom concludes that letting the actors themselves produce common rules can generate a sustainable management of common resources insofar as certain principles are respected. These principles of co-production of rules and self-management echo the foundations of the SSE: they also raise questions for it in terms of its governance and its concrete application of management autonomy and internal democracy. On the other hand, works on the SSE underscore the political dimension of this institutional work of producing norms, which cannot be confined solely to the issue of trust.

Apprehending and understanding the diversity of institutional forms: an analysis of property regimes

Since the mid-1970s, we have seen a deployment of various approaches which aim to underline the existence of a real "third sector" in our economies, distinct from the capitalist private sector and the public sector – the nonprofit sector, the social economy, the solidarity economy, social enterprise, etc. A strong European tradition sees the third sector as bringing together cooperatives, associations, mutual societies and increasingly foundations, or in other words, all not-for-profit organizations (organizations not owned by shareholders) that are also labelled the "social and solidarity economy" in some European countries. This legal–institutional approach is usually combined with a normative or ethical approach which underlines the essential common features of these different types of organizations: their aim is to provide a good or service to their members or to a community, rather than generating profits, and their specific governance rules (independent management, democratic decision-making process and primacy of people and labor over capital in the distribution of income) thereby express a long historical quest for economic democracy.

The emergence of this type of concept requires us to move beyond a representation of the economy based on the state–market dichotomy.

Ostrom's works on common resources belong to this perspective. She shows that many institutional arrangements distinct from the traditional public and private sectors are possible and sustainable:

> Some scholarly articles about the "tragedy of the commons" recommend that "the state" control most natural resources to prevent their destruction; others recommend that privatizing these resources will resolve the problem. What one can observe in the world, however, is that neither the state nor the market is uniformly successful in enabling individuals to sustain long-term, productive use of natural resource systems. Furthermore, communities of

individuals have relied on institutions resembling neither the state nor the market to govern some resource systems with reasonable degrees of success over long periods of time.

(Ostrom 1990, p. 1)

Ostrom starts out from the principle that, in traditional theories, the actors are seen as being caught up in a set of constraining rules that influence their behavior and over which they have no control. For her, (local) actors are capable of self-organizing to "govern" common resources by producing a system of rules, adapted to the local context, which allows sustainable exploitation of these resources. Her approach thus also contributes in a fundamental way to recognizing and understanding an "eco-diversity" seen as a necessary plurality of institutional forms. In this regard, she in a way confirms Laville's (2006) statement of an indispensable recognition of institutions capable of ensuring a "pluralization of the economy":

The answer to this question can be sought only through institutional inventions anchored in social practices; it is these practices that can point to the pathways for reinserting the economy in democratic norms.... It is a question of looking to practices to inform ourselves about their existence and analyse them, in other words to start from the "real economic movement" and not from a project for social reform imposed on reality.

(Laville 2006, p. 257)

This is a first point of convergence between Ostrom and the SSE analyses.

A second point of convergence between the SSE and Ostrom's works flows directly from this recognition of institutional diversity. It is a matter of questioning the traditional conception of the ownership of an enterprise. As Weinstein (2013, p. 3) underscores, for Ostrom, "the question of the commons is not separable from questions about the place of ownership and the forms of ownership in the economy." Whether it be a matter of the ownership of common resources or of SSE organizations, these institutional forms indeed challenge economic theory in several regards.

Ownership is generally defined in terms of the joint possession of two formal rights: the rights to control and the rights to residual earnings (Hansmann 1996). The residual character refers to rights not previously assigned in a contract. Thus residual earnings consist of the financial surpluses, including the realization of the assets by a possible sale of the rights, once all financial commitments have been honoured. The rights to control consist of those rights that have not been assigned by law or contract to other stakeholders (in particular the managers of the enterprise) and may be limited to the right to elect the board of directors and a restricted range of decisions such as transferring the enterprise to a third party or dissolving it.

The institutional forms studied by Ostrom and those of the SSE diverge fundamentally from this representation. On the one hand, the investors are not the owners of the organization although, according to the ownership rights school, this is the optimal situation; on the other hand, the property rights regimes are much more varied than the one presented by the dominant theory. These points will be developed successively.

First, in the field of SSE, the investors are not the owners of the organizations. In the case of associations, various categories of stakeholders may sit in the organs of governance: the direct beneficiaries of the activity, the employees, the volunteers, the public authorities, donors or the local community; however, these stakeholders do not have the right to individually appropriate the financial surpluses of the organization, in view of the constraint of non-distribution of profits. In the case of cooperatives, the twofold character of the associates is fundamental. While the cooperators hold one or more shares, they are there because they have a relationship with the cooperative either as employees, users or suppliers.

In the case of the governance of common resources, Ostrom is interested in systems where the "appropriators," i.e., those who may withdraw units of resources, self-organize. The appropriators may be:

> herders, fishers, irrigators, commuters and anyone else who appropriates resource units from some type of resource system. In many instances, appropriators use or consume the resource units they withdraw.... Appropriators also use resource units as inputs into production processes.... In other instances, the appropriators immediately transfer ownership of resource units to others, who are then the users of the resource units.
>
> (Ostrom 1990, p. 31)

These appropriators do not generally have the relationship of investors in the strict sense (investing financial capital with a view to maximizing its financial return) but are either consumers (fishers who take fish for their own consumption) or producers (fishers who sell their catch, irrigators who use the water for their own fields).

Second, the property regimes of the SSE and those of common resources also deviate from the principle of joint possession of the rights to residual control and residual earnings.

In an association, no one has the right, in the strict sense, to appropriate the earnings, which leads some authors to declare that "Nonprofit organizations do not have owners" (Glaeser 2003, p. 1). However, these organizations are indeed constituted by a set of assets for which the rights to residual control, such as the right to elect the members of the board of directors, are assigned to one or several agents. The idea of assets is used here in a broad sense to designate any potential flow of earnings or future services. The persons who have control in the organization, following the principle "one person, one vote," are "collectively" tasked with reinvesting the residual earnings in the organization. Ultimately, these residual earnings, collectively assigned, return in multiple forms to what Gui (1991) calls the "beneficiary category," which will vary according to the purpose of the organization: for example, the users of the service (e.g., persons being socially integrated), but also the persons who control the organization, as in the case of mutual interest organizations such as sports clubs, or common-resource organizations such as those studied by Ostrom. While an individual distribution of the net financial surplus is forbidden in non-profit organizations, an assignment of residual benefits nonetheless takes place.

In a cooperative, a part of the earnings is channelled towards the non-shareable reserves, the collective fund of the organization; the capital, when it is remunerated, is done so in a limited way. The shares cannot be sold on the stock market and are only transferrable on certain conditions laid down in the statutes. The principle "one person, one vote" means that the number of shares held by a member does not influence his or her weight in the control of the organization.

Drawing on theorists who define property as a "bundle of rights" that are divisible, separable and alienable (see esp. Commons 1893 and Alchian and Demsetz 1973), Ostrom and her colleagues (Ostrom 2010; Schlager and Ostrom 1992) stress the separability of the right to have access to the resource, the right to appropriate the products of the resource, the right to manage the resource, the right to determine who will have an access right and how that right may be transferred, and finally the right to sell these last two rights. The first rights and the last one are akin to the residual earnings and the others to the right to residual control. According to Ostrom, property regimes are plural because these rights are independent and can be combined in different ways.

Ostrom's position is not to identify a specific property regime as the most effective *a priori*: "the valid question is how various types of institutional arrangements perform comparatively when confronted with similarly difficult environments" (Schlager and Ostrom 1992, p. 260).

She answers this question through principles derived from hundreds of specific case studies. Rather than identify recurrent rules, she thus extracts principles of conception common to durable institutions managing common resources, which we shall detail below. Moreover, the appropriators often do not possess the right of alienation, which has generally contributed to the success of collective management by strengthening the cohesion of local communities (Poteete *et al.* 2010, p. 47).

Regarding analysis of the forms of ownership of the SSE and commons, institutional diversity is impossible to ignore, and it calls into question both the classic state–market dichotomy and the classic definition of property. These forms testify to the plurality of property regimes, particularly through the possible separation of different property rights and the multiple combinations that can result from this, and call into question the supremacy of private property in the strict sense.

Between public good and private good: mutual interest or general interest?

Common resources, as examined by Ostrom, are characterized by the fact that it is difficult but not impossible to exclude beneficiaries from access to them. But the access is limited, i.e., subject to competition in its consumption, as in the case of water, forests or ocean fisheries. The problem lies in over-exploitation, with each individual having a personal interest in using the common resource in such a way as to maximize his individual use while distributing the operating costs over the collectivity. These situations are described, in Ostrom's terms, as "social dilemmas" inasmuch as the short-term maximization of individual interests leads to a suboptimal outcome for the whole group and hence for each participant (Ostrom 1998).

The type of production stemming from SSE organizations can be described, in many cases, as "quasi-collective" goods and services: childcare services, social integration through economic activity, short-circuit cooperatives, social finance, etc. In addition to the direct benefits for the users, these initiatives simultaneously generate benefits for the collectivity as a whole (a better-functioning labor market, social cohesion, local development, public health, sustainable development, etc.). These goods or services are described as quasi-collective because while the user and his/her consumption can be clearly identified, the benefits created are collective. These benefits are not always taken into account in agents' consumption or production choices, which leads to suboptimal situations in terms of the general interest.

While common resources and quasi-collective goods are comparable in the need to integrate, through collective action, collective externalities that would not be taken into account in agents' individual decisions, some important differences must nonetheless be stressed.

In the case of common resources, management needs to be entrusted to a specific category of more or less homogeneous stakeholders, the appropriators, who are generally direct beneficiaries of the resource (as consumers or producers). A "sub-group" for Ostrom is a group potentially capable of collective action because its members have similar rights, responsibilities and interests in the resource (Poteete *et al.* 2010, p. 92). Ostrom does indeed acknowledge a certain heterogeneity (ibid., p. 54) in these groups in economic terms (wealth), or socio-cultural terms, but all generally have the same kind of relation to the resource as appropriators.

Ostrom envisions a move from a situation in which "individuals act independently, to one in which they coordinate activities" to produce benefits "shared by all appropriators" (Ostrom 1990, p. 40). This reflects the configuration of a mutual benefit organization, exactly as in the case of producer or consumer cooperatives, which are based on a dynamics of self-organization by the actors, even if there is a general interest dimension, inasmuch as society has an interest in the resource being managed in a way that guarantees its sustainability.

However, the notion of collective benefit or social utility in SSE analyses goes far beyond a conception of the collective interest. This social utility, which is multiform (Gadrey 2006), is generally mobilized by SSE organizations as part of their mission: lower cost for public bodies, contribution to the fight against inequality, environmental profit, etc. For SSE organizations, these benefits are no longer a phenomenon induced by the economic activity ("an externality") but are at the core of the objectives they promote (Laville and Nyssens 2001).

In the case of these quasi-collective goods produced by the SSE, the day-to-day management is often entrusted to professionals, possibly alongside volunteers, under the aegis of a board of directors and a general assembly. In contrast to Ostrom's commons, these collectives are generally more heterogeneous. They represent a diversity of stakeholders (members of civil society, employees, users, the public authorities, etc.), reflecting the general interest dimension that characterizes this type of organization. This is the framework in which the European literature on the social enterprise introduces the possibility of the involvement of a diversity of stakeholders in the very structure of governance of the organization (see Chapter 6 by Borzaga and Depedri in this volume; Defourny and Nyssens 2010; Petrella 2008). Although these actors pursue interests that are at least partially divergent, the aim is to construct a collective interest from their adherence to a common social purpose. The question of the construction of the collective interest arises from a compromise among different action logics that are sometimes contradictory or in tension.

So for Ostrom, organizations are driven by the appropriators of the resource, who organize collective action to secure common benefits. In the case of the SSE, the construction of a social finality goes beyond a narrow definition of the interests of the direct beneficiaries and often requires dialogue among a heterogeneity of stakeholders, which gives, among other things, another position to the public actors in the name of their contribution to the general interest.

Indeed, an important difference emerges here between the SSE and the governance of common goods, since the state or local governments generally contribute to the production of quasi-collective goods and services by the SSE, through various forms of financing and regulation and even, in some cases, through the presence of public authority representatives in the decision-making bodies of the organizations. State participation takes its place in a historical context of compromise between the state and associations in offering these services, resulting in close interactions between these two actors.

For Ostrom, the role of the state is to give institutional legitimacy to the systems set up by the appropriators. They must be recognized by the state. She also stresses in her works the need to develop polycentric institutions (a situation in which several decision-making centers coexist, at different scales, and are at least formally independent while contributing to the supply and production of the common resource); the state may be involved in some of these levels, especially the higher ones (Ostrom 2010). However, fundamentally, the role of the state is to "recognize" and so legitimate the agreements as deployed by the local actors.

Because in the case of common resources there is open access to appropriation of the resource, the question of financing is not central, even if the question of the implicit price arises when the rules for sharing exploitation and maintaining the resource are discussed. By contrast, the question of fixing the price emerges more directly in the case of the provision of quasi-collective goods, since the financing of the collective benefits by the collectivity is a matter of the highest importance.

Although both approaches address the difficulty of providing goods and/or services that have a collective dimension, the nature of the collective interest clearly differs between the two. In the case of common resources, the collective interest is essentially the interest of a group, which is more a case of mutual interest, even if the sustainable management of a resource includes a general interest dimension. By contrast, in the production of collective goods or services, the collective interest is that of the society as a whole and is more akin to the general interest. This general interest dimension means that more importance is given to the role of the state in the production of these goods and services and to a stronger hybridization of commercial, public and voluntary resources.

Co-producing rules in an environment of trust: the institutional dimension of organizations

Questions of trust and imperfect information are as central to Ostrom's works as to works on the SSE.

In response to the postulates of perfect information and perfect rationality of the neoclassical model, Ostrom stresses that, in reality, actors are very often in situations of profoundly imperfect information characterized by great uncertainty (Kiser and Ostrom 2000, p. 61). If economic theory addresses the question of trust in situations of imperfect information, these are reduced to a probabilizing uncertainty and says little about the institutional forms favoring this trust. Faced with these blind spots, Ostrom's essential questioning is the analysis of the mode of governance of common resources and therefore the rules, i.e., the institutional framework, that allow sustainable exploitation of these resources. On the basis of analysis of hundreds of cases of commons management around the world, she shows that appropriators are capable of creating local, sustainable institutional arrangements, which take account of the specific context, make possible an effective management of common resources and prevent over-exploitation. She derives from them some general principles for sustainable management of common resources. For an agreement to be effective and sustainable and to engender trust and reciprocity among the members, several general principles must be collectively defined and applied by the members themselves, taking account of the local conditions and the long-term preservation of the resource (Ostrom 1990):

- rights to extract the resource must be clearly defined;
- appropriation and provision rules must be congruent with local conditions and benefit must be proportional to the costs undertaken;
- collective-choice arrangements must be set up;
- there must be rules for monitoring users and resources;
- graduated sanctions must be applied;
- conflict resolution mechanisms must be set up;
- the state must recognize the organization in place, i.e., the right of local users to make their own rules;

- the whole system must be organized in multiple layers of nested enterprises in the case of common resources connected to a larger system.

Ostrom thus shows that it is important to set up a hierarchical system of rules that includes operational rules (determining the conditions of access to and use of a resource), "collective choice" rules (to deal with conflicts and dysfunctions) and "constitutional choice" rules which frame collective choices, for example by determining who may modify these rules (Weinstein 2013, p. 7).

A central conclusion of Ostrom's works with regard to economic theory thus concerns the bringing to light of the importance of letting the actors discuss among themselves in order to draw up their own rules (Holland and Sene 2010). Ostrom does not stop with the analysis of property regimes but also analyzes the institutional work of the appropriators. This analysis relates to the instituting capacity of organizations, i.e., their ability to collectively produce rules of decision and operation. Involving the actors in the institutional arrangements that they have created is primordial, especially in the mechanisms for monitoring the application of the rules so as to prevent opportunist behaviors.

Trust is also a central issue in the production of many quasi-collective goods: information is fundamentally imperfect, the product being marked by "the uncertainty of service relationships" (Gadrey 1996, p. 7). It is indeed difficult to evaluate the quality of quasi-collective services whose objectives are multidimensional, with quality being based on a co-construction between the supplier and the user (Laville 2005). While the imperfect nature of the information may partially explain the existence of associations (Hansmann 1980), it is generally agreed that the constraint of non-redistribution of profits does not suffice to protect the users (Nyssens 2008). In this context, it is therefore important to consider the modalities that make it possible to create a relation of trust.

The involvement of a diversity of stakeholders in the ownership of organizations is one way of dealing with the imperfect character of the information and creating a relationship of trust among them, whether they be the users, the public authorities or the employees (see Chapter 6 by Borzaga and Depedri in this volume; Nyssens and Petrella 2009).

However, Ostrom draws our attention to the importance of creating norms to ensure the durability of collective action. The principles she invokes echo the foundations of the association and more generally of the SSE. They are relevant to the SSE in terms of its governance and its concrete application of the principles of independent management and internal democracy.

These observations question the positioning of associations and the SSE vis-à-vis the institutional environment, which is viewed as given and as a constraint for many SSE organizations. What then becomes of the capacity of the associative actors and the SSE to produce their own operating rules and norms and indeed, through these rules, to contribute to institutional change by playing a part in reshaping the modalities of public action?

While Ostrom underlines the importance of drawing up norms in the framework of the management of uncertainty and the production of trust, analyses of the SSE highlight the fact that institutional work relates to the political dimension of the SSE. It is a matter of recognizing the political embeddedness of organizations, defined as the set of interactions between the public authorities and the SSE, reflected in mutual effects whose intensity and modalities vary considerably in time (Laville 2006). While the SSE cannot be apprehended without integrating analysis of the public regulation to which it is subject and whose isomorphic pressures it has to cope with, at the same time the forms it takes cannot be determined by public regulation alone. SSE organizations play a part in the co-construction of the norms and in this case of public policies. It is indeed necessary to recognize the "institutional work" of the actors at the meso-economic level, which Lawrence and Suddaby (2006) term "institutional entre-preneurship." Ostrom concludes that letting the actors themselves produce common rules can generate a sustainable management of common resources insofar as certain principles are respected. On the other hand, her works say very little about the role of these local institutional arrangements at the level of the social and political transformation of our economies, in contrast to some approaches to the SSE and the solidarity economy in particular.

Conclusion

Although the starting points are different, our analysis confirms the heuristic interest of pursuing the dialogue between SSE analyses and those of the governance of common resources. Our analysis leads us to identify the common points and divergences in terms of analysis of property regimes, the nature of goods and services that are neither public nor private, and the collective production of norms, giving rise to some reciprocal questionings.

These approaches have in common the fact that they underscore the importance of examining the forms of governance of goods and services with a collective dimension, which differ from public and for-profit private forms. These approaches contribute to the recognition of a necessary "eco-diversity," i.e., a plurality of institutional forms (Ostrom, 2005) which challenges the classic state–market dichotomy and thereby promotes an approach to property in terms of bundles of rights that can be combined in multiple ways. These analyses thus show the great diversity of the property regimes that contribute to the construction of a common interest. In these property regimes, the right of alienation – rarely granted in the case of the services studied – or the right to residual earnings are subject to specific rules reflecting in some sense the fundamentally collective heritage underlying these regimes and questioning the supremacy of capitalist property as put forward by the property rights school.

However, the nature of the collective interest clearly differs between the two approaches. In the case of common resources, the collective interest is essentially the interest of a group, the appropriators, making it more of a mutual interest, even if the sustainable management of a resource includes a general interest dimension. By contrast, in the case of the production of quasi-collective goods or services, the collective interest concerns the whole society and is more a matter of the general interest, requiring a dialogue among a variety of stakeholders. This general interest dimension leads to a more important place being given to the state, whose role cannot be limited to "recognizing" the local institutional arrangements, as envisaged by Ostrom, but includes an essential role in the financing and regulation of these goods and services. This is one of the major divergences between Ostrom's works and those on the SSE, since she ultimately remains ambiguous on the question of the role of the state.

Finally, from an institutional standpoint, the two approaches also insist on the need for the stakeholders to produce – collectively, transparently and in a negotiated way – the rules governing decision-making, operation and the allocation of any surplus. These analyses are therefore not limited to an analysis of property regimes. Ostrom particularly stresses the involvement of the actors in the institutional arrangements they have created, especially in the arrangements for monitoring the proper application of the rules defined, so as to prevent opportunistic behaviors and create a climate of trust. This may explain why many initiatives implemented "top-down" by public authorities have failed to secure the commitment and mobilization of the local actors. The creation of grassroots public spaces capable of constructing institutional arrangements is one of the essential conditions for producing a lasting agreement among the stakeholders concerned; this may be of concern to SSE organizations, which are often locked into systems of constraints with the public authorities. Ostrom subtly analyzes the set of rules – to be deployed by the actors themselves – required for the sustainability of systems of governance. However, according to the SSE analyses, beyond their function of producing effective rules and relations of trust, these institutional local arrangements have a public dimension contributing to the construction of regulations. Recognizing the institutional dimension of the SSE also means analyzing its participation in the deployment of norms and regulations both at the level of the organization and beyond and so asserting its public dimension, which remains a blind spot in Ostrom's works. These norms and regulations in fact shape the fundamental equilibria of our societies, in particular the place of the market, the state and civil society. To recognize the institutional dimension is to recognize the contributions of SSE organizations to shaping a more sustainable society. Here there is a major issue for the present time, particularly around the question of the political dimension of the management of both common resources and collective goods.

Note

1 This research benefits from a grant, "If Not For Profit, For What?," funded by the Interuniversity Attraction Poles Program initiated by the Belgian Science Policy Office.

References

Alchian, A. and Demsetz, H. (1973). The Property Right Paradigm. *Journal of Economic History* 33(1), pp. 16–27.
Commons, J. (1893). *The Distribution of Wealth*. London: Macmillan and Co.

Defourny, J. and Nyssens, M. (2010). Conceptions of Social Enterprise and Social Entre-preneurship in Europe and the United States: Convergences and Divergences. *Journal of Social Entrepreneurship* 1(1), pp. 32–53.

Gadrey, J. (1996). *Services: la productivité en question.* Paris: Desclée de Brouwer.

Gadrey, J. (2006). Utilité sociale. In Laville, J. -L. and Cattani, A. (eds) *Dictionnaire de l'autre économie, édition revue et augmentée.* Paris: Gallimard, pp. 641–651.

Glaeser, E. (2003). *The Governance of Not-For-Profit Organizations.* Chicago and London: University of Chicago Press.

Gui, B. (1991). The Economic Rationale for the "Third Sector": Nonprofit and other Non-capitalist Organizations. *Annals of Public and Cooperative Economics* 62(4), pp. 551–572.

Hansmann, H. (1980). The Role of Nonprofit Enterprise. *Yale Law Journal* 89(5), pp. 835–901.

Hansmann, H. (1996). *The Ownership of Enterprise.* Cambridge, MA: Harvard University Press.

Holland, G. and Sene, O. (2010). Elinor Ostrom et la gouvernance économique. *Revue d'économie politique* 120(3), pp. 441–452.

Kiser, L. and Ostrom, E. (2000). The Three Worlds of Action: A Metatheoretical Synthesis of Institutional Approaches. In McGinnis, M. (ed.) *Polycentric Games and Institutions.* Michigan: University of Michigan Press, pp. 56–88.

Laville, J. -L. (2005). *Sociologie des services: entre marché et solidarité.* Toulouse: ERES.

Laville, J. -L. (2006). Economie plurielle. In Laville, J.-L. and Cattani, A. (eds) *Dictionnaire de l'autre économie, édition revue et augmentée.* Paris: Gallimard, pp. 250–258.

Laville, J. -L. and Nyssens, M. (2001). The Social Enterprise: Towards a Theoretical Socio-economic Approach. In Borzaga, C. and Defourny, J. (eds) *The Emergence of Social Enterprise.* London and New York: Routledge, pp. 312–332.

Lawrence, T. and Suddaby, R. (2006). Institutions and Institutional Work. In Clegg, S., Hardy, C., Lawrence, T. and North, W. (eds) *Handbook of Organization Studies*, 2nd edition. London: Sage, pp. 215–254.

Nyssens, M. (2008). Les analyses économiques des associations. In Hoarau, C. and Laville, J. -L. (eds) *La gouvernance des associations.* Toulouse: ERES, pp. 27–49.

Nyssens, M. and Petrella, F. (2009). Finalité sociale et partenariat public-privé dans l'offre de services quasi-collectifs locaux: une forme innovante de propriété. *Economie et Sociétés, série EGS* 10(4), pp. 747–774.

Ostrom, E. (1990). *Governing the Commons: The Evolution of Institutions for Collective Action.* Cambridge: Cambridge University Press.

Ostrom, E. (1998). A Behavioral Approach to the Rational Choice Theory of Collective Action: Presidential Address, American Political Science Association, 1997. *American Political Science Review* 92(1), pp. 1–22.

Ostrom, E. (2005). *Understanding Institutional Diversity.* Princeton: Princeton University Press.

Ostrom, E. (2010). Beyond Markets and States: Polycentric Governance of Complex Economic Systems. *American Economic Review* 100(3), pp. 641–672.

Poteete, A., Janssen, M. and Ostrom, E. (2010). *Working Together: Collective Action, the Commons, and Multiple Methods in Practice.* Princeton: Princeton University Press.

Petrella, F. (2008). Organizations non lucratives et partenariat: avantages et risques dans le cas des services de développement local en Belgique. In Enjolras, B. (ed.) *Gouvernance et intérêt général dans les services sociaux et de santé.* Brussels: CIRIEC, Peter Lang, pp. 107–127.

Schlager, E. and Ostrom, E. (1992). Property-Rights Regimes and Natural Resources: A Conceptual Analysis. *Land Economics* 68(3), pp. 249–262.

Weinstein, O. (2013). Comment comprendre les "communs": Elinor Ostrom, la propriété et la nouvelle économie institutionnelle. *Revue de la régulation* [online] 14, second semester/autumn, http://regulation.revues.org/10452.

11 Democratic governance and citizenship

Bernard Enjolras and Kari Steen-Johnsen

Introduction

The term "democratic governance" denotes forms of governance that involve citizens through one or another form of democratic mechanism; in this, civil society organizations (CSOs) have traditionally played central roles. There are three ways in which CSOs have been thought to contribute to active citizenship: through shaping identities and the sense of belonging; through creating possibilities for participation and empowerment; and through allowing for representation in a public sphere (Warren, 2001). The importance of CSOs in relation to citizenship thus resides first in *internal* factors, that is, in internal democratic governance. A central question in this context is how CSOs forge links to their members and what form of participation they facilitate. Second, the impact of civil society depends on *external* factors, that is, the role of CSOs in the democratic governance of society.

In modern welfare states, the representation of CSOs has traditionally tended to be institutionalized through a variety of corporatist and neo-corporatist arrangements, where organizations in different areas of society have forged links to government and spoken on behalf of their members as part of these arrangements (Kuhnle and Selle, 1992; Hill, 1997). Over the last decade most European countries have reformed their local governments: the competencies and powers of local authorities, and relations between center and region, have been modified considerably, favoring a process of decentralization (John, 2001). The growing involvement of civil society associations and business organizations in government at different levels has led to network-based forms of coordination (Cohen and Sabel, 1997).

In relation to the question of active citizenship, a pivotal point is the type of representation and participation in democracy that these new forms of societal governance allow citizens – through CSOs or other forms of emerging collectives. In our perspective, the question of whether citizenship is enhanced hinges on the institutional framework shaping relationships between civil society and local public authorities in policy-making processes. Traditionally, policy-making in democratic representative systems has been understood as a result of parliamentary activity. However, the role of civil society in policy-making was acknowledged by Rokkan as early as 1966. In a seminal article, Rokkan identifies three channels of political influence: the numerical-democratic (through representative institutions); the corporatist (through civil society organizations); and the mass media (Rokkan, 1966). Hill (1997) defined two classical institutional models for the relationship between civil society and government, the neo-corporate and the pluralist. In his comparison of 19 democracies, Wilensky (2002) defines neo-corporatism (democratic corporatism) as a structure that allows for the interplay of strongly organized interest groups with a centralized government. In contrast, pluralism does not provide an institutional structure for interest representation or for the interplay of government and organized interests (Dahl, 1982). Neo-corporatist structures have been challenged in recent decades by the multiplication of interests and identities that characterizes late-modern societies and by an increase in networking. New approaches to governance, policy networks and policy communities have emphasized these changes and provided conceptual tools for understanding them. Based on this perspective, there is a need, we suggest, to distinguish between different forms of new societal governance modes. In the latter part of this chapter we therefore argue that a distinction should be made between what we have termed "network governance" and "partnership governance." Only the latter form of governance implies a reference to civic collectives.

The chapter proceeds as follows. First, we present three theoretical perspectives on democracy and discuss the challenges they pose to modern democracies. As part of this we also describe the potential internal democratic effects of CSOs and their relationship with internal governance. In the next section we present a typology of new and old societal governance forms and relate them to different conceptions of citizenship. The last part of the chapter is devoted to a discussion of the implications for citizenship of network governance and partnership governance. We point out some of the particular challenges to democracy from network governance. More generally, our analysis points to two paradoxes. First, CSOs may have an impact on governance even when their internal governance is not democratic. Second, the role of CSOs in democratic governance is conditioned on the prevailing institutional governance regime. The increasing reliance of new forms of network governance on CSOs may paradoxically undermine the very principles of liberal democracy.

Three dimensions of democracy

Theories of democracy are manifold and the concept of democracy contested, leaving space for several different "models of democracy" (Held, 1987). Despite such diversity, it is common to distinguish three normative conceptions (Allern and Pedersen, 2007): competitive democracy; participative democracy; and deliberative democracy. Competitive democracy emphasizes voting as a mechanism of aggregating political preferences, choice between rival interests, and selection and accountability of leaders. Participative democracy focuses on the active participation of all citizens in political activities and decision-making.

Deliberative democracy seeks to solve conflicts of interest through rational discussion and deliberation in the public space. Instead of preference aggregation (as in the case of voting) deliberation leads to preference transformation.

To each of these models of democracy is attached a set of conditions, suggesting different ideals and challenges for democracy, related to representation, participation and competition among interests. Common to the *competitive* approach to democracy is the centrality of elections as the means of aggregating individual interests or selecting leaders. In economic theories of democracy, citizens are seen as having fixed preferences and the political system as an arena where conflicting interests struggle for power. From this viewpoint, elections and vote procedures are conceived as aggregative mechanisms of individual preferences. On the other hand, it has also been argued that the aggregation of preferences through voting may lead to irrational results, as shown by Arrow's (1951) "impossibility theorem," and may fail to produce a conception of the common good (Ricker, 1982). And as Schumpeter (2008) also stresses, the empirical reality of representative democracies is not that the electorate makes decisions on public affairs. Elections, he argues, do not express any popular will concerning policies. In a representative democracy, he claims, people do not govern indirectly "by choosing individuals who will assemble to put their will into action." The people merely select, from among a number of competitors, those who will make political decisions.

Despite these concerns, competition still remains a basic mode of democracy, both in societies and within CSOs. The theoretical understanding of democracy as a form of competition was challenged, however, at the beginning of the 1980s by scholars who emphasized instead the importance of *deliberation*. The 1984 publication of Habermas's *Theory of Communicative Action* spurred several scholars to launch a critique of the politics-as-competition hypotheses, sparking renewed interest in deliberation. Deliberation, by which Habermas meant discussions of issues involving different points of view, can facilitate consensus, he maintained, by transforming preferences or clarifying alternatives, which can then be submitted to the vote. To function properly, deliberative processes require a fair communicative process that leads to mutual understanding (Gutmann and Thompson, 1996, p. 17). This potential problem is recognized by Habermas: "reaching mutual understanding through discourses indeed guarantees that issues, reasons, and information are handled reasonably, but such understanding still depends on contexts characterized by capacity for learning, both at the cultural and the personal level" (1996, p. 324)." Due to the complexity of the issues at stake and unequal access to resources, deliberation may lead to the appropriation of power by specialists and passivity among citizens.

A third understanding of democracy emphasizes the *participation* of citizens and organizations in setting the direction of political systems and how they operate in practice (Pateman, 1972). The direct participation of citizens is thought to resolve some of the problems related to indirect representation, in particular the disconnection between the political system and society. Active participation is thought to empower citizens, individually and in groups, that are affected by given policies. However, the active involvement of some citizens in these different forms of democracy can be problematic. Dissymmetry of resources between representatives and represented can encourage the formation of oligarchies and undermine the legitimacy of representative democracy. According to Michels (1949), leaders have an advantage over members insofar as the latter have neither the time nor the resources to compete with the leaders who control organizational resources (knowledge, means of communication, skills in the art of politics). Similarly, active participation in deliberations or decision-making is unequally distributed and conditioned on social, educational and economic resources. Indeed a requirement for participative and deliberative democracy, i.e., active participation, is "enlightened understanding" (Dahl, 1982; Gutmann and Thompson, 1996; Habermas, 1996; Young, 1999), which supposes that each citizen (or organization member) enjoys equal access to the resources necessary to make an informed choice on an issue. The unequal distribution of political skills and cultural resources may lead a minority to seek to dominate political processes by intimidating those who feel unqualified to participate.

We can use these three conceptions of democracy as descriptions and yard-sticks for an evaluation of the roles of CSOs in democratic governance, both in the relationship between citizens and the state and in the relationship between members and CSOs. The three conceptions are also useful for characterizing the relationship between CSOs and the state. For example, in relation to the competitive view of democracy, Dahl's pluralist theory introduces the idea of competition among organized interests as a feature of the political system (Dahl, 1982). But connected to each of the concepts of democracy a number of obstacles to democratic processes may be identified, the most important of which are lack of representativeness; lack of adequate communication structures; and unequal distribution of information and skills. The manner in which CSOs are governed internally and the way state governance regimes are set up and practiced can either increase or decrease the effect of these obstacles.

In this chapter the main thrust is the discussion of the latter set of conditions, i.e., how various state governance regimes facilitate or impede citizenship either through their impact on CSOs or directly as an effect on citizens. As a basis for this argument we need to look very briefly into the potential effects of CSOs on democracy. The democratic effect of associations or CSOs, in Warren's view, resides in three factors. First, associations are loci of democratic self-rule and hence allow for citizens to take part in making decisions that are of direct relevance to them. Second, CSOs may have a skills effect on individuals in the sense that they allow them to develop their political skills and their civic virtues. Finally, CSOs may have a public sphere effect. They may ensure representation of different interests within the public sphere, and they may also contribute by enforcing public deliberation in itself. This, in turn, depends on a well-functioning internal competitive democracy.

These internal democratic effects of CSOs, however, rely on a set of factors such as the degree of bureaucracy and professionalization, power distribution in the organizations, and the knowledge, competence and activity of members.

Even though several authors have pointed out a clear connection between the development of democratic skills and participation in CSOs (Almond and Verba, 1963; Wollebæk and Selle, 2009), effects related to self-rule, to the representation of interests and to the establishment of well-functioning public spheres are less certain. Among the central challenges to the internal democratic effects of CSOs are the problems of oligarchy (Lipset *et al.*, 1962; Michels, 1949). Due to the complexity of the matters to be dealt with and unequal access to resources, deliberative democracy within organizations may lead to the appropriation of power by specialists and to member passivity.

Another important factor is that organizations meet pressures from the environment through isomorphic processes (Amis *et al.*, 1995; Di Maggio and Powell, 1983; Vercher and Chemin, 2011). Coercive, mimetic and normative isomorphism may lead to increasing bureaucracy and professionalization and play in favor of an oligarchic structure. But still, the need to secure internal and external support may counteract this tendency to oligarchic governance and put a limit on the degree of bureaucratization and professionalization. In this sense, the requirements posed by societal governance regimes could prove to be of high importance.

The internal democratic effects of CSOs provide a yardstick for whether governance is democratic. If CSOs do not have the assumed democratic effects, this will undermine their legitimacy as democratic agents in systems of societal governance and in society as a whole. In the next part of this chapter we ask whether different modes of societal governance imply different democratic effects, both in their presumptions and aims and in the institutional arrangements that they entail.

Governance regimes and citizenship

What is termed "societal governance" or "external governance" describes the relationship between the state and different sections of society in processes of policy-making and policy implementation. A regime of governance may be characterized along three dimensions: the types of actors involved; the types of policy instruments used for the implementation of the policy; and the types of institutional coordination used for policy-making (Enjolras, 2009). In current debates, various new forms of governance that involve networks and cooperation are at times confused with one another. In the following we try to systematize the differences between what we have termed public, corporative, network and partnership governance. We then focus specifically on how these forms of governance conceptualize the policy-making process, and we show how these are related to different conceptions of citizenship and democracy. The regimes of governance that we describe are ideal types of distinct forms of interaction between the state, civil society and citizens (see Table 11.1).

Public governance involves only public actors, relies on direct government and public ownership and supposes a technocratic policy-making process through voting. This type of governance is best exemplified by the way public services have been traditionally run.

Table 11.1 Types of governance regimes (ideal types)

	Public governance	*Corporative governance*	*Network governance*	*Partnership governance*
Actors' institutional form	Public	Public Nonprofit	Public For-profit Nonprofit	Public For-profit Nonprofit
Policy-making	Technocracy	Corporatism	Policy network	Institutionalized partnership

Corporative governance gives the state a monopoly of representation and delegates implementation to a nonprofit umbrella organization within a policy field (for example health or social services). Policies are implemented through the use of coercive instruments; usually public bodies fund and regulate the activities whereas nonprofits provide them. One example is the way nonprofit hospitals operate in many countries. They receive funding from the state and deliver health services based on specific state-defined criteria. The state relates only to a limited set of actors and new nonprofit actors may find it difficult to set up operations from within the system.

In *network governance*, public authorities make use of open policy networks to develop policies, while implementation is achieved by the creation and regulation of (quasi-) "markets" through the use of incentives. For example, when comparing the transformations of local governance of care services in Europe, Petrella and Richez-Battesti (2012) identify common trends such as the decentralization of authority and the multi-level institutional structure of governance; the diversification of the actors involved in the conception and implementation of public policies, with growing recourse to private providers, whether profit-making or non-profit; and significant changes in the public policy instruments mobilized, particularly when it comes to the funding of these services.

Whereas network governance in this respect relies on competitive, market-like mechanisms both in policy-making and implementation, in *partnership governance* institutional partnerships used political mechanisms to regulate the potential competition between actors (negotiation, deliberation). In implementation, public authorities may choose to use direct and coercive policy instruments in order to achieve agreed goals. An example of such partnership governance is given by Polizzi (2012) in his analysis of Social Area Plans (Piani Sociali di Zona) in Italy. With the introduction of Social Area Plans, district administrations were required to create participatory governance arenas, where all local actors connected to the local welfare sector were asked to take part in planning social services (2012, p. 108). The intention was to increase their mutual knowledge and to create a common ground for cooperation.

Each of these four types of governance implies a certain conception of the role of different parts of society in making policy, and hence a certain idea of citizenship. Citizenship may be conceptualized as a "repertoire of action" (Boltanski and

Thevenot, 2006) with three main constituents: (1) the pre-eminence of collectives (collective good, general will, public interest, solidarity, etc.); (2) the prevalence of democratic rules of governance (representation, participation, deliberation, election); and (3) the qualification of the persons and the regulation of relations between persons according to their rights and legal rules (law, citizenship, civil rights, social rights, etc.). When citizenship is invoked as part of a process, the process must therefore involve some sort of collective, the application of democratic rules and regulations in terms of rights or laws. But the types of collective, the democratic rules, and the rights and laws applied may vary. According to variations along these criteria we can construct a set of ideal types that describe the concept of citizenship embedded in our four governance regimes (Table 11.2).

As we can see, each governance regime entails a given conception of citizenship and citizens' roles, which is embedded in the prevailing institutional logic characterizing it. Each regime therefore varies in how it conceptualizes the collectives that underpin it, the rules of governance, and the recipients of the policy. For example, public governance is based on public interest as expressed through voting. Here, governance is understood as encompassing political representation in the policy-making process, and social rights and a public service ethos in the policy implementation process. Within this form of governance, citizens take the role of voters (in policy-making) and users (of public services).

When it comes to conceptions of democratic policy-making, the differences among the alternative governance regimes may be conceptualized along three dimensions. First, there is a distinction between governance regimes that see policy-making as proceeding through the electorate channel as opposed to the corporate channel. Here, public governance is distinguished from the three other forms of governance. Traditionally, policy-making in democratic representative systems has been understood to be a result of parliamentary activities. However, the role of civil society in policy-making has been acknowledged by Rokkan (1999). Rokkan identifies three channels through which political influence can be brought to bear: the electorate channel through representative institutions; the corporate channel through CSOs; and the mass media.

Table 11.2 Governance regimes and dimensions of citizenship

	Public governance	*Corporative governance*	*Network governance*	*Partnership governance*
Basis for the collective	Public interest	Collective interest	No collective	Solidarity
Rules of governance	Indirect voice/political representation	Indirect voice/interest representation	Quasi-market competition between interests	Direct voice, direct participation, empowerment
Qualification of the persons/ participants	Voters	Members	Stakeholders	Active citizens

Second, within the corporate channel two classical institutional models of relationship between civil society and government have traditionally been distinguished: the model of neo-corporatism and the model of pluralism (Hill, 1997). In his comparison of 19 democracies, Wilensky (2002) defines neo-corporatism (democratic corporatism) as a structure providing the interplay of strongly organized interest groups with a centralized government. In contrast, pluralism does not provide an institutional structure for interest representation and for the interplay between government and organized interests (Dahl, 1982). Network governance and partnership governance are examples of pluralist institutional arrangements.

The third dimension refers to the normative conceptions of democracy and is related to the three views of democracy that were described in the introduction to this chapter: competitive democracy; participative democracy; and deliberative democracy (Allern and Pedersen, 2007; Bohman and Regh, 1997; Mansbridge, 1992). Competitive democracy emphasizes the role of voting as a mechanism enabling the aggregation of political preferences; the choice among interests in competition; and the selection and accountability of the leaders. Deliberative democracy underscores the possibility of resolving conflicts of interest through rational discussion and deliberation in the public space. Instead of entailing preference aggregation (as with the case of voting), deliberation leads to preference transformation. Participative democracy, in contrast, focuses on the active participation of all citizens in political activities and decision-making processes.

In our typology of governance regimes, public governance emphasizes competitive democracy that operates within the electorate channel. Corporative governance is associated with a deliberative conception of democracy through the corporate channel and within an institutional structure providing the interplay between organized interests and government. Both network governance and partnership governance entail a pluralist institutional setting for policy-making, but they differ according to the conception of democracy they presuppose.

Partnership governance involves both participative and deliberative conceptions of democracy by establishing institutional settings and arenas where non-profit actors have the possibility to participate in the development of policy as well as in implementation. Network governance, on the other hand, is at best based on a competitive conception of democracy. If deliberative arenas and principles of representation are not defined, the impact and influence of each civil society actor will depend on the relative power and position of each actor. As shown by Morgan-Trimmer (2012) in her study of policies promoting citizens' participation in an urban regeneration program in Britain, the lack of formal governance structures can become an impeding factor. While there were initiatives that encouraged local residents to participate, as a rule, only a limited number of residents became very involved in the partnership, and most actors had very few links to strategic decision-making structures in the local authority area. Residents therefore faced significant challenges in their efforts to influence public services and public decision-making on a broader scale.

A final distinction between partnership governance and network governance is that, within network governance, policy can be implemented only through market-based mechanisms. This will be the situation in cases in which the government relates to each possible provider or stakeholder separately, and includes them in policy implementation solely on the basis of what they can offer in terms of service delivery.

Distinctions within the "new" forms of governance

In the literature on "new governance" (Levy-Faur, 2012; Osborne, 2010; Pierre, 2000; Rhodes, 1997; Stoker, 2004), the network governance model and the partnership model are often conflated (Sørensen and Torfing, 2007). This is a result of two simultaneous trends in public-sector reform in recent years. On the one hand, customer orientation and efficiency were the main catchwords of fundamental transformations in public service delivery. The introduction of market logic to public service delivery made ideas of competition and choice seem the optimal approach to achieving local goals, blurring the boundary between the state and the market. On the other hand, as new ways of coordinating activities – by means of networks, partnerships and the creation of deliberative devices – emerged, they have replaced centralized and hierarchical forms of representation.

Network governance embraces a wide range of actors: labor unions, trade associations, firms, local authority representatives, social entrepreneurs, CSOs and community groups (Osborne, 2010). Here, enhancing responsiveness to an increasingly differentiated economic and social environment has been the main rationale. "One-size-fits-all" policies and actions – characteristic of the welfare era – gave way to more localized and specific policy solutions. An essential part of service delivery strategy therefore involved the pooling of local knowledge of local actors in the private, public and third sectors.

Social and economic networks play a new role in these policy processes. According to Rhodes, new governance refers to "self-organizing, inter-organizational networks," including interdependent organizations, that interact continuously using reciprocally negotiated rules, rooted in trust (1999, p. xvii). With this understanding, a network is a particular form of public–private interaction based on coordination and representing an alternative to hierarchical or market systems. Networks are seen as a

> set of relatively stable relationships which are of non-hierarchical and inter-dependent nature linking a variety of actors who share common interests with regard to a policy and who exchange resources to pursue these shared interests acknowledging that co-operation is the best way to achieve common goals.
>
> (Borzel, 1997: 1)

Traditional forms of public management are known in particular for their focus on the operation of public agencies; command and control as the main instruments by which public programs operate; rule compliance as the main logic of action; and hierarchy as the predominant line of interaction. In contrast, new governance emphasizes the central role of networking and network relationships. New governance means that governments, rather than acting alone, increasingly engage in co-regulation, co-steering, co-production, cooperative management and other forms of interaction that blur the boundaries between government and society and between the public and the private sectors (Kooiman, 2003). These governance-promoting shifts are reflected in policies based on "partnerships" that seek "joined-up solutions" to complex social problems. These solutions, according to the new paradigm, depend on a wide range of actors – including civil society actors – working together across boundaries.

The main distinction between what we have termed partnership governance and network governance concerns the institutional mechanisms through which governance proceeds. These mechanisms, in turn, affect whether citizenship will be enhanced by this particular form of governance. A major difference between the two forms is that in partnership governance the state institutionalizes the relationship to networks and actors, forming relationships of cooperation and exchange that are to a certain extent formalized. The state thus creates an institutional space for representation and negotiation with defined boundaries and with certain criteria for participation. These criteria refer to the representation of different types of organized or unorganized groups within civil society, according to either their membership size, their competence or the citizen rights that they represent. Through this institutionalization partnership governance thus assumes the representation of citizens in one way or the other and refers to an idea of collectivities with given rights within civil society.

In contrast, network governance does not imply institutionalization on the part of the state but rather presumes that influence networks are open and fluid, depending on the field. Within network governance, participation and influence by civil society or market actors are not defined according to specified criteria. As a result, the influence of different parties – or stakeholders – may be determined not in terms of their representativeness but in terms of their resources, expertise and power. This power may result from either political or market mechanisms. The main issue then is to determine what differentiates political behavior from market behavior. In answering that question, Jon Elster (1997), in his essay "The Market and the Forum," emphasizes that politics involves a public activity that cannot be reduced to the private choices of consumers in the "market." Political engagement requires citizens to adopt a civic standpoint, an orientation toward the common good, when they consider political issues in the forum. The lack of a public activity and of a civic standpoint both lead to the absence of collectives (a common good) that characterizes the competitive governance regime. From this viewpoint, pure network governance – as well as pure consumerism and managerialism – leaves no space for citizenship. The inner logic of market-based governance is individualism and atomism, a logic which is opposed to that of citizenship based on social rights, community, and collectives.

Concluding discussion: challenges to citizenship and democracy within network forms of governance

The modalities of state action are changing and governance networks can be seen as an attempt on behalf of public authorities to increase the efficiency and effectiveness of public action by harnessing the untapped potential that emerges from cooperating with civil society and market actors through diverse mechanisms (networks, participatory forums, hybrid organizational forms) for the making and implementing of public policies. Our main thesis in this chapter is that governance is a mix of coordination mechanisms, which therefore necessarily generates ambiguities. In their outline of the network governance paradigm, Sørensen and Torfing (2005, 2007) emphasize that such networks are self-regulating and characterized by bargaining and deliberation.

However, this model of network governance is not neutral in terms of citizenship, the political function of governance and institutional arrangements insofar as they affect decision-making, democracy, and power relations. The institutional settings in which governance takes place appears as normative frameworks regulating power relations and defining the processes of public deliberation, decision-making, and democratic participation. In turn, these regulative frameworks may have broader social and political effects by empowering certain actors (such as experts) and disempowering others, through the valorization of certain forms of knowledge and skills, thereby raising issues of democracy and accountability.

In the literature, governance arrangements are interpreted variously as a fruitful development that empowers citizens, or a menacing development that threatens citizens' ability to exercise control over collective decision-making. Our contribution in this chapter is to show in a more specific way how different governance regimes presuppose different types of democracy and citizenship. While the public governance regime addresses citizens as voters, and corporative governance addresses them as members of organized civil society, the new governance regimes address them intermittently as stakeholders or citizens, depending on the premises. We have argued for the necessity of distinguishing partnership governance from network governance by their respective democratic effects. While partnership governance presumes participatory and deliberative democracy, network governance will often not include a democratic element.

In an ideal-typical manner of description, the neo-corporatist system of governance was an integrated system that ensured a certain representativeness, from the individual member of an organization with their assigned democratic rights to the representation of the organization in an organized relationship with the state. This type of arrangement promoted citizenship by stimulating individual participation, by defining interest groups and by ensuring empowerment of these groups through representation. Still, one may argue, neo-corporatism implied a limited impact on the state on the part of a restricted group of actors within civil society. In this sense, new forms of democratic and network-based governance may be conceived as increasing the impact of CSOs on the state, by accommodating more actors, allowing stronger involvement and supporting more symmetrical relationships.

However, network governance is problematic for democracy and citizenship. First, it decouples participatory practices at the local level from the hierarchical institutions of competitive democracy that have traditionally linked local members to national level political systems. This results in a biased representative system, where there is a lack of consultative contact between different levels of government and grassroots organizations and their members. Second, network-based democracy challenges the basic principles of liberal democracy (Sørensen and Torfing, 2005), since it blurs the boundaries that define a political community and fails to guarantee equal democratic rights to different groups of citizens. Even though partnership governance may imply the institutionalization of certain principles of representativeness and of certain rights, this does not guarantee such equality. Since network-based representation is based neither on elections nor on representativity criteria (Pitkin, 1967), it undermines the principles of representative democracy according to which representatives are supposed to "act for" their constituencies, and it fails to guarantee the equality of formal democratic rights to each citizen. By emphasizing the outputs of the policy-making process, new forms of governance therefore legitimize recourse to democratic institutions that are in conflict with the principles of liberal representative democracy. In the same vein, new developments in democracy theory, i.e., post-liberal approaches to democracy, stress the inability of liberal principles to guarantee whether democracy works well in practice. Outcome-oriented theory (Fung and Wright, 2003), for example, assesses democratic institutions on the basis of their ability to solve given problems (their outcomes), not on the basis of their basic principles.

In order to assess the impact of the new forms of governance on citizenship, there is a need to consider how they affect the different aspects of democracy: representation; participation; competition among interests; and deliberation inside organizations, among CSOs, and in the relationship between the CSOs and the state. Both the intra- and interorganizational level and the societal level must be considered when evaluating how new governance forms affect citizenship and democracy. A crucial element in this discussion is how network relationships are set up and institutionalized. Embedded in new forms of governance is a transformation of citizenship in the sense that new forms of civil collectivities, such as local residents, marginalized citizens or hospital clients, are taken into account and given a potential role in policy-making. On the one hand, this implies a pluralization of the policy-making processes and a potential enhancement of deliberative and participatory democracy. On the other, it risks effacing the principles of liberal democracy. This dilemma lies at the heart of the search for new governance forms in complex societies.

References

Allern, E. H. and Pedersen, K. (2007). The impact of party organizational changes on democracy. *West European Politics*, 30(1), pp. 68–92.

Almond, G. A. and Verba, S. (1963). *Civic Culture: Political Attitudes and Democracy in Five Nations*. Princeton: Princeton University Press.

Arrow, K. J. (1951). *Social Choice and Individual Values*. New Haven: Yale University Press.

Bohman, J. and Regh, W. (eds) (1997). *Deliberative Democracy: Essays on Reason and Politics*. Cambridge, MA: MIT Press.

Boltanski, L. and Thévenot, L. (2006). *On Justification: Economies of Worth*. Princeton: Princeton University Press.

Borzel, T. (1997). What's so special about policy networks? An exploration of the concept and its usefulness in studying European governance. *European Integration online Papers (EIoP)* 1(16), http://eiop.or.at/eiop/texte/1997-016a.htm.

Cohen, J. and Sabel, C. (1997). Directly-deliberative polyarchy. *European Law Journal*, 3(4).

Dahl, R. A. (1982). *Dilemmas of Pluralist Democracy*. New Haven: Yale University Press.

Elster, J. (1997). The market and the forum. In Bohman, J. and Regh, W. (eds) *Deliberative Democracy: Essays on Reason and Politics*. Cambridge, MA: MIT Press.

Enjolras, B. (2009). A governance-structure approach to voluntary organizations. *Nonprofit and Voluntary Sector Quarterly*, 38(5), pp. 761–783, doi: 10.1177/0899764008320030.

Gutmann, A. and Thompson, D. (1996). *Democracy and Disagreement*. Cambridge, MA: The Belknap Press of Harvard University Press.

Habermas, J. (1984). *The Theory of Communicative Action*. Boston: Beacon Press.

Habermas, J. (1996). *Between Facts and Norms*. Cambridge, MA: MIT Press.

Held, D. (1996). *Models of Democracy*. Cambridge: Polity Press.

Hill, M. (1997). *The Policy Process in the Modern State*. London: Prentice-Hall.

John, P. (2001). *Local Governance in Western Europe*. London: Sage.

Kooiman, J. (2003). *Governing as Governance*. London: Sage.

Kuhnle, S. and Selle, P. (eds) (1992). *Government and Voluntary Organizations*. Aldershot: Avebury.

Levi-Faur, D. (ed.) (2012). *The Oxford Handbook of Governance*. Oxford: Oxford University Press.

Mansbridge, J. J. (1992). A deliberative theory of interest representation. In Petracca, M. P. (ed.) *The Politics of Interests*. Boulder, CO: Westview Press, pp. 32–57.

Michels, R. [1949] (1962). *Political Parties*. New York: The Free Press.

Olson, M. (1965). *The Logic of Collective Action: Public Goods and the Theory of Groups*. Cambridge, MA: Harvard University Press.

Osborne, S. P. (ed.) (2010). *The New Public Governance?* London: Routledge.

Pateman, C. (1972). *Participation and Democratic Theory*. Cambridge: Cambridge University Press.

Pierre, J. (ed.) (2000). *Debating Governance*. Oxford: Oxford University Press.

Pitkin, H. F. (1967). *The Concept of Representation*. Berkeley: University of California Press.

Rhodes, R. A. W. (1997). *Understanding Governance: Policy Networks, Governance, Reflexivity and Accountability*. Buckingham: Open University Press.

Rhodes, R. A. W. (1999). Foreword: governance and networks. In Stoker, G. (ed.) *The New Management of British Local Governance*. Macmillan: London.

Riker, W. H. (1982). *Liberalism Against Populism*. Long Grove: Waveland Press.

Rokkan, S. (1966). Numerisk demokrati og korporativ pluralisme: To beslutningskanaler i Norsk politick. In Rokkan, S. (ed.) *Stat, Nasjon, Klasse*. Oslo: Universitetsforlaget, 1966.

Rokkan, S. (1999). *State Formation, Nation-building and Mass Politics in Europe*. Oxford: Oxford University Press.

Schumpeter, J. [1942] (2008). *Capitalism, Socialism and Democracy*. New York: Harper Collins.

Sørensen, E. (2005). The democratic problems and potentials of network governance. *European Political Science*, 4, pp. 348–357, doi: 10.1057/palgrave.eps.2210033.

Sørensen, E. and Torfing, J. (2007). Governance network research: Towards a new generation. In Sørensen, E. and Torfing, J. (eds) *Theories of Democratic Network Governance*. New York: Palgrave.

Stoker, G. (2004). *Transforming Local Governance*. Basingstoke: Palgrave Macmillan.

Walzer, M. (1983). *Spheres of Justice: A Defence of Pluralism and Equality*. Oxford: Basic Books.

Warren, M. E. (2001). *Democracy and Association*. Princeton: Princeton University Press.

Wilensky, H. L. (2002). *Rich Democracies*. Berkeley: University of California Press; London: Sage.

Wollebæk, D. and Strømsnes, K. (2008). Voluntary organizations, trust and civic engagement: A multi-level approach. *Nonprofit and Voluntary Sector Quarterly*, 37(2), pp. 249–263.

Young, I. M. (1999). Justice, inclusion and deliberative democracy. In Maced, S. (ed.) *Deliberative Politics*. Oxford: Oxford University Press.

12 Differing perspectives on civil society and the state[1]

Lars Hulgård

Introduction

In this chapter I will go through some of these battles fought by theorists as well as practitioners, both groups trying to get hold of balances and causes of imbalances in the relationship between civil society initiatives by individuals and communities and by the state.

The role of the state will be discussed with respect to the possibility of a vibrant civil society. This will be done in four steps. First the chapter will discuss the relation between civil society and state in the social science tradition. Second, it will identify a dominant American discourse that emphasizes a voluntaristic and communitarian approach to civil society and leaves a very limited space, if any, for the role of government. Third, the chapter will introduce a mix of theories that stresses a complex relation between state and civil society. Fourth, it will discuss the relation between civil society and the welfare state in the Scandinavian countries and how this trajectory is endangered by decades of privatization and a more recent introduction of entrepreneurial thinking in civil society. Finally it will be concluded that the complex relation approach in particular could be a generator of a new space for an institutional–reciprocal model of welfare. This is more sensitive to the political dimension of civil society than what was seen in the heyday of the Scandinavian welfare state and is now seen in today's homage to civil society as a provider of welfare services.

Civil society and state in the tradition: a matter of the individual and the community

A core element in the civil society tradition within the social sciences is the relation between the individual and the larger community. The individual seems to be the basic entity in civil society in the sense that civil society is a space for individuals to associate with others (Post and Rosenblaum, 2002: 3), but scholars disagree in their evaluation of the links between individuals, their groups, communities and the larger society. Thus from Hobbes to Hegel the solution of this conflict between the civil society of individuals and the sphere of common interests was to look upon the state as the highest possible achievement in the direction of mediating between the civil society of private persons and the interests of the entire national community. In the Hegelian tradition the "good society was presented as one erected on the blueprint of a rational law" (Habermas, 1996: 43). To Marx the solution was to engage in a struggle to overturn the contradictory relationship between bourgeois and citizen and to further the upheaval of that social order where people primarily enter social relations as a means.

The concept of a civil society appeared in history at a time marked by comprehensive "crisis in the social order and a breakdown of existing paradigms of the idea of order" (Seligman, 1992: 15). The societies of the late seventeenth century and the eighteenth were confronted with a tremendous break with the traditions and customs of the past "as the binding forces of society" (Seligman, 1992: 16). The break with old bonds and traditions led to a long-lasting search for new principles of moral unity. The "contract" itself served as a strong unifier between the individual and common interests:

> The obligations implied by contract and the necessary and complementary idea of the agentic and autonomous individual upon which the contract rested were both formidable concepts in the seventeenth and eighteenth century for a new model of the social order.
>
> (Seligman, 1992: 16)

In the liberal tradition "the individual is perceived as sacrosanct and autonomous – a universal value in itself" (Seligman, 1992: 120). If so, what are the possibilities of linking the individual to the community? In other words, what are the possibilities of developing solidarity among individuals, if each individual is an autonomous economic and moral agent in itself? Habermas (1996) contests such "economistic" views (based upon individual rational choice) because evidence speaks against "all models that were premised on egocentric decision making and that disregarded how changes in interests and value orientations relate to social context" (Habermas, 1996: 334).

If the contrary were the case, and decision-making was purely based upon the exposure of individual calculations of costs and benefits, then the main way of linking individuals to each other would be through contracts. If individuals are conceptualized as cost–benefit analyzing persons, broader forms of solidarity seem impossible "beyond the calculus of mutual self-interest" (Seligman, 1992: 120). But the "contract" never stood unchallenged as the only principle of uniting the private individual to the public interest. Durkheim's critique of the utilitarian tradition is an important cornerstone in the debate on citizenship and further in the making of a civil society theory. For Durkheim the idea of the "precontractual" served as the "locus" of solidarity and social bond. The precontractual form of uniting individuals is based upon the idea that there exist rules, norms and forms of regulation which are prior to any given contract and independent of the contract. In this perspective "each person is defined not just alone but in relationship to others" (Wilson, 1997: 756) and the condition for communities to be sustainable in the long run is not based upon "a collection of atomistic individuals bumping into each other's self-interest, but rather is a network, a web of individuals-in-community" (Wilson, 1997: 756). A similar emphasis on solidarity or the possibility of mutual trust was Durkheim's answer to utilitarian and contract political theories:

> This "precontractual" trust was, for Durkheim, based on the governing terms of social solidarity ... a vision of the individual where the social is contained in the person, the universal embodied in the particular, and where the sources of moral action rest on the cognizance of the individual sanctity of each member of society.
>
> (Seligman, 1992: 120)

Refering to these classical theories, two significantly different ways of conceptualizing the relation between state and civil society have emerged since its reintroduction in the wake of the velvet revolutions in 1989. These two approaches will be dealt with in the following two sections of the chapter. First, the volunteerism and familism argument that a civil society can only blossom without interference will be introduced. Second, a complex relation approach will be presented by departing from Habermas's notion of the public sphere, deliberative democracy and the sluice model followed by other scholars who have emphasized the necessity of an active, dynamic and complex relationship between civil society and state.

Civil society as familism, volunteerism and one unit at a time

When influential actors talk about the necessity of restoring civil society, the role of the state is seldom addressed or praised. In the volunteerism tradition of civil society, the state and its institutions have appeared as persona non grata both in the days of the American "Thousand Points of Light" discourse during the late 1980s and early 1990s and in the "Everyone is a Changemaker" (Elkington and Hartigan, 2008; Mawson, 2008) that dominates the social entrepreneurship discourse on a global scale today. As early as 1992 Nancy Fraser labeled the volunteer tradition of civil society a bourgeois model that "supposes the desirability of a sharp separation of (associational) civil society and the state" (Fraser, 1992: 134).

The anti-state approach to civil society that was dominant in the volunteerism approach to civic renewal has been refined and supplemented by dominant approaches to social entrepreneurship as a way to replace the welfare state with social entrepreneurship originating in civil society and underpinned by corporate philanthropy. In the dominant discourse on social entrepreneurship, the welfare state "is ill-equipped to deal with many of the modern social problems it has to confront" (Leadbeater, 1997). Thus social entrepreneurs are needed to promote a new type of leadership that can combine social purpose activities in poor constituencies with capital, knowhow and managerial structures developed in the for-profit market sphere of society. Apparently, the social entrepreneur is a kind of civil society agent who combines virtues of community with the spirit of free enterprise, and such agents are needed for "creating a fit between investor values and community…. When feasible, social entrepreneurs create market-like feedback mechanisms to reinforce this accountability" (Dees, 2001: 5). In the social entrepreneurship discourse the collective and public dimensions of civil society have been replaced by the entrepreneurial spirit of the individual changemaker. Proponents of the "Everyone is a Changemaker" strategy in social change and social entrepreneurship have claimed that social innovation is generated through effective alliances between commercial entrepreneurs and social entrepreneurs as alternatives and usually in opposition to "the megastate" that "has not delivered on a single one of its components" (Drucker, 1994).

Within this "tradition" civil society is understood as family values and voluntarism as the only path to community improvement. As a strategy influenced by libertarian thought, it perceives the state and government sector as being opposed to the realization of civil society. It is based upon "a bourgeois assumption that a sharp separation of civil society and the state is necessary" for a liberal constitutional democracy to be operational (Fraser, 1992: 133). In unison the volunteerism approach to civil society and the anti-welfare state approach to social entrepreneurship form a strong discourse that have slowly but steadily changed civil society from being a category related to political philosophy, the enhancement of citizenship and the possibility of democratic governance to a question of training business leaders to better identify and serve the markets at the bottom of the pyramid (Elkington and Hartigan, 2008). Accordingly, as a critique of this trend, Skocpol has asked the question: why should professional and economic elites participate in broad endeavors of civil society when they can use their managerial skills "on the boards of their favorite charities?" (Skocpol, 2003: 219).

But during the two decades spanning the turn of the millennium, civil society in the sense of the relation between the individual and the community has been reintroduced by a number of scholars who from various perspectives have examined the complex relations between civil society and state. Perhaps this is because citizens in (post-) modern liberal democracies are facing similar kinds of problems confronted with a breakdown, not only in the steering capacity of the modern state but also in the moral forces of modernity.

The complex relation between state and civil society

The complex relation discourse avoids simple statements based upon *a priori* homage to either volunteerism or statism. Though major differences exist among the theorists within the frames of this approach, they share one common view: they do not consider the public sector and civil society as necessarily being opposed to each other. In what follows, three different perspectives from the complex relation discourse will be analyzed.

The Habermasian understanding of state and civil society

From Habermas (1981), we know that system (state and economy) institutions primarily interact with the lifeworld (civil society) through two kinds of media: money and power. This way of interaction may lead to processes of colonization that finally end in a situation of social pathology. In 1996, however, Habermas presented civil society in a somewhat different way. In his revised version, civil society has a much more constituting power in a liberal democracy than in the case he presented in 1981. Now the representative political system is open to influence by civil society when transmitted through the public sphere (Habermas, 1996/1992). The public sphere is that part of civil society which can ensure that civil society can "fight back," stop the colonization and even increase its importance, as suggested by Habermas. In the center of his new argument stands the application of a sluice model of problem solving and communication that is a crucial part of his own version of deliberative democracy. The legitimacy of political decisions is secured only by "communication flows that start at the periphery and pass through the sluices of democratic and constitutional procedures" (Habermas, 1996: 356). Thus in a constitutional democracy the political system

> is internally differentiated into spheres of administrative and communicative power and remains open to the lifeworld. For institutionalized opinion- and will-formation depends on supplies coming from the informal contexts of communication found in the public sphere, in civil society, and in spheres of private life. In other words, the political action system is embedded in lifeworld contexts.
>
> (Habermas, 1996: 352)

According to Habermas and particularly the sluice model, the civil, politically oriented public sphere serves as an important mediator between the citizenry and its elected officials, since the public sphere is "rooted in the communication of civil society" (Cohen, 1997).

Civil society in the volunteerism and familism tradition, where civil society is based upon voluntary belonging to associations with network relations and face-to-face interaction, carries the danger of lending itself to a project aimed at dismantling the role of democratic governance from civil society and related areas such as third-sector and social enterprise: "Minus the public sphere, civil society talk all too easily lends itself to projects that have little to do with democratization" (Cohen, 1997: 8) – and thereby dissociates itself from its conceptual origin in the history of political philosophy.

As we have seen in the Habermasian version of the complex relation discourse, the public sphere is the resource – or locus – which connects democratic regimes with their citizens. The public sphere is an indispensable resource for civil society inputs to the democratization of society. Inspired by Fraser (1992), Habermas distinguishes between weak publics and strong publics. The interrelation between both of these and the state apparatus is that whereas weak publics relate to processes of deliberation outside the political system, strong publics relate to processes of deliberation in parliamentary and formally organized institutions (Eriksen and Weigård, 2002: 273; Fraser, 1992: 132ff.). Whereas weak publics are limited to opinion formation, strong publics are also engaged in decision-making (Fraser, 1992: 134). With this approach to the public sphere it is possible to fully comprehend the potential of civil society to be both an agent of social service in the third-sector tradition and an agent of democratic governance and decision-making (Defourny *et al.*, 2014; Evers, 2013). Thus it is possible to pinpoint not only the connection and sluices between weak and strong publics but also the locus where communicative actions are present, important and related to the preconditions for large-scale democratic governance:

> The civil, politically oriented public, rooted in the communication processes of civil society, presumably has a communicative connection to the legislature and thereby serves as the most important mediation between the citizenry and its elected officials in a constitutional democracy.
>
> (Cohen, 1997: 8)

Skocpol's notion of diminishing democracy

Skocpol (1996; 2002; 2003) attacks the conception put forward by communitarian and libertarian thinkers who claim that the transactions in society can be seen as a zero sum game, where the impact of civic responsibility cannot exist in collaboration with the impact of the welfare state. The zero-sum proposition is based upon the assumption that when the state and institutions related to the public sector grow in number and importance it necessarily leads to the diminishing of the voluntary sector – the civil society and civic responsibility:

> On the right, civic responsibility means drastic reductions in the role of the national government.... Conservatives may imagine that popular voluntary associations and the welfare state are contradictory opposites, but historically they have operated in close symbiosis. Voluntary civic federations have both pressured for the creation of public social programs, and worked in partnership with government to administer and expand such programs after they were established.
>
> (Skocpol, 1996: 21, 22)

According to Skocpol, the role of a universally oriented welfare state that worked in unison with large voluntary associations has been replaced by the evolution of the enabling state and accordingly a managerial culture is simultaneously replacing a type of civic engagement that has played a crucial role in the US version of a public welfare state:

> well-educated and economically better-off citizens have been key founders, leaders, and sustaining members of voluntary associations. The commitment of business people and professionals, and of women married to them, has

been especially important for the great cross-class and cross-regional associations – such as veterans' groups, fraternal bodies, temperance associations, ethnic benefit societies, and women's federations – that played such a major role in US civic life from the nineteenth through the mid-twentieth century.

(Skocpol, 1996)

The important lesson is that the vision of a universal orientation of an institutional and intrinsic welfare state was not restricted to Scandinavian or European countries. Research undertaken by Skocpol (2003) and Gilbert (2002) bears witness to the fact that the universal horizon of the welfare state was more similar on both sides of the Atlantic in the decades after World War II than has been assumed by generations of welfare theorists. Skocpol has documented that the universal orientation of the welfare state was not restricted to European countries as European welfare theorists have often argued (Esping-Andersen 1990). On the basis of several large-scale empirical studies of how government and civil society institutions have related to each other, Skocpol stresses that "the US version of the modern welfare state" was thoroughly intertwined with voluntary membership associations, and that, even in the post-World War II era,

popular social programs in the United States were never "welfare" hand-outs for the poor alone. They were inclusive benefits or services, exactly the kinds of government activities likely to be favored by massive voluntary federations that spanned places and bridged classes.

(Skocpol 2003, p. 72)

With this, Skocpol questions an assumption held by many welfare state theorists, that a modern welfare state with a universal and institutional orientation never existed in the USA.

Somers and the problem of the third sphere

Political sociologist and historian Somers has addressed the relation between civil society and state (Somers, 2001, 2008). A cross-cutting dimension in her work is the claim that "democratic and socially inclusive citizenship regimes rest on a delicate balance of power among state, market, and citizens in civil society, which is mediated through collective adjudications in the public sphere" (Somers, 2008: 2). This view is based upon historic institutionalism and argues that of the three spheres that constitute modernity, civil society is the most fragile, and in permanent danger of being squeezed in the great dichotomy (Somers, 2008: 32). Somers argues that the burden on civil society as a third realm separate from state and market has been too great. The consequence of this overload has been that the civil society concept has been increasingly subsumed by a "private, anti-political, free market" ideology (Somers, 1998: 2). Civil society may very well be a third sphere separate from state and market; but it is also the most fragile sphere since its capacity to become an agent of political decision-making depends upon a specific institutional configuration or institutional environment involving at least one of the other two spheres that constitute contemporary liberal democracies. This fragility is based upon a historic analysis which suggests that modernity has developed more as a bi-polar (state and market/civil society) than as a tri-polar entity (state, market and civil society), and due to the recent decades of privatization this is a main reason for neoliberalism's successful attempts to "privatize the public sphere of citizenship, demonize the state, and undermine the promise of a third sphere" (Somers, 1998). Normatively, Somers is a strong believer in the third sphere. But she claims that the fragility of the third sphere becomes obvious when the aim is

> fitting three conceptual pegs into only two available conceptual holes. On the one hand we have the only recently rejuvenated and still somewhat fragile idea of civil society as one of three spheres; and on the other hand – and here is where the problem surfaces – we have classical liberalism's entrenched and historically hegemonic dyadic framework.
>
> (Somers, 1998: 5)

Civil society is not only fragile due to its position vis-à-vis the power of states and markets under contemporary neoliberalism, but also due to the evolution of modern society which has been framed by the hegemony of a bi-polar or a "binary spatial divide between public and private" that goes back to Locke's narrative of a separate and pre-political space "as the sole realm of true freedom" (Somers, 1998: 31). This narrative has gradually turned into a political principle that is based upon the "fear and loathing of the public sphere" (another of Somers' illuminating notions) as analyzed in the second section of this chapter in the case of the straightforward rejection of the welfare state as a way of improving the argument for investing resources and interests in social entrepreneurship. For instance, Drucker (2004), Leabeater (1996) and Mawson (2008) consider government to be "run by well-qualified civil servants who rarely get hold of the pieces themselves and whose approach has so failed many of our poorest communities". Hence, these civic-minded entrepreneurs adopt a business approach because they have "discovered that business has a considerable amount to teach them. They like business because business operates in the real world" (Mawson, 2008: 8). According to Somers this fear and loathing has been "driven by a fear of the tyranny of the state" that can be traced back to Locke's invention of a private anti-political sphere inhabited by free citizens trading and interacting with each other beyond the realm of the state (Somers, 2008: 282).

Donati on relational goods and the third sector

Donati promotes "relational sociology" as a new paradigm for the social sciences (2011). Its main cornerstones are civil society, relational goods and social capital, and he weaves them together in a highly complex and sophisticated fashion. He rejects the tendency to interpret society in simple black-and-white terms, divided between the market and the state, and he argues that the third sector plays an independent and unique role. Relational sociology also challenges a single-minded focus on either micro or macro aspects of society. Donati considers both a micro focus or "methodological individualism" and a macro focus on collective structures or "methodological holism" to be insufficient for understanding civil society (2013). Furthermore, like Skocpol, Selle, Rothstein and others, he argues that de Tocqueville's and Putnam's view of the relation between associational democracy and social capital are unsatisfactory.

Relational goods are not "things" that can be appropriated by any single actor or bought and sold on the market. Rather they consist of social relations that are produced together by those who participate in them, e.g., the professional providers and users of these services who co-produce them. Donati considers this an emergent effect which benefits the participants of such relations in the form of social capital, as well as benefiting those on the outside, such as the participants' families and friends, who share in its repercussions. Moreover, relational goods have a democratic character that distinguishes them from goods and services produced by bureaucratic organizations such as public administration (2014). Thus they are goods that are not available on the basis of private ownership nor accessible to everyone indiscriminately.

Moreover, Donati argues that primary relational subjects are characterized by intersubjective, face-to-face relations, including self-help groups at the micro level. Secondary relational subjects are created in social networks that are not purely functional. The latter are found in third-sector organizations, civil associations and some social enterprises at the meso level, while secondary and tertiary level organizations that affiliate lower-level relational subjects are found at the macro level. Thus he clearly sees the third sector as a supplement to both the market and state, not merely as a complement to them nor one that can be combined with or subsumed by either of them.

State and civil society in the Scandinavian countries

Is the fearing and loathing of the state necessary if the goal is to build a strong and resilient civil society, as suggested by the volunteerism discourse of civil society? Or is the active and dynamic interrelation between organized civil society and the state on the contrary a precondition for civil society to become a powerful third sphere not only in terms of opinion formation but also in terms of decision-making? If we look at evidence from the history of American social policies as presented by Skocpol it seems as if social integration and redistribution was granted by a mix of organized civil society and the enduring capacity of government. And according to Donati, public goods and added social value are generated through a variety of social actors and relations from all spheres of society (Donati, 2014: 2).

In the Scandinavian states the impact of organized civil society grew in the years of welfare state expansion in the decades after World War II; however, this balance has been challenged by more recent decades of privatization. Thus the changes in the relation between the (welfare) state and civil society can be framed in an individual–market version, where citizens' relations with the market are unmediated, versus a collective relation with the state, where citizens' relations with the state are mediated by civil society, i.e., a classical pluralist relationship.

Civil society in the institutional–redistributive welfare state

Historically the typical Scandinavian welfare state facilitates a relationship between civil society and state that nourishes bridging social capital that is more related to citizens than to members and volunteers. The institutional–redistributive welfare state (Titmuss, 1987) in the Scandinavian countries was based upon institutions that encouraged people to perceive themselves as being members of a broader national community rather than merely worrying about their own family, their immediate neighbors and their individual benefits. To understand the positive correlation between civil society and the Scandinavian welfare states, it is helpful to delve deeper into the institutional aspect rather than the redistributional aspect of the so-called institutional–redistributive model of welfare (Titmuss, 1987). This model of welfare is based upon a conception of social justice that sees man not merely as an individual or as belonging to specific local communities or associations but as a citizen with social rights (Titmuss, 1987: 264). The historical legacy of an institutional welfare state model is to stimulate bridges of solidarity between groups and across otherwise segregated communities. Much macro-oriented theory has scrutinized the redistributional aspects of various welfare state regimes while neglecting to pay similar attention to the institutional capacity and specific institutional configurations. Such theories have partly failed to understand the *sociology* of the welfare state in terms of examining relations, relational goods (Donati, 2014), and patterns of co-production and collaboration between public and private actors (Pestoff, 2009), and and civil society-based institutions and public institutions in specific local welfare production (Hulgård and Andersen, 2012). However important the redistributional and de-commodifying capacity of a welfare state may be, this does not say much about specific institutional configurations of actors and institutions involved in the co-productive and interrelational character of welfare.

Research from Sweden, Norway and Denmark displays remarkably similar findings concerning the relationship between type of welfare state and civil society. In Sweden, Rothstein (2001) found that the expansion of the welfare state was based upon "an unusually close collaboration between the state and major interest organizations in the preparation as well as in the implementation of public policies" (Rothstein, 2001: 207). The "universal welfare state did not wipe out" social capital, and the results from two studies show that people in the 1990s were generally more interested in socializing than they were in the 1950s before the expansion of the welfare state (Rothstein, 2001: 224).

There have been changes, however, from the collective mass movements of the heyday of the universal welfare state towards "organized individualism"

(Rothstein, 2001: 220). This transition reflects a change from a "mass-organizational" society in the direction of a new type of collectivity, where the individual is more prominent. This change can be found in all Scandinavian countries in the behavior of citizens engaged in organizations in civil society (Selle, 1999). Although there are no indications of dramatic decline in the social capital or impact of civil society, people are turning away "from traditional channels for political participation, such as political parties and interest organizations, and are turning toward temporary and 'one issue' organizations" (Rothstein, 2001: 210).

Measured quantitatively, we do find a weakening of collective ideological movements, e.g., membership of political parties, free churches, temperance movement and the labor movement, while both the organizational landscape and the way people get involved is much more diversified today than it was in the peak period of the welfare state. Thus the close historical connection between social movements and the public sector in state-friendly Scandinavian countries may be about to change. Whereas the typical "hybrid character" of civil society in the twentieth century "could be described in terms of 'half movement' half government," the character of the more recent civil society developments could maybe instead be understood as a drive towards organizational solutions being of " 'half charity, half business' character" (Wijkström, 2011: 46).

Decades of privatization

Thus in recent decades, there have been moves towards individualization and privatization of welfare and citizenship in the Scandinavian countries. The transition from a "mass-organizational" society in the direction of organized individualism has been accompanied by a rather drastic surrender of public responsibility for welfare (Gilbert, 2002) and the generation of bridging social capital. The changes are reflected both in the organizational behavior of citizens engaged in organizations in civil society (Selle, 1999) and in a gradual change of the "traditional" social democratic welfare regime (Esping-Andersen, 1990) towards "rampant privatization" (Pestoff, 2009). This may indicate a fundamental alteration of the existing framework for social policies. Indeed, policies previously framed by a universal approach to publicly delivered benefits, designed to protect labor against the vicissitudes of the market and firmly held as social rights (Titmuss, 1987), are currently evolving into policies framed by a selective approach to private delivery of provisions designed to promote labor force participation and individual responsibility (Gilbert, 2002: 4). More specifically, what is occurring is a shift towards work-oriented policies, with a privatization of the responsibility for social welfare and an increase in the targeting of benefits. In terms of citizenship and the composition of civil society, it is a shift from an emphasis on the social rights linked to citizenship to the civic duties linked to being a community member, providing space for active citizens to become active volunteers and successful social entrepreneurs.

Accordingly, Evers (2013) observes a general societal trend towards the economic dimension of civil society as a third sector for service provision that may lead to a re-traditionalization and paternalization of welfare. A few pieces of evidence may indicate the level of change towards general privatization and accordingly towards more entrepreneurial and service-providing paradigms for civil society as experienced in Scandinavian countries. In Sweden, the government's share of GDP, measured as public spending, reached as high as 67 percent in 1993. And as early as 1974 the Swedish prime minister had declared that "The era of neo-capitalism is drawing to an end.... It is some kind of socialism that is the key to the future." His lookout point was several decades of almost complete social democratic hegemony with the party ruling uninterrupted between 1932 and 1976. Since then the Scandinavian countries have changed course in the composition of welfare policies. In Sweden in 2013, the government's share of GDP, "which has dropped by around 18 percentage points, is lower than France's and could soon be lower than Britain's" (*The Economist*, 2013); in Denmark, CEVEA (a think tank) has stressed that the country's position as the most equal country in the world lies in the past. Between 2004 and 2011, apparently, Denmark was the country in Western Europe where inequality rose the most. Still, in a longer perspective Denmark is one of the most equal societies measured by the Gini coefficient – but nevertheless in 2014 it was only the fourteenth most equal society in Europe.

Towards a new reconciliation between state and civil society?

The Scandinavian countries form a unique background and a laboratory for a new reconciliation between an empowered civil society and a continuation of the universal orientation of the welfare state.

On the one hand Scandinavia has followed the international trend of privatization and decline in the universal welfare state. This has been described as a process towards rampant privatization, with for-profit providers having "become quite strong in the past 20 years" (Jeppsson Grassman, 2014: 156) and a welfare state that may be ill equipped to protect its citizens unless a better defined role for the third sector can be determined (Pestoff, 2009). On the other hand, Scandinavian history is marked by unique collaboration between the three spheres of modern society: state, market and civil society. With its origin in the institutional–redistributive (Titmuss, 1987) or social democratic welfare model (Esping-Andersen, 1990), Scandinavia has a tradition of active intervention in the lives of citizens and communities for the sake of comprehensive risk coverage and the generation of high and full employment (Jeppsson Grassman, 2014).

Thus it seems urgent to ask if the tendency towards a continued downsizing and privatization of the welfare state can be challenged by systematic investments in programs for co-production and mixed types of welfare provision, where civil society is equally recognized for its political dimension in matters of decision-making (Fraser, 1992) and for its capacity for service provision delivered by volunteers and social entrepreneurs. Resources should be devoted to understanding the potential of an *institutional–reciprocal model of the welfare state*. So far this model is a pure construction in the sense that it is neither the depiction of an actual welfare state nor a coherent political strategy. It is yet to be defined and realized. However, it is not utopian since we have several indications of its potential and practical characteristics. The strategy is to give civil society a much stronger societal position without losing the objectives of social justice, redistribution and the institutional mechanisms of "the old" universal welfare state. As we have seen in this chapter, the complex relation discourse provides a good conceptual framework and sources for such a project.

Whereas Titmuss (1987) distinguishes between the residual model of welfare, the achievement–performance model of welfare and the institutional–redistributive model of welfare, we will address the residual model and achievement–performance model as one under the label "the residual model of welfare" and argue that a future for a reinforced civil society lies in innovating the third model, the redistributive–institutional model of welfare, by bridging the big historic divide between mass organization, as adopted especially by socialist and social democratic parties, and active participation in the civil society. The institutional–reciprocal model of welfare is inspired equally by the tradition for equality and bridging social capital, as realized by the Scandinavian countries, and by the insights from the complex relation discourse that draws upon experiences across welfare models and scholarly disciplines. The bridge between the universal welfare state and reciprocity as a core principle in civil society may be the cornerstone of a welfare model that will make societies and citizens more resilient and competent to face the negative consequences of marketization and privatization without losing the objectives of entrepreneurship, enterprise and innovation (see Table 12.1).

The residual and the institutional–redistributive type are related to the classical distinction between the regimes and clusters of the welfare state, whereas the third type, *the institutional–reciprocal model*, is the suggestion of a new model (Laville, 2010, 2014). The institutional–redistributive model of welfare was functioning well as a political project after World War II, but it has proved inadequate to challenge the power of neoliberalism and to produce a vision for how to expand the space of social justice and participation, not least in the wake of the financial crisis. From the literature on social and solidarity economy we know that a much more differentiated understanding of economic integration is required than what is usually understood by the term "market economy" (Laville,

Table 12.1 Three models of welfare

Type of welfare state	Economy	Welfare state
Residual	Market, reciprocity	Market, civil society
Institutional–redistributive	Market, redistribution	State
Institutional–reciprocal	Reciprocity, market, redistribution	Civil society/solidarity economy, market, state

2014). In a solidarity economy, a pluralistic society is based upon a full recognition of three economic principles: market, redistribution and reciprocity that is manifest in relational goods and co-produced services. From the complex relation discourse and the trajectory of civil society in the Scandinavian welfare states, we see that there are several perspectives, where the state has an explicit role to play for the generation of an empowered civil society that is recognized both for its capacity as a service provider and as a cornerstone in a strong public sphere that has the potential of becoming the vehicle for the institutional–reciprocal welfare state.

Note

1 I wish to thank Professor Victor Pestoff for his comments to an earlier version of this chapter.

References

Alexander, J. C. (ed.) (1998) *Real Civil Societies – Dilemmas of Institutionalization*. London: Sage Publications.

Barber, B. R. (1997) *Clansmen, Consumers and Citizens: Three Takes on Civil Society*. The National Commission on Civic Renewal, Working Paper no. 4., University of Maryland.

Baynes, K. (2002) "A Critical Theory Perspective on Civil Society and the State," in Rosenblum, N. L. and Post, R. C. (eds) *Civil Society and Government*. Princeton: Princeton University Press.

Brandsen, T., Dekker, P. and Evers, A. (2010) *Civicness in the Governance and Delivery of Social Services*. Baden-Baden: Nomos Verlagsgesellschaft.

Calhoun, C. (1995) *Critical Social Theory*. Cambridge: Blackwell Publishers.

Cohen, J. L. (1997) *American Civil Society Talk*. The National Commission on Civic Renewal, Working Paper no. 6., University of Maryland.

Cohen, J. L. and Arato, A. (1992) *Civil Society and Political Theory*. Cambridge, MA: MIT Press.

Defourny, J., Hulgård, L. and Pestoff, V. (2014) *Social Enterprise and the Third Sector: Changing European Landscapes in a Comparative Perspective*. New York: Routledge.

DiIulio, J. J. (1997) "The Church and the Civil Society Sector," *The Brookings Review*, 15(4), www.brook.edu/pub/review/oldtoc.htm# FAL97.

Di Maggio, P. J. and Powell, W. W. (1983) "The Iron Cage Revisited: Institutional Isomorphism and Collective Rationality in Organizational Fields," *American Sociological Review*, 48(2/April), pp. 147–160.

Dionne, E.J. (1997) "Why Civil Society? Why Now?" *The Brookings Review*, 15(4), www.brook.edu/pub/review/oldtoc.htm# FAL97.

Donati, P. (2011) *Relational Sociology: A New Paradigm for the Social Sciences*. London and New York: Routledge.

Donati, P. (2013) "Social Capital and Associative Democracy: A Relational Perspective," *Journal for the Theory of Social Behavior*, 44(1), pp. 24–45.

Donati, P. (2014) "The Ferment of a New Civil Society and Civil Democracy," in Donati, P. and Calvo, P. (eds) *New Insights into Relational Goods*, Bologna: Department of Philosophy and Sociology; *Recerca Revista de Pensament i Analisi*, 14, pp. 19–46.

Elkington, J. and Hartigan, P. (2008) *The Power of Unreasonable People*. Boston: Harvard Business Press.

Elshtain, J. B. (1997) "Civil Society Creates Citizens; It Does Not Solve Problems," *The Brookings Review*, 15(4), www.brook. edu/pub/review/oldtoc.htm# FAL97.

Eriksen, E. O. and Weigård, J. (2002) *Kommunikativt demokrati: Jürgen Habermas' teori om politik og samfund*. Copenhagen: Hans Reitzels Forlag.

Esping-Andersen, G. (1990) *The Three Worlds of Welfare Capitalism*. Cambridge: Polity Press.

Evers, A. (2013) "The Concept of 'Civil Society': Different Understandings and their Implications for Third-sector Policies," *Voluntary Sector Review*, 4(2), pp. 149–164.

Fraser, N. (1992) "Rethinking the Public Sphere: A Contribution to the Critique of Actually Existing Democracy," in Calhoun, C. (ed.) *Habermas and the Public Sphere*. Cambridge, MA: MIT Press.

Galston, W. A. and Levine, P. (1997) "America's Civic Condition: A Glance at the Evidence," *The Brookings Review*, 15(4), www.brook.edu/pub/review/oldtoc.htm# FAL97.

Gilbert, N. (2002) *Transformation of the Welfare State: The Silent Surrender of Public Responsibility*. Oxford: Oxford University Press.

Habermas, J. (1969) *Vitenskap som ideologi*. Oslo: Gyldendal Norsk Forlag.

Habermas, J. (1975) *Legitimationsproblemer i senkapitalismen*. Copenhagen: Fremad.

Habermas, J. (1981) *Theorie des kommunikativen Handelns*, volumes 1 and 2. Frankfurt am Main: Suhrkamp Verlag.

Habermas, J. (1992) *Faktizität und Geltung: Beiträge zur Diskurstheorie des Rechts und des demokratischen Rechtsstaats*. Frankfurt am Main: Suhrkamp Verlag.

Habermas, J. (1996) *Between Facts and Norms*. Cambridge: Polity Press.

Hulgård, L. (1997) "Ildsjælen mellem staten og det civile samfund" [The Social Entrepreneur between State and Civil Society], in Hegland, T. J., Henriksen, L. S., Kristensen, C. J. and Krogstrup, H. K. (eds) *Sammenbrud eller sammenhold – nogle udviklingstendenser for velfærdssamfundet*. Århus: Akademisk Forlag.

Hulgård, L. and Andersen, L. L. (2012) "Social entreprenørskab – velfærdsarenaer eller afvikling af solidaritet?" [Social entrepreneurship – arenas for welfare or decrease in solidarity?], *Dansk Sociologi*, 4(23/December).

Janoski, T. (1998) *Citizenship and Civil Society*. Cambridge: Cambridge University Press.

Jeppson Grassman, E. (2014) "The Question of Civil Society in a Scandinavian Welfare State: Focusing on Older People in Sweden," in Suzuki, N. (ed.) *The Anthropology of Care and Education for Life*, Senri Ethnological Studies 87.

Kickul, J. (ed.) (2013) *Social Entrepreneurship*. Cheltenham: Edward Elgar.

Laville, J.-L. (2010) "Solidarity Economy," in Hart, K., Laville, J.-L. and Cattani, A. D. *The Human Economy*. Cambridge: Polity Press.

Mawson, A. (2008) *The Social Entrepreneur: Making Communities Work*. London: Atlantic Books.

Pestoff, V. (2009) *A Democratic Architecture for the Welfare State*. London and New York: Routledge.

Post, R. C. and Rosenblum, N. L. (2002) "Introduction," in Rosenblum, N. L. and Post, R. C. (eds) *Civil Society and Government*. Princeton: Princeton University Press.

Potucek, M. (1999) "Havel vs. Klaus: Public Policy-making in the Czech Republic," *Journal of Comparative Policy Analysis: Research and Practice*, 1, pp. 163–176.

Powel, C. L. (1997) "Recreating the Civil Society – One Child at a Time," *The Brookings Review*, 15(4), www.brook.edu/pub/review/oldtoc.htm# FAL97.

Putnam, R. D. (1993) "The Prosperous Community: Social Capital and Public Life," *The American Prospect*, 13(Spring).

Putnam, R. D. (1995a) "Bowling Alone: America's Declining Social Capital," *Journal of Democracy*, 6(1/January), pp. 65–78.

Putnam, R. D. (1995b) "Bowling Alone: An Interview with Robert Putnam about America's Collapsing Civic Life," American Association for Higher Education, http://xroads.virginia.edu/~ HYPER/DETOC/assoc/aahe.html.

Putnam, R. D. (1996a) "The Strange Disappearance of Civic America," *The American Prospect*, Winter.

Putnam, R. D. (1996b) "Unsolved Mysteries. The Tocqueville Files," *The American Prospect*, 25(March–April), pp. 26–28.

Putnam, R. D. (2000) *Bowling Alone*. New York and London: Simon and Schuster.

Putnam, R. D. (ed.) (2002) *Democracies in Flux*. Oxford: Oxford University Press.

Rappaport, J. (1985) "The Power of Empowerment Language," *Social Policy*, 16(2).

Rifkin, J. (1996) *The End of Work: The Decline of the Global Labor Force and the Dawn of the Post-Market Era*. New York: G. P. Putnam's Sons.

Rosenblum, N. L. and Post, R. C. (eds) (2002) *Civil Society and Government*. Princeton: Princeton University Press.

Rothstein, B. (2001) "Social Capital in the Social Democratic Welfare State." *Politics and Society*, 29(2/June), 206–240.

Rothstein, B. (2002) "Social Capital in the Social Democratic State." In Putnam, R. D. (ed.) *Democracies in Flux*. Oxford: Oxford University Press.

Rothstein, B. and Stolle, D. (2002) *How Political Institutions Create and Destroy Social Capital: An Institutional Theory of Generalized Trust*. Paper presented at the 98th Meeting of the American Political Association, Boston, MA, 29 August – 2 September.

Schambra, W. A. (1997) "Local Groups are the Key to America's Civic Renewal," *The Brookings Review*, 15(4), www.brook.edu/pub/review/oldtoc.htm# FAL97.

Seligman, A. B. (1992) *The Idea of Civil Society*. New York: The Free Press.

Selle, P. (1999) "The Transformation of the Voluntary Sector in Norway: A decline in Social Capital?" in Van Deth, J. W., Maraffi, M., Newton, K. and Whiteley, P. F. (eds) *Social Capital and European Democracy*. London: Routledge.

Skocpol, T. (1996) "Unravelling From Above (Unsolved Mysteries. The Tocqueville Files)," *The American Prospect*, 25(March–April), pp. 20–25.

Skocpol, T. (1997) "Building Community Top-down or Bottom-up?" *The Brookings Review*, 15(4), www.brook.edu/pub/review/oldtoc.htm# FAL97.

Skocpol, T. (2002) "From Membership to Advocacy," in Putnam, R. D. (ed.) *Democracies in Flux*. Oxford: Oxford University Press.

Skocpol, T. (2003) *Diminished Democracy: From Membership to Management in American Civic Life*. Norman: University of Oklahoma Press.

Solo, P. (1997) "Beyond Theory: Civil Society in Action," *The Brookings Review*, 15(4), www.brook.edu/pub/review/oldtoc.htm# FAL97.

Somers, M. R. (1995) "Narrating and Naturalizing Civil Society and Citizenship Theory: The Place of Political Culture and the Public Sphere," *Sociological Theory*, 13(3/November).

Somers, M. R. (1998) "Romancing the Market, Reviling the State: Historizing Liberalism, Privatization, and the Competing Claims to Civil Society," in Crouch, C., Eder K. and Tambini, D. (eds) *Citizenship, Markets, and the State*. New York: Oxford University Press.

Somers, M. R. (2008) *Genealogies of Citizenship*. Cambridge: Cambridge University Press.

Sullivan, W. M. (1997) *Making Civil Society Work: Democracy as a Problem of Civic Cooperation*, The National Commission on Civic Renewal, Working Paper no. 3, University of Maryland.

The Economist (2013) "Special Report: The Nordic Countries – The Next Supermodel," 2 February.

Titmuss, R. M. (1987) *The Philosophy of Welfare: Selected Writings of Richard M. Titmuss*, edited by Abel-Smith, B. and Titmuss, K. London: Allen and Unwin.

Torpe, L. (2001) "Folkets foreninger? De frivillige organizationsers folkelige forankring I Skandinavien," in Henriksen, L. S. and Ibsen, B. (eds) *Frivillighedens udfordringer – nordisk forskning om frivilligt arbejde og frivillige organizationer*. Odense: Odense Universitetsforlag, pp. 107–124.

Torpe, L. (2003) "Social Capital in Denmark: A Deviant Case?" *Scandinavian Political Studies*, 26(3).

Trägårdh, L., Selle, P., Henriksen, L. S. and Hallin, H. (eds) (2013) *Civilsamhället klämt mellan stat och capital*. Stockholm: SNS Förlag.

Wijkström, F. (2011) "Charity Speak and Business Talk. The Ongoing (Re)hybridization of Civil Society," in Wijkström, F. and Zimmer, A. (eds) *Nordic Civil Society at a Cross-Roads*. Baden-Baden: Nomos Verlagsgesellschaft.

Wijkström, F. and Zimmer, A. (eds) (2011) *Nordic Civil Society at a Cross-Roads*. Baden-Baden: Nomos Verlagsgesellschaft.

Wilson, P. (1997) "Building Social Capital: A Learning Agenda for the Twenty-first Century," *Urban Studies*, 34(5–6), pp. 745–760.

Wolfe, A. (1989) *Whose Keeper? Social Science and Moral Obligation*. Berkeley: University of California Press.

Wolfe, A. (1997) "Is Civil Society Obsolete?" *The Brookings Review*, 15(4), www.brook. edu/pub/review/oldtoc.htm# FAL97.

Wuthnow, R. (1997) *The Role of Trust in Civic Renewal*. The National Commission on Civic Renewal, Working Paper no. 1, University of Maryland.

13 Social management and para-economy

Genauto Carvalho de França Filho and
Rosanna de Freitas Boullosa

Introduction

In the necessary effort to renew the analytical framework of the study of CSOs, the more recent francophone sociological studies deserve attention, especially those of Laville and Sainsaulieu (2013), Laville and Hoarau (2008), and Laville (2010). Here we hope to enrich the debate with a Brazilian contribution. This chapter seeks to reveal the analytical potential of two quite original theoretical perspectives. The first is more recent and can be observed in the critical debate on the concept of social management in Brazil. The second perspective is older and can be traced to the concept of para-economics introduced by the Brazilian sociologist Guerreiro Ramos in the final parts of his last major work. The objective is to point out new ways of analyzing CSOs.

The critical power of the social management concept: from public sphere to public action

Social management is a new concept or approach that has been underway in Brazil since the 1990s. It found root in the experiences of Latin American professors in a training course offered by the Inter-American Development Bank. In the Brazilian context, however, this expression gains a different meaning from the one originally proposed in the course. This new meaning has a critical dimension, rejecting the initially proposed understanding of social management as management of social government programs with a neoliberal orientation. This rejection, however, admits the critical and propositional potential of the term in rethinking the management and administration of everything that concerns the public sphere and public action. At the end of the 1990s, at least three Brazilian research groups were working with this concept. Each one explored or helped build this concept by integrating it into their own lines of research: democracy, territory and the third sector.

The concept of social management expanded very rapidly, winning over professors, practitioners, scholars and students, especially in the field of administration, who appreciated its denial of more generalist explanations of decision-making processes. They also embraced its proposals for more dialogue-orientation and democratic management of state–society relations, as explained in theoretical essays on the increasing popularity of the term (Boullosa and Schommer 2008; 2009). The main evidence of this growth are the expanding national meetings of social management researchers held in Brazil every year since 2007, the academic courses now offered throughout the country on undergraduate and graduate levels, and the vast bibliographic production on the subject, including specialized periodicals and a dedicated dictionary.

Faced with such growth, researchers (Araújo, 2012; Cançado, 2011) have begun to discuss and question the nature of social management as a field of knowledge or as a discipline. Constructing an up-to-date map of this theoretical discussion is no easy task, but we can say it has two major starting points: on the one hand the concept of the public sphere, and on the other the concept of public action.

Social management and the public sphere

Concerning the first strand of research, the public sphere concept is always linked to the work of Arendt and Habermas. Researchers in this line, led by Tenório (1998, 2008a, 2008b, 2012), frequently assume that the public sphere is the space where individuals meet to deal with matters relating to their own society (Habermas, 2003) and that social management seeks to somehow consolidate these spheres, to reconnect people with politics so that "private persons can meet in a public space in order to deliberate about their needs and the future" (Cançado, 2001, p. 172). From this point of view, social management can:

> be presented as collective decision-making, without coercion, based on the intelligibility of language, on dialogicity and on an enlightened understanding of the process, on transparency as a prerequisite and on emancipation as an ultimate goal. This synthesis is not of a prescriptive nature. In other words, social management can go further. The objective here is to delimit the field not to "enclose what's inside," but to create boundaries that can be moved with the advances of research and experiences in the field.
>
> (Cançado *et al.*, 2011, p. 697)

The latest research in this line discusses what could be the main engine of social management, which, in turn, should occur within the public sphere. According to these researchers, this engine would be "interests rightly understood," a concept proposed by Toqueville (1998) and taken up by Cançado (2011). The doctrine of interests rightly understood is the conception that the realization of private interests is itself intimately linked to the realization of the common interest. From this perspective, social management is driven by the rightly understood interests of actors that interact in the public sphere, which would lead the individual to his own emancipation as a political subject. This interest instigates a virtuous circle that can only be interrupted when the private interests cease to have the characteristics of interests rightly understood, or when the public sphere itself changes its configuration – a reason why social management can be considered as a process in constant (re)construction, as Cançado warns.

In the second approach, social management as management for public action stems from the conceptual approximation of social management with the idea of co-production of public goods and services within the new public service framework proposed by Denhardt and Denhardt (2011). It assumes a certain centrality of more institutional government processes in public affairs, in which public management is seen as governmental management (with greater emphasis, it would appear, on municipal government). The public sphere means the space for socio-political organization and public action, for criticism and transformation of the political order, with its spaces extended beyond the limits of organized power groups, with reasonably well-defined political and communicative dimensions, and with a decentralized and decentralizing outlook on government action. The public sphere is the locus of social innovation, the latter being understood as new approaches that seek to solve concrete socio-environmental problems in the public sphere. The relationship between co-production and social innovation to redefine the social management concept seems to be one of the main focal points, interpreted as a factor that mediates co-production relationships, drives innovation and fosters and enriches the public sphere (Schommer *et al.*, 2011).

Social management and public action

This second line of theoretical studies on social management prioritizes the congruence of the social management concept with the public action concept, and it seems more useful for an understanding of CSOs. As is the case with the first line of research described, the public action concept is not understood in a single way, but in two ways. On the one hand, the public quality of the action is derived from the public quality of the actor who promotes the action, i.e., the action is public because the actor is the government in its different spheres and combinations with organized civil society. On the other hand, the action is public because the event generating the action is of public importance.

In the first approach, social management is defined as a complex concept (França-Filho, 2003 and 2008) that goes beyond the organizational question. Social management is also understood as a societal issue, i.e., it concerns "the management of demands and needs of the social" (França-Filho, 2003) or of the *socius*. In this dimension, the social management concept can be confused with the public management concept itself by emphasizing the possibilities in the management of societal demands and the needs of society itself. The debate is one about the limits and possibilities of the public management of society, which therefore expands the concept of public action and public policy itself. The conceptual innovation here consists in the choice for a more socio-political approach to organizational analysis. From this perspective, the social management concept embraces the possibility of conceiving the role of civil society and popular organization initiatives as self-governed mechanisms linked to the demands and services of society itself. Among the numerous challenges that arise from this debate is the risk of instrumentalization of social management – either through the market, as a rationale for hollowing out its more political public action dimension through business philanthropy processes, or through the state, via the risk of autonomy loss due to the appropriation of processes by public authorities. In any case, the theoretical possibilities in a debate on the regulatory mechanisms of society are very distinct from those offered by a functional outlook on the role of the third sector.

In the second approach, social management begins to take on new contours based on a triangle involving the concepts of public policy, political co-production and public action. For starters, the proximity between the public policy concepts within the policy inquiry school (Fisher, 1998; Regonini, 2002), and in alignment with the "mirada ao revés" approach (Boullosa, 2013) and the public action concept, has led the latter to be modelled as if it were superimposed over the collective action concept. This superposition is justified by assuming that all collective action would occur in a government context of problems or goods with public relevance, further emphasizing the multi-actor nature of public policy processes. This was based on Cefaï's definition (2007, p. 8), in which collective action is the result of "any attempt to establish a more or less formalized and institutionalized collective by individuals seeking to meet a shared goal, in contexts of cooperation and competition with other collectives."

Social management began to be seen, therefore, as a special way of framing the problem and managing complex socio-interactive realities, along with a newly configured pattern of relations between the state and society to cope with contemporary challenges (Boullosa and Schommer, 2008, 2009), including different expressions of CSOs. Because such realities would always occur in the context of public policies, the actors that would help shape these arenas would be seen as public policy actors, whose more systematized and complex actions could be framed as public policy instruments (Boullosa, 2012, 2013). The social management question would therefore be framed as specifically associated with the production of a limited set of public policy instruments that would be based on or justified by the notion of political co-production. Political co-production does not refer to just any form of shared production of goods and services between government and society. It refers to the process in which the actors that activated it reach an understanding in a social co-production process, or to put it differently, in a multi-actor flow of public policies. By reaching an understanding of this flow, they make a political choice for combined action. Each action on the initiative of an actor or social group, as in the case of CSOs, has its own framework, development dynamic, characteristics, resources, timing, motivations and internal governance systems. In all cases, however, collective processes are triggered. From this perspective, social management can be understood as a set of processes and dynamics that activate and shape this collectivity (or the desire to act collectively) of actors that operate in the public policy flow, acting by and in the public interest, to handle publicly relevant problems or to preserve public goods.

Another look at governance

In the way described above, social management concepts lead to redefining the very idea of governance from a perspective of democratic radicalization. By emphasizing new mechanisms for public action and the quest for emancipation as the ultimate goal of the management process itself, we see the possibility for another type of governance that seems more appropriate to the reality of CSOs, in addition to enabling, on the macro level, new relationships between society, the state and the market. The assumption in this approach is that individuals have the right to a voice in decisions (of all kinds) that will impact their lives in all dimensions (socially, economically, environmentally, culturally or politically). The perspective of interest rightly understood coupled with emancipation as the ultimate goal seems therefore to lead us beyond the classical discussion of sustainable development, as it introduces to this debate the people who will suffer the impacts of this development. In this sense, thinking about social management as a new form of governance is betting on the possibility that individuals will have the autonomy to decide their own fate without the tutelage of experts, who also have their own interests. In the context of social management, their role is to clarify the discussion, not to make decisions for other people.

Even if the social management concept is a significant advance in relation to the governance concept, especially in recognizing the essentially political nature of organizational action when dealing with CSOs, this concept still brings little to bear on the economic dimension of this reality. In a way, there is a gap in the understanding of the economic sphere in these practices, or at least it takes the back seat in the analysis. It is precisely to cover this conceptual gap in the above-mentioned debate that we now turn to the concept of para-economics.

The concept of para-economics in Ramos: addressing the shortcomings of social management

Para-economy is a term used by Guerreiro Ramos that refers to the need for an analytical model of organizational dynamics that is not restricted to the self-regulated market. To understand the para-economics concept we must first re-edify at least two related arguments:

- the first concerns a proposed theory to delimit social systems, understood as a multi-centric analytical model of such systems, which Guerreiro Ramos describes as the "para-economic paradigm";
- the second refers to the law of "appropriate requirements," which establishes a given value of certain basic factors (such as technology, size, cognition, space and time) that can vary significantly depending on the nature of the social system under analysis.

An original proposal for a theory to delimit social systems

Taking up Marcuse, Guerreiro Ramos starts with the assumption that the prevailing analytical and planning models of social systems – not only in the field of administration, but also in political science, economics and social sciences in general – are one-dimensional in nature. Confronted with this diagnosis, he proposes a multidimensional model "for the analysis and the formulation of social systems, in which the market is considered a legitimate and necessary social enclave, but one that is limited and regulated" (Guerreiro Ramos, 1981, p. 140). It is precisely this model, which he called the "para-economic paradigm," in which anomy, economy, isonomy and fenonomies are differentiated.

Economy refers to "a highly ordered organizational context, established for the production of goods or for the provision of services" (pp. 147–148). As a typical organization of a marked-centered society, it tends to "transform into an all-encompassing category regarding the ordering of individual and social life" because of its freedom (in this type of society) "to shape the minds of its members and the lives of its citizens, in general" (p. 148).

The term "anomy" is borrowed from Durkheim to point out that "one of the reasons why the referred institutions generally aggravate the anomic condition of people for whom they care, is the fact that their model and management are systematically seen as belonging to a specific social enclave" (p. 147).

But there are also isonomies, referring to an organizational context of free association of people marked by the absolute equality of its members. Some characteristics highlighted by the author are: (1) the primacy of the actualization of its members at the expense of the imposed requirements, which are minimal and, where unavoidable, are established by consensus; (2) their self-gratifying nature, in the sense that "people do not earn a living in an isonomy; rather, they participate in a generous type of social relationship in which they give and receive" (p. 150); (3) hence, their activities are defined not as jobs but as vocations (in other words, maximizing utility loses importance as an individual's higher objective); (4) in addition, it is based on a decision-making system characterized by the non-differentiation of leadership, management and subordinates, distinguishing isonomy from a democracy; (5) effectiveness relies on the prevalence of primary interpersonal relations between its members, assuming a size limit. Finally, a fenonomy is defined as

> A social system of a sporadic or more or less stable nature, initiated and directed by an individual, or by a small group, and that allows its members maximum personal choice and minimum subordination to formal operational requirements.... Although the result of the activities undertaken in a fenonomy might be considered in market terms, the economic criteria are incidental in relation to the motivation of its members.
>
> (p. 152)

In short, this para-economic perspective suggests that the different natures of the social systems we deal with in society must be understood to determine to what extent each one is conducive to the development or emancipation of people. The more conventional forms of organization are not central from an analytical point of view, that is, based on market logic as summarized in the economy category. The challenge is at the same time analytical and practical in order to think about the possibilities for human actualization and development contained in different forms of organizational expression, such asisonomies and fenonomies, based on the action of an individual or a small group dedicated to what they do by vocation, and affirming the principle of free human association based on values. Such forms of organization, understood as social systems, mobilize resources as exemplified by different cooperatives and membership organizations in different societal contexts. The main challenge is that in many cases they still deal with market logic, but they always look to subordinate it to other economic rationales in an attempt to preserve the goal of actualization of their members. This outlook stresses the need for valuing other forms and mechanisms of resource management through practices of human association while facing a series of dilemmas that affect contemporary societies, such as the attrition of meaningful work and shortages.

A discussion of the requirements for a delimiting design of social systems

After describing the categories that make up the para-economic paradigm, it remains to construct it in practice. And this is primarily a political effort, requiring an assessment of the more appropriate requirements for each type of social system. Therefore, the effectiveness of a multi-centric society as portrayed in the para-economic paradigm involves a vigorous political resistance to the trends in a market-centered society in order to contain its encroachment on vital human space. This does not mean that the goal of the para-economy is to suppress the market mechanism. According to Guerreiro Ramos, the unprecedented capabilities created by the market, "even if for the wrong reasons ... can ... meet the goals of a multidimensional model of human life in a multi-centric society" (p. 155).

Starting, therefore, with the assumption that the existence of a variety of requirements constitutes an "essential qualification of any society sensitive to the actualization of the needs of its members" (p. 156), the task at hand is precisely to define the planning requirements inherent to each social system. For this, Guerreiro Ramos examines the five main dimensions of such systems: technology, size, space, cognition and time.

Technology constitutes an essential part of the support structure inherent to any social system. The challenge of harmonizing the technology in a given social system with its own specific objectives, particularly present in the socio-technical system concept, should be assimilated "by planners of social systems of confrontation" (p. 157). This reflection seeks to emphasize the necessary technological development not driven by market ends and can be backed up today by the concept of social innovation itself, understood as appropriate solutions to the reality of certain groups and local populations, whose purpose is other than to meet market demands. The reflection leads us to look more carefully for solutions in the field of technology and innovation that come from other social systems, such as isonomies. Examples of this type can be recognized in popular self-organization practices for managing services and other demands in the social context of poverty, such as solidarity finance initiatives through community development banks in Brazil, whose innovations surface at different levels because they can relate to financial resources management tools offered as well as to the institutional management model itself.

The size dimension refers to the number of people that should constitute a social scenario. This is a subject that has received very little attention in the theory because of the prevalence our culture puts on "the bigger, the better." In contrast to this principle, Ramos (p. 158) stresses that

> the effectiveness of a social scenario in achieving its goals and in making optimal use of its resources does not imply, ultimately, an increase in size ... we need to learn the art of planning social scenarios that are able to endure.

In summary, the required size depends fundamentally on the nature of each social system and on its basic requirements. It raises the question of limits in terms of scale and size for effectively managing certain goods or services that society needs. An emblematic question in this respect can be formulated as follows: under what conditions should the demands and needs of society be best managed by private market, public–state or public–societal mechanisms? The first two are based on large-scale cases and the last considers mostly small- or medium-scale cases, according to the different examples of isonomy. In practice, different types of arrangements between the three enclaves are of course possible in this understanding. Once again, examples of community self-organization initiatives for managing common services in contexts of poverty in Latin America prove in many cases more effective because they reach those who need it most, they avoid side effects, or they are simply more reliable and therefore obtain greater legitimacy in their respective contexts.

As concerns the cognition dimension, Ramos stresses the direct correlation between the variety of forms of knowledge and the nature of each social system. His greatest concern is trying to show "the all-encompassing nature of the market system ... which continuously involves individuals in its intrinsic cognitive patterns, and can make them unsuitable for action as efficient members of fenonomies or isonomies" (p. 161). He underscores the effort required to "provide the appropriate conditions to individuals for their specific and dominant cognitive interests" (p. 161). In other words, the different social systems cannot prioritize the rationale of functional knowledge or they risk losing their purpose and becoming inefficient. Both technical–formal know-how and cultural knowledge and wisdom are valued in local self-organization initiatives of the community, as this emphasizes the concept of popular education in the Latin

American tradition. Taking into account, therefore, that many local initiatives in different territorial contexts, especially in more impoverished regions, are characterized by a public with a very distinct socio-educational profile, the aspect of cognition, in the sense of the forms of knowledge, know-how and learning processes that are more appropriate to the reality of this public, becomes an element of extreme importance in the planning of actions to strengthen local initiatives.

With respect to the space dimension, the expansion of the market system in the last two centuries ended up progressively occupying the spaces reserved for social systems, turning it into the main driving force in the lives of individuals. The clearest example in this respect is precisely the architecture of contemporary cities, which caters mainly to the needs of the market. Guerreiro Ramos explores the economic, social and architectural consequences of the industrial revolution, indicating both the influence of space on human mental development and "some implications of the space dimension for the planning of social environments" (p. 163). He assumes that "specific spatial dimension requirements are inherent to each type of social scenario" (p. 163). As such, it is necessary to give pre-eminence to the anthropological point of view in the analysis of important aspects of the vital human space, emphasizing the distinction between socially converging and socially dispersing spaces, i.e., those that keep people separated, on the one hand, and those that encourage living together, on the other, with each being necessary for different reasons. However, "what should be avoided is the careless aggravation of socially-dispersing dimensions in social systems, where these should actually be socially converging" (p. 164). The perspective invites us to think about the importance of social-approximating relationships in the context of the organization of human labor. This dimension maintains a close relationship with the others, since it assumes small-scale organizational processes with socially appropriate technologies and based on knowledge systems distributed to fit each situation. An example is provided by popular and solidarity economy initiatives where the management of services uses mechanisms of solidarity, based on relations of trust or cooperation, pooling of resources and self-help rationales among people.

Finally, the time dimension entails a multidimensional approach of time as a category for the planning of social systems, as opposed to the time of economic market systems that is predominant in analyses. For this, Guerreiro Ramos draws on the typology of temporal dimensions of social systems developed by Gurvitch to suggest the following categories: serial, linear or sequential time; convivial time; leap time; and wandering time. These time categories have a direct correlation with the social systems proposed in his paradigm. Serial time prevails in social systems of the economy type because these are "incapable of fulfilling human needs whose satisfaction involves an experience of time that cannot be established in terms of series" (p. 168). Convivial time, on the other hand, is characteristic of isonomic scenarios and constitutes "an experience of time in which what the individual gains through his relationships with other people is not measured quantitatively, but represents a profound gratification for seeing himself released from pressures that prevent his personal actualization" (p. 169). Leap time, in turn, is characteristic of fenonomies, according to the author. It is "a very personal temporal experience, whose quality and pace reflect the intensity of the desire of the individual for creativity and self-clarification" (p. 169). It is also not quantifiable and constitutes "a certain trace of intimate personal life, when involved in self-exploratory days and efforts that culminate in important advances" (p. 169). Finally, wandering time is defined by Ramos as "time with an inconsistent direction," in which the people have an "inaccurate experience of their existential agenda" (p. 170).

In this discussion, the author seeks to deconstruct the one-dimensional tendency of time, which is particularly present in organizational and economic theories. His concern resides in the risk of mental deformation of social subjects living in a world where the market's logic of social time tends to determine the nature of social temporality as a whole. The high incidence of "apathy, alcoholism, drug addiction, insomnia, nervous breakdowns, stress, suicides, anxiety, hypertension, ulcers, and heart disease" are, therefore, seen as symptoms of a "normal pathology" that is characteristic of contemporary industrial societies, since within them a "synchronization of human life to the demands of the market system" is at work (p. 172). A society centered on the market deprives "the individual of the variety of temporal experiences that he has always had at his disposal until the emergence of this society" (p. 172). A reversal of the synchronization process is proposed by "adjusting the market to operate in line with the requirements of the social systems that raise the quality of life of the community in general, of coexistence, and the personal actualization of individuals" (p. 173).

In summary, it is worth highlighting a complementary argument concerning the political implications that derive from use of the para-economy concept, understood as a resource allocation paradigm and multi-center model. In fact, the para-economy was conceived as "a provider of the structure for a substantial political theory of resource allocation and of functional relationships between social enclaves, necessary for the qualitative stimulation of the social life of citizens" (p. 177). The para-economist can be every citizen who seeks to implement alternative scenarios to market-centered systems. This paradigm presupposes, for analysis and planning of social systems, the idea of "a sufficiently diverse society to allow its members to take care of the substantive issues of life, in accordance to their respective intrinsic criteria" (p. 178). A para-economic policy, therefore, would assert the necessary legitimacy of isonomies and fenonomies as agencies through which labor and resources should be executed and allocated, in order to make society viable as a whole.

Conclusion

This chapter has introduced the reader to the concept of social management as applied to the Brazilian context. The emphasis of this concept on the reconfiguration processes of public action, in terms of civil society itself and its relationship with public authorities, raises more effective possibilities for understanding CSOs. Moreover, social management seems to better frame the economic aspect of the management of these forms of organization, which is why the chapter introduced the ideas of para-economics proposed by Guerreiro Ramos. One can see how much this approach converges with the Polanyan perspectives of an institutional model that also emphasizes the multi-centric nature of society, with special emphasis on the plurality of forms and rationales of economic action. Despite the different times and contexts of the two approaches, they appear to be complementary in the sense that they reflect more extended organizational scenarios, and offer specific viewpoints on the singular characteristics of certain social systems including various forms of association.

References

Araújo, E. T. (2012). *(In)consistências da gestão social e seus processos de formação: um campo em construção*. PhD thesis, Pontifícia Universidade Católica de São Paulo, São Paulo.

Boullosa, R. F. (2013). Mirando ao revés as políticaspúblicas: Notas sobre um percurso de pesquisa. *Pensamento and Realidade*, 28, pp. 68–86.

Boullosa, R. F. and Schommer, P. C. (2008). "Limites da natureza da inovação ou qual o futuro da gestão social?," paper presented at the 32nd Encontro da Associação Nacional de Pós-Graduação e Pesquisa em Administração, Anais. Rio de Janeiro: ANPAD.

Boullosa, R. F. and Schommer, P. C. (2009). "Gestão social: Caso de inovação em políticas públicas ou mais um enigma de Lampedusa?," paper presented at the 3rd Encontro Nacional de Pesquisadores em Gestão Social. Juazeiro: NIGS/UNIVASF. Available at www.anaisenapegs.com.

Cançado, A. C. (2011). *Fundamentos teóricos da gestão social*. PhD thesis, Universidade Federal de Lavras, Lavras.

Cançado, A. C., Tenório, F. G. and Pereira, J. R. (2011). Gestão social: Reflexões teóricas e conceituais. *Cadernos EBAPE.BR*, 9(3), pp. 681–703.

Cefaï, D. (2008). Une écologie des publics: Park, l'opinion publique et le comportement collectif, in Guth, S. (ed) *La modernité de Robert Ezra Park*. Paris: L'Harmattan, pp. 155–188.

Denhardt, J.V. and Denhardt, R.B. (2011). *The new public service: Serving, not steering*. New York: M.E. Sharpe.

Fischer, F. (1988). Beyond empiricism: Policy inquiry in postpositivist perspective. *Policy studies journal*, 26(1), pp. 129–146.

Fischer, T. D. and Melo, V. P. (2006). Programa de desenvolvimento e gestão social: Uma construção coletiva, in Fischer, T. D., Roesch, S. and Melo, V. P. (eds) *Gestão do desenvolvimento territorial e residência social: Casos para ensino*. Salvador: EDUFBA, pp. 13–41.

França Filho, G. C. de (2003). "Gestão social: Um conceito em construção," paper presented at the 9th Colóquio Internacional Sobre Poder Local, Salvador, Anais. Salvador: CIAGS/UFBA.

França Filho, G. C. de. (2008). Definindo gestão social, in Silva Júnior, J. T., Mâish, R. T. and Cançado, A. C. (eds) *Gestão social: Prática sem debate, teorias em construção*. Fortaleza: UFC, pp. 27–37.

Guerreiro Ramos, A. (1981), *A nova ciência das organisações – uma reconceituação da riqueza das nações*. São Paulo: FGV.

Habermas, J. (2003). *Mudança estrutural na esferapública: Investigações quanto a uma categoria da sociedade burguesa*. Rio de Janeiro: Tempo Brazileiro.

Laville, J. -L. (2010). *Politique de l'association*. Paris: Seuil.

Laville, J. -L. and Hoarau, C. (2008). *La gouvernance dês associations*. Toulouse: Érès.

Laville, J. -L and Sainsaulieu, R. (1997). *Sociologie de l'association*. Paris: Desclée de Brouwer.

Polany, K. (2011). *La subsistance de l'homme*. Paris: Flamarion.

Regonini, G. (2001). *Capire le politiche pubbliche*. Bologna: Il Mulino.

Schommer, P. C., Andion, C., Pinheiro, D. M., Spaniol, E. L. and Serafim, M. C. (2011). Coprodução e inovação social na esfera pública em debate no campo da gestão social, in Schommer, P. C. and Boullosa, R. F (eds) *Gestão social como caminho para a redefinição da esfera pública*. Florianópolis: UDESC, pp. 31–70.

Tenório, F. G. (1998). Gestão social: Uma perspective conceitual. *Revista de Administração Pública*, 32(5), pp. 7–23.

Tenório, F. G. (2008a). *Um espectro ronda o terceiro setor, o espectro do mercado*. Ijuí: Unijuí.

Tenório, F. G. (2008b). *Tem razãoa administração?* Ijuí: Unijuí.

Tenório, F. G. (2012). Gestão social um conceito não idêntico? Ou a insuficiência inevitável do pensamento, in Cançado, A. C., Tenório, F. G., Silva, J. R., and Jeová, T. (eds) *Gestão social: Aspectosteóricos e aplicações*. Ijuí: Unijuí, pp. 23–36.

Tocqueville, A. de. (1998). *Democracia na América*. Rio de Janeiro: Biblioteca do Exército.

14 The theory of social enterprise and pluralism

Solidarity-type social enterprise

*José Coraggio, Philippe Eynaud,
Adriane Ferrarini,
Genauto Carvalho de França Filho,
Luis Inácio Gaiger, Isabelle Hillenkamp,
Kenichi Kitajima, Jean-Louis Laville,
Andrea Lemaître, Youssef Sadik,
Marilia Veronese and Fernanda Wanderley*

Introduction

The international debate on social enterprise is at present mainly driven by English-language research. But there is also an important European contribution. Based on the results of surveys since the 1990s, the European network EMES (a European Association for Social Enterprise Research) has proposed an ideal type for social enterprise. It identifies nine characteristic criteria of social enterprises in economic, social and governance domains. However, the definition proposed by EMES has been influenced by North American research in some of its wording. For example, the political dimension is not approached directly but through the concept of governance.

While the debate goes on, it is important to keep it inclusive by bringing in configurations of social enterprise coming from new realities in Europe and from outside Europe. The aim of this chapter is to work with data from Africa, South America, Asia and Europe and to create an ideal type of solidarity social enterprise (see Chapter 8) with an intercultural perspective. Such social enterprise will be defined in this text as solidarity enterprise. The intent here is to enrich the mapping of social enterprise by approaching solidarity enterprise on the basis of nine criteria. The question is: does this new ideal type sharpen the terms defined in previous research by EMES, or is it a distinct approach?

Approaches to social enterprise

What differentiates social enterprise approaches from dominant approaches in the economics and management sciences is that they address the purposes of the enterprise and of the economic activity. Regardless of the sensibilities and currents of thought within these approaches, they agree on emphasizing a social purpose behind the enterprise, such as reinserting the unemployed into the job market, proposing new local services, revitalizing territories starting with mutual assistance among inhabitants, or promoting innovative approaches to sustainable local development. These approaches are therefore a step forward compared to those that focus on maximizing profit and value creation for shareholders.

Within these approaches, there are currents of thought that correspond to specific characteristics distinguishing between North American and European contributions, respectively.

North American and European contributions

North American currents of thought are positioned with regard to the market and social innovation. A first current, systematized in particular by Austin and his colleagues (2006) from the Harvard Business School, highlights the use of market resources as a means for nonprofit companies to fulfill their social mission. The second, inspired by the figure of the entrepreneur innovating to meet social needs, considers from the start that different types of companies can contribute to a social objective, be they nonprofits or not (Dees 1998; Salamon and Young, 2002). Perhaps as these two currents of thought have become closer, social enterprise in North America is now approached via its social mission. In this approach, an increase in market resources is recommended for the fulfillment of the mission, not necessarily linked to the type of economic activity, governance structure or social innovation dynamics. The criterion of non-redistribution of profits that was central for the third sector has thus been gradually diminished or even abandoned for the social enterprise. The dynamics of social innovation are understood primarily as linked to the actions of individual social entrepreneurs and are viewed as a function of creating "social value." From this point of view, companies, civil society and the public sector are seen as complementary and the distinction between social enterprises on the market and those creating economic equilibrium by mobilizing non-market resources may be underestimated (Ferrarini 2013).

In comparison, the European contribution from the EMES network of researchers has the originality of combining the social purpose of the enterprise with its internal governance structure. The historical trajectory of European social enterprises, which links them to organizations of the social economy, thus explains the importance of criteria of participation, decision-making not related to capital ownership and the limits of profit distribution.

There is therefore common ground in all of these currents of thought with regard to social purpose, autonomy and economic risk. However, two sizeable differences between the North American and European approaches result from the different conception of the link between social mission and the internal governance structure. First, in the European contribution, the importance granted to more democratic management methods is at odds with private-sector for-profit management methods that prevail in the North American approach. Second, the European emphasis on internal economic democracy legitimizes social enterprises as partners in public policies having a certain degree of interaction with their institutional environment. Therefore, these policies are a channel for spreading the social innovations. Alternatively in the United States, the spread of social innovation is considered to be the result of the expansion or multiplication of social enterprises through market resources, the support of foundations and entrepreneurs' dynamism (Defourny and Nyssens 2013).

Limits of the existing approaches to the social enterprise

On the whole, these various approaches to social enterprise view it as a private organization. However, social enterprise is arguably positioned between the private and public spheres, in that it can contribute to defining public issues that become open to debate. This public dimension must be taken into account. For this, we follow Arendt and Habermas in their definition of the public, while distancing ourselves from the separation they draw between political and economic spheres. In our perspective, it is clear that the economic activities of the social enterprise are inseparable from the institutional dimension, understood here in terms of meaning and legitimacy. This dimension involves two aspects: first, that of the *instituting logics* by which actors create and consolidate the activity by issuing rules, thus demonstrating their ability to generate commons (Ostrom, 2005) and even their desire for transformation; and second, that of the *institutional framework*, a set of pre-established norms on different scales and in different registers, enacted by law or not, that influence their action. These considerations must be accounted for to reinsert the institutional aspect into the analysis. This aspect is what makes collective action possible, but also what limits it.

The mission of social enterprises is best examined with respect to its instituting logic. By concentrating on the categories of "enterprise" (defined with regard to the "economic" activity) and "social," and the relationships between these two categories, we risk neglecting critical considerations regarding the mission of the social enterprise and the process of creating social value. The possibility of positive interaction between the economic sphere and the social sphere is stated without being questioned. The "social" is defined as a default category resulting from "needs" that are not satisfied by the state or the market. The choice of a mission within this vast space can be made by a social entrepreneur or by other decision-makers in the enterprise. Analysis is not centered on the nature and legitimacy of the actors, on their political project, nor on the social relationships in which they participate. Social enterprises claim that they contribute to a social mission, and thus to the creation of social value, but the relationship between these companies and public debate is avoided. Of course, the European definition includes the notion that the initiative stems from a group of citizens, but limits democratic functioning to formal statutory equality between the members without explaining the way these equal relationships become reality.

More generally, these approaches do not question the place of the economy and the enterprise in society. The economy is defined as the activity of continuously providing goods and services. This idea makes it possible to distinguish between social enterprises and other types of organizations with a social mission but no "economic" activity, such as foundations. However, it does not allow us to examine the way in which production, exchange, consumption and financing are *instituted*, or to analyze the political order in which social enterprises operate.

Moreover, this view may, among other things, reduce the various forms of institutionalization of social enterprises to the existing legal forms – cooperatives, associations, mutual societies and new specific forms of social enterprises recognized in the laws of some countries. In this framework, informal social enterprises that do not fit into any legislation are neglected. They tend to be seen as a mere "variation" of the modalities of reference (Fonteneau *et al.*, 2011, p. 2 quoted in Gaiger, 2013, p. 10), while in many contexts, they in fact represent the most important cases (Gaiger, 2013). The importance of informal social enterprises is due to their number but is also intrinsic, considering that these enterprises do not necessarily intend to formalize but have their own instituting logic through their internal management rules (ibid.), manifested in their capacity to self-organize (Veronese, personal communication). By completing the organizational analysis by an institutional approach that is not limited to the existing legal framework, it is possible to restore the meaning and overall logic that crystallize in particular organizational forms, whether legally recognized or not. If one does not consider the instituting logic, which may be found in the informal or formal economy, then analyzing social enterprises risks becoming a reflex of the neo-modernizing approach, implicitly assuming a trend towards formalizing informal social enterprises.

Lastly, this approach does not focus on the relationships between the political and economic spheres. It develops a different vision of the enterprise, but it does not question the institutional framework in which the activity of the enterprise is conducted. It allows for a division between three spheres of activity – economic, social and political – the boundaries and interactions of which are only partially questioned. Questioning the "social" and "enterprise" categories from the perspective of the place of the economy in society, public debate and democracy is, therefore, a complementary line of research on social enterprise.

Solidarity enterprises

The foregoing theoretical concerns resonate with empirical observations: there are various initiatives on different continents that can be considered to be social enterprises, created as part of a desire to transform the economic and political spheres. They emerge as a reaction against the dominant economic order, their creators being aware that "between capitalism and democracy, there is an insurmountable tension" (Habermas 1998, p. 379). In Europe, after the "Thirty glorious years" during which the perception of this tension became blurred, it has again gained credence with the appearance of new social movements, crucibles of alternative ideas and, starting in the 1970s, solidarity practices. These experiences, which sought for example to protect the environment or to oppose patriarchy, claimed to "overrun the usual field of democracy, i.e., the political, to enter the economic domain" (Sousa Santos and Rodriguez, 2013, p. 141). Then in the 1980s, they were jostled by the wave of deregulation and flexibility measures recommended by the Washington Consensus, which resulted in more defensive actions such as buy-outs of companies by their workers (Paton, 1989) or economic integration for the unemployed (Gardin *et al*, 2012). In Latin America, experiments are emerging from the inability or unwillingness to adapt to the conditions of peripheral capitalism and the forms of sociability it leads to (Gaiger, 2013). They usually take place in a context of social vulnerability and they are primarily intended to create incomes needed to survive. But at the same time, they reactivate solidarity, based on old and new communities in populous areas. Solidarity enterprises thus generate a shift towards a stronger mobilization of solidarity and cooperation, with a transition from survival tactics to strategies (De Certeau, 1990) of solidarity enterprises. Razeto (1993, p. 40) asserts that cooperation and collaboration, which he calls the "C factor," allow economies of scale, and positive externalities in the course of collective action, which leads to redefining the concepts of efficiency and effectiveness.

In Europe today, various types of initiatives affirming their political dimension also exist among social enterprises. In southern Italy social cooperatives and in France *Régies de quartier* experimented with participative dynamics with local authorities. In Portugal, the local development network Animar encourages the democratization of the economy through local experience. In Latin America, social enterprises inspired by North American approaches (for example, the Social Enterprise Knowledge Network linked to the Harvard Business School) have only a minor place in public and political debate. On the other hand, networks of popular solidarity enterprises that link the democratic organization of economic practices with positioning in the public arena (França Filho, 2006) play a role in institutional change and social transformation. Particularly in Brazil, Bolivia, Ecuador and Nicaragua, these enterprises have given rise to new public policies and new frameworks of laws and norms that try to redefine the meaning of modernity via a pluralistic vision of the economy (Wanderley, 2009), which is of course not exempt from contradictions or excesses. In South Africa, a new movement called the "solidarity economy" bringing together various types of cooperatives was formed in order to push transformative policies, as the participants felt that the traditional social economy and the current policy of Black Economic Empowerment were insufficient (COPAC, 2011).

To avoid a methodological bias by basing the reality of social enterprises only on certain analytical frameworks proposed in the North, this text aims to employ the conceptual requirements above as well as practices such as those mentioned here to create a model of social enterprise in a solidarity economy perspective (to wit, a solidarity enterprise).

Criteria for defining the solidarity enterprise

In this second part, a model is built according to a methodology similar to the one used for the EMES definition, as it is based on criteria in the social, economic and *political* fields. The ideal type of social enterprise in a solidarity economy perspective is hence consistent with the definition proposed by EMES, while suggesting certain criteria with reference to diverse realities. Thus, in the methodological perspective of EMES, the "criteria" discussed below are indicators of different dimensions that constitute the ideal type of solidarity enterprise as an abstract construction (see Table 14.1), and not as properties that each individual solidarity enterprise should check off a list. In order to take into account the socio-political aspects that characterize solidarity enterprises via their instituting logic, the political domain widens the scope of governance compared to the previous EMES approach, which focuses more on organizing enterprises internally.

Economic indicators

Hybridization of economic principles and solidarity logic

In order to distinguish between social enterprises and nonprofit organizations aiming only at defending interests or redistributing resources (such as foundations), the EMES social enterprise model defines the continuous production of goods or services as an indicator based on the substantive economy approach of Polanyi (1975 [1957]). However, this indicator does not distinguish between enterprises whose production of goods and service follows market logic exclusively and those that involve other principles. This choice, which makes it possible to include social enterprises founded on the North American model of mobilization of market resources, tends to leave out an essential specific characteristic of solidarity enterprises, which is the plurality of economic principles and a logic of solidarity.

Investigations carried out regarding the economy do in fact converge to refute an economic rationale that could be reduced to individual material interests, the

Table 14.1 The ideal type of social enterprise in a solidarity economy perspective

Indicators	Solidarity enterprise
Economic	Hybridization of economic principles and logic of solidarity Consistency of economic, social and environmental commitment Valorization of work
Social	Objective of transformation and repair Democratic solidarity Autonomy
Political	Public dimension Intermediate public spaces Institutional entrepreneurship and political embeddedness

coordination of which would result from market mechanisms only. In agreement with Braudel (1985, p. 45), who suggests that we should not be obsessed with the market economy "as it is only a fragment of a vast whole," it is important to recognize along with Polanyi (2011) the plurality of resources: not only market resources but also non-market and non-monetary resources. In addition to resources drawn from the market, there are also those that come from redistribution (taxation by a central authority and allocation based on rules emanating from that authority), reciprocity (symmetrical groupings whose members practice a kind of mutualism) and householding (production for use within the domestic unit). In addition, these principles of economic integration may be considered not as simple resources but rather as types of interdependence, making up the fundamental element of economic analysis as a process instituted, as per Polanyi. Reciprocity therefore does not only refer to resources that are made available, but to a principle of complementarity instituted at different levels. Redistribution corresponds to interdependence in centralized systems, also at different levels. Householding describes changing types of interdependence within domestic-type units founded on self-sufficiency (Hillenkamp, 2013; Servet, 2013). Finally, the market corresponds to types of interdependence that are automatically created between buyers and sellers via price fluctuations.

This interpretation re-establishes the principles of Polanyi in a political economy vision. It requires us to seek out the institutional and political frameworks that social enterprises are a part of when they mobilize various types of resources. Each of the principles is indeed ambiguous. Like householding in patriarchal systems, the principle of reciprocity, in particular, is not an automatically positive category from the standpoint of democratization. It may be implemented coercively, as for example in community-type structures. It is only when reciprocity is voluntarily instituted that it can take on an egalitarian character and become the basis of a participative or deliberative democratic process. In the same way, public redistribution via taxation and reallocation of resources can be associated with methods of representative democracy, including at a local level, just as it can be managed in an authoritarian manner.

In this logic, the solidarity enterprise tends to replace householding, which takes priority in the popular economy, with reciprocity voluntarily instituted on an egalitarian basis. This type of social enterprise is also based on a mix of economic principles under the aegis of egalitarian reciprocity as a "mixture of formal and informal agreements" (Nyssens 1996).

Consistency of economic, social and environmental commitment

In order to distinguish between social enterprises and public administrations, one of the EMES indicators of the social enterprise concerns the level of risk taken by its founders. This criterion, which measures the economic commitment of the founders of the enterprise, appears insufficient if it is not considered as part of a whole – including the social and environmental commitment.

The minimal consensus on the sustainable development agenda, from the Brundtland report (1987) to the Earth Summits in 1992, 2002 and 2012, has come from the recognition of the urgency of integrating the economic, social and environmental dimensions of human activities. It is difficult to imagine that social enterprises should ever engage in economically risky activities or activities that are harmful from a social or environmental standpoint and then reinvest the profits thus generated in their social mission.

The founders of solidarity enterprises, and certainly more generally many creators of social enterprises, aim for consistency between their activities in various domains. Even in informal solidarity enterprises, such as groups of craftsmen or farmers, considering the social and environmental impact of the activity is important and generates real responses, such as a preference for natural pigments or for agro-ecology, even if they increase production costs at first (later, they can be recuperated on specific markets). By submitting these choices to internal spaces for democratic discussion, these enterprises can also develop methods for *prioritizing* economic, social and environmental objectives at the local level, offering a practical response to the main criticism of ecologists, which is the insufficiency of the paradigm of the *integration* of different domains without an actual decision-making principle (van Griethuysen 2010).

Valorization of work

The EMES model identifies a "minimum" level of paid work as the last economic criterion of social enterprises. Here again, the experience of solidarity enterprises, in particular those from the popular economy (see below), requires us to take a step further by positing the valorization of work as the common principle.

The popular economy has been defined as "economic activities and social practices developed by popular groups in order to guarantee, by the use of their own work force and available resources, the satisfaction of basic needs, both material and immaterial" (Sarria Icaza and Tiriba, 2006, p. 259). This approach has the merit of reviving these forms of popular organization that have an economic component embedded in social and cultural relationships, as they have been invalidated for two centuries as archaic, outdated and condemned to disappear due to modernization. This popular economy cannot be conceptualized as a simple dependency on the formal economy, the mandatory complement to rampant capitalism or the voluntary expression of "barefoot" capitalism (De Soto 1997). For Coraggio (2002–2006), popular economy is an economy of work as opposed to an economy of capital because it is implemented based on the logic of work and reproduction of life within the domestic unit.

The solidarity enterprise, which is anchored in this popular economy of work, takes a position against the social division between capital and labor. It focuses on labor relations between associates (or members) and limits the use of hired workers who are not members of the organization. It tends to manage the organization of work and determine its remuneration via democratic decision-making, irrespective of shares of capital, as illustrated particularly by the self-management and cooperative models.

Social indicators

Objective of transformation and repair

The social mission of social enterprises, referred to in the EMES model as a service to the community or a group of beneficiaries, can be specified and examined in the case of solidarity enterprises via a double objective of transformation and repair. Motivated by the desire to move towards a different, more equal world and to resolve emergency situations, solidarity enterprises are both transformative and reparative. The "protest logic (protest current rules and values)" within them cannot be isolated from a "palliative logic (improve what is already there)" (Blanc, Fare 2012, p. 76). This ambivalence comes from the importance for their proponents of democratizing the economy via citizen commitments, based on the observation that the excessive predominance of financial and patrimonial capitalism is now an essential cause of unemployment, precarious living conditions and poverty.

This desire for long-term transformation combined with short-term pragmatism yields a conception of social change that does not claim to be "a new whole, broken away from current determinations" but rather is careful to provide "an improvement in living conditions" (Gaiger 2006, pp. 350–353). This attention to the human consequences of change is also inspired by alter-globalism, in which the other world to be invented is already present in this one. Its motto, "resist and build," transposed economically supposes that we do not rely on another global system, but rather anchor the perspective of another economy in popular practice and "invent (plural) alternatives" (Sousa Santos and Rodriguez, 2013, p. 129). This perspective is congruent with that of social innovation and social value creation, provided that the processes of the innovation – participatory or not – and its purpose – transformative or not – are taken into account (Ferrarini, 2013).

Democratic solidarity

From a democratic perspective, the vision of transformation and repair in solidarity enterprises cannot be interpreted only via mechanisms for limiting the distribution of benefits. More generally, it is the desire to democratize, expressed in practice through solidarity from the ground up, that maintains and legitimizes the purpose of these companies.

*   With regard to the forms adopted, solidarity is not traditional solidarity in which belonging to certain groups can bolster hierarchies founded on age or sex. This being said, it also differs from philanthropic solidarity based on a vision of an ethical society where altruistic citizens fulfill their duties towards the poor on a voluntary basis.

• With regard to the people concerned, it is solidarity that is both immediate, which is aimed at currently living social groups, and future-oriented, which includes successive generations. There is therefore a desire to fight against inequalities and for social justice, integrating environmental aspects in particular.

The solidarity enterprise is based on solidarity that can be qualified as democratic in that it comes from a postulate of equality in the political order, and as such it can be transposed in social and economic life. As a corollary, the fight against poverty is not the priority, unlike in other configurations of social enterprises. It is not about showing compassion and kindness to its beneficiaries, as is the case of charities. It exists so that people affected by a problem can take control of solving it, as in "friendly societies," "self-help" and "community development." The criterion is the active participation of beneficiaries in the definition and implementation of the mission of the enterprise.

Thus, the protection obtained by collective action is worthwhile because it is a vector of emancipation, in other words self-realization. The analysis of Fraser (2013) makes it possible to clearly explain this special configuration. Based on Polanyi, who laid bare the devastating effects of the market society and showed how society protects itself from this danger, Fraser's analysis rightly observed that this protection can promote domination or, on the contrary, emancipation. She makes the double movement (marketization–protection) of Polanyi more complex by converting it into a triple movement (marketization–protection–emancipation). In this theoretical framework, all social enterprises organize forms of protection. The solidarity enterprise, for its part, tries to bring together protection and emancipation. In other words, the solidarity perspective emphasizes the importance of emancipation and implementing of actions leading to protection and emancipation, rather than choosing between one or the other.

Autonomy

Finally, the chosen structuring principle is that of self-organization by instituting logic that mixes mutual assistance and social transformation dynamics. The self-management claimed in the internal functioning is inextricably linked to autonomy in decision-making and access to strategic knowledge. If solidarity enterprises maintain relationships with other organizations and receive resources that enable them to access markets, funding, or technical or managerial knowledge, this aid must not cause them to relinquish control of their organization. Solidarity enterprises should not become mere implementers of government programs nor social projects initiated by private foundations. As highlighted by Defourny and Nyssens, social enterprises are "created by a group of people on the basis of a specific project and are controlled by these people.... They have the right to make their voices heard (voice), as well as to put an end to their activities (exit)" (Defourny and Nyssens, 2013, p. 7).

Political indicators

One of the primary traits of the solidarity enterprise is that it does not see itself as a private organization, but instead carries out an activity in the public domain. Political criteria therefore appear absolutely necessary to characterize solidarity enterprises, in addition to the governance structure indicators of the EMES model.

Public dimension

The role of the solidarity enterprise is not only economic. It participates in the formulation of public issues according to a political approach that recognizes the role of public spaces in which citizens can express their concerns and ask their questions. Social needs are not identified using marketing processes such as those promoted for the "bottom of the pyramid" (Prahalad, 2004). They are apprehended thanks to autonomous micro public spaces (Eme and Laville, 1994) in which deliberation makes it possible to redefine the interests and values of the participants (Hillenkamp and Bessis, 2012, p. 93). This iterative creation, via direct contacts and well-argued exchanges, is particularly relevant in situations where the information held by the protagonists is radically incomplete and where it is the social structuring of the situation that allows the creation of collectively validated activities (Laville and Nyssens, 2001, pp. 313–332). Such autonomous public spaces, based on proximity, characterize the participative dynamics of solidarity enterprises, which go beyond legal equality among the members. Their sustainability over the long term requires special awareness of the threat of institutional isomorphism that the pressures of economic activity create, as shown by the abandonment, in the past, of the self-management movement (Singer, 2006, p. 294).

Intermediate public spaces

Autonomous micro public spaces at the level of singular experiences can survive only if the institutional framework is changed to address the extant pressures against them. Territorial and sectoral groupings and the creation of forums and wider arenas are therefore essential to stimulate such developments through intermediate-level public spaces. Institutions for mediation with public authorities, representation, and support are even more useful for solidarity enterprises, as they generate learning yield material results and extra-economic gains (França Filho, 2006; Gaiger, 2006, p. 345).

It is essential to inject dynamism into autonomous micro public spaces and intermediate public spaces to implement non-capitalist economic strategies, handled by the popular and middle classes confronted with the excesses of the dominant economy. These public spaces are decisive for the revival of citizen involvement which representative democracy alone cannot ensure.

Institutional entrepreneurship and political embeddedness

It would be naive to believe that solidarity enterprises can succeed solely based on their economic performance. They constantly suffer from opposing forces that are part of the institutional framework in the broad sense. A change at this level is absolutely necessary, mainly in legal frameworks and public policies, which need to be deconstructed (by delegitimizing instituted hierarchies and powers) and reconstructed (by recognizing activities that were previously ignored). This activity in favor of an institutional change has been dubbed "institutional entrepreneurship" (Lawrence, Suddaby 2006) and its importance highlighted by UNESCO, which stipulated in its universal declaration on cultural diversity in 2001 that "faced with an oligopolistic concentration, states must closely associate the various sectors of civil society." While the literature on institutional entrepreneurship has focused on organizations as a whole, case studies in the medical and environmental sectors (respectively, Levy and Scully, 2007, and Quéinnec, 2007) emphasize the role of associations (Rival *et al.*, 2008). Solidarity enterprises are certainly one of the areas to be explored in this connection.

Finally, it is crucial to analyze political embeddedness, meaning the interactions between civil society initiatives for the common welfare and legislation and public policy. Solidarity enterprises, like other initiatives, can influence methods of public action while being simultaneously standardized by public authorities, via institutionalization processes that are neither pure reproductions nor pure innovations from existing forms.

Conclusion

The indicators of the solidarity enterprise reflect stylized behaviors. As an ideal type,

> the concept of the solidarity enterprise is a heuristic instrument, useful in the search for causal, not accidental, connections that are at work within the experiences of the solidarity economy and that constitute them as a specific category of economic initiatives.
>
> (Gaiger 2006, p. 355)

Putting solidarity enterprise in perspective with other approaches to social enterprise also stimulates reflective feedback on these approaches. The criteria that have been selected show the simultaneous social, economic and political dimensions of solidarity enterprises, which are linked to each other through an explicit normative core. In contrast, the normativity of market resources and social innovation in American currents of thought are implicit.

Technically, the market resources school of thought supports what Polanyi (2007) calls "the economic fallacy," or an abiding confusion between economy and market. The increase in market resources is evaluated positively here, without questioning the effects induced, based on a formal approach to the economy that, unlike the substantive approach, does not recognize the plurality of economic principles. However, on an empirical level, formalism and this focus on market resources have already produced pernicious effects: the example of microcredit shows how the search for self-financing through the market led to the skimming of the affected populations, a preference for individual loans to the detriment of group solidarity loans (Servet 2006, p. 455) and a risk of over-indebtedness (Guérin *et al.*, 2013). This propensity to make a simple tool the subject of belief, which is symptomatic in the example of microcredit, should make us pause and reflect when faced with the heroic depiction of social entre-preneurs who have "the ability to transform the world" (Bornstein 2004) by spreading a "social business" that works, according to Yunus (2008) "in com-pliance with management principles that are used in a traditional company" and with the purpose of "completely covering its costs." North American literature about social enterprise intertwines analytical and promotional dimensions, which can lead to market isomorphism by recommending private management methods or by favoring a psychological approach to social entrepreneurship.

In this context, the model of the solidarity enterprise, due to its more institu-tional register, widens the range of possible variations of the social enterprise, enriching debates that would benefit from critical perspectives from outside the English-speaking world, such as those of Foucault (2004), speaking against the doctrine purporting that the company is the only legitimate form of collective activity, or Laval (2007, p. 333), studying how the company is currently pre-sented "as a universal form of activity."

Due to the multiple dimensions of its criteria and its emphasis on internal governance, the solidarity enterprise extends the work began by the EMES network with, however, traits such as the objective of transformation and repair, the plurality of economic principles and the public dimension that reflect observ-able realities in very different contexts. These realities should not be ignored in the ongoing theorization of social enterprise. The model presented in this chapter seeks to integrate the thought processes on these practices in an open and multi-cultural way.

References

Austin, J. E., Leonard, B., Reficco, E. and Wei-Skillern, J. (2006) "Social Entrepreneur-ship: It's for Corporations too," in Nicholls, A. (ed.) *Social Entrerpreneurship, New Models of Sustainable Social Change*, Oxford: Oxford University Press, pp. 169–180.

Blanc, J. and Fare, M. (2012) "Les monnaies sociales en tant que dispositifs innovants: Une évaluation," *Innovations sociales*, 38.

Bornstein, D. (2004) *How to Change the World: Social Enterpreneurs and the Power of New Ideas*, New York: Oxford University Press.

Braudel, F. (1985) *La dynamique du capitalisme*, Paris: Arthaud.

Certeau, M. de (1990) *L'invention du quotidien*, Paris: Gallimard.

Co-operative and Policy Alternative Center (COPAC) (2011) *Beyond the Social Economy: Capitalism's Crises and the Solidarity Economy Alternative*, conference report, University of Witwatersrand, Johannesburg.

Coraggio, J. L. (2002) *La gente o el capital: Desarollo local y economia del trabajo*, Buenos Aires: Espacio editorial.

Coraggio, J. L. (2006) "Economie du travail," in Laville, J. -L. and Cattani, A. D. (eds) *Dictionnaire de l'autre économie*, Paris: Gallimard Folio.

Dees, J. -G. (1998) "Enterprising Nonprofits," *Harvard Business Review*, January–February.

Defourny, J. and Nyssens M. (2013) "L'approche EMES de l'entreprise sociale dans une perspective comparative," SOCENT Working Paper 2013/01, in partnership with EMES network.

Defourny, J. and Nyssens, M. (2013) "Les conceptualisations internationales de l'entreprise sociale," in Gardin, L., Laville, J. -L. and Nyssens, M. (eds) *L'insertion par l'économique au prisme de l'entreprise sociale: Un bilan international*, Paris: Desclée De Brouwer.

De Soto, H. (1997) *El otro sendero*, French translation: *L'autre sentier: La révolution informelle*, Paris: La Découverte.

Eme, B. and Laville, J. L. (1994) *Cohésion sociale et emploi*, Paris: Desclée de Brouwer.

Eme, B. and Laville, J. L. (2006) "Économie solidaire (2)," in Laville, J. L. and Cattani, A. D. (eds) *Dictionnaire de l'autre économie*, Paris: Gallimard.

Ferrarini, A. V. (2013) "O ethos da inovação social no ambiente das lutas populares e da economia solidária," Anais do XVI Congresso Brazileiro de Sociologia, Salvador.

Fonteneau, B., Neamtan, N., Wanyama, F., Pereira Morais, L. and Poorter, M. de. (2011) *Economía social y solidaria: Nuestro camino común hacia el trabajo decente*, Turin: Centre international de formation de l'OIT.

Foucault, M. (2004) *Naissance de la biopolitique*, Paris: Gallimard.

França Filho, G. C. (2006) "Políticas públicas de economia solidária no Brazil: Características, desafios e vocação," in França Filho, G. C., Laville, J. L., Siqueira Medeiros, A.J. and Magnen, J. P. (eds) *Ação Pública e economia solidária – uma perspectiva internacional*, Salvador, Porto Alegre, EDUFRGS/EDUFBA, pp. 259–267.

Fraser, N. (2013) "Marchandisation, protection sociale, émancipation: Vers une conception néo-polanyienne de la crise capitaliste," in Hillenkamp, I. and Laville, J. L. (eds) *Socioéconomie et démocratie: L'actualité de Karl Polanyi*, Toulouse: Erès, pp. 39–63.

Gaiger, L. I. (2006) "Entreprise solidaire," in Laville, J. L. and Cattani, A. D., *Dictionnaire de l'autre économie*, Paris: Gallimard Folio.

Gaiger, L. I. (2013) "O Mapeamento Nacional e o Conhecimento da Economia Solidária," *Revista da ABET* (online) 12, pp. 7–24.

Gardin, L. (2006) *Les initiatives solidaires: La réciprocité face au marché et à l'Etat*, Ramonville Saint-Agne: Erès.

Gardin, L., Laville, J. L. and Nyssens, M. (2012) *Entreprise sociale et insertion: Une perspective internationale*, Paris: Desclée de Brouwer.

Guérin, I., Morvant-Roux, S. and Villarreal, M. (eds) (2013) *Microfinance, Debt and Over-indebtedness: Juggling with Money*, London: Routledge.

Habermas, J. (1998) *Théorie de l'agir communicationnel*, Paris: Fayard.

Hillenkamp, I. (2013) "Le principe de *householding* aujourd'hui: Discussion théorique et approche empirique par l'économie populaire," in Hillenkamp, I. and Laville, J. L. (eds) *Socioéconomie et démocratie: L'actualité de Karl Polanyi*, Toulouse: Erès, pp. 215–239.

Hillenkamp, I. and Bessis, F. (2012) "L'innovation sociale par l'économie solidaire en Bolivie: Une démocratisation des conventions de production et de genre," *Innovations sociales*, 38.

Lautier, B. (2006) "Economie informelle," in Laville, J. L. and Cattani, D.A. (eds) *Dictionnaire de l'autre économie*, Paris: Gallimard Folio.

Laval, C. (2007) *L'homme économique: Essai sur les racines du néolibéralisme*, Paris: Gallimard.

Laville, J. L. and Nyssens, M. (2001) "The Social Enterprise: Towards a Theoretical Socio-economic Approach," in Borzaga, C. and Defourny, J. (eds) *The Emergence of Social Enterprise*, London and New York: Routledge.

Lawrence, T. -B. and Suddaby, R. (2006) "Institutions and Institutional Work," in Clegg, S. R. (ed.) *Handbook of Organization Studies*, 2nd edition, London: Sage.

Lévy, D. and Scully, M. (2007) "The Institutional Entrepreneur as Modern Prince: The Strategic Fact of Power in Contested Fields," *Organization Studies*, 28(7), pp. 971–991.

Nanteuil, M. de and Laville, J. L. (2013) "Crise du capitalisme et économie plurielle: Une perspective anthropologique," *Revue Option*, Brussels, Confrontation Europe.

Nyssens, M. (1996) "Popular Economy in the South, Third Sector in the North: Seeds of a Mutually Supportive Sector?," in Sauvage, P. (ed.) *Reconciling Economy and Society: Towards a Plural Economy*, Paris: OECD, pp. 91–115.

Ostrom, E. (2005) *Understanding Institutional Diversity*, Princeton and Oxford: Princeton University Press.

Paton, P. (1989) *Reluctant Entrepreneurs: The Extent, Achievements and Significance of Worker Takeovers in Europe*, Milton-Keynes and Philadelphia: Open University Press.

Polanyi, K. (1975 [1957]) "L'économie en tant que procès institutionnalisé," in Polanyi, K., Arensberg, C. M. and Pearson, H. (eds) *Les systèmes économiques dans l'histoire et dans la théorie*, Paris: Larousse université, pp. 239–260.

Polanyi, K. (2007) "Le sophisme économiciste," *Revue du MAUSS semestrielle*, 29, *Avec K. Polanyi, contre la société du tout marchand*.

Polanyi, K. (2011) *La subsistance de l'homme: La place de l'économie dans l'histoire et la société* (translated and edited by B. Chavance), Paris: Flammarion.

Prahalad, C. K. (2004) *The Fortune at the Bottom of the Pyramid*, Paris: Village Mondial.

Quéinnec, E. (2007) "La croissance des ONG humanitaires, une innovation devenue institution," *Revue française de gestion*, 33(117), pp. 83–94.

Razeto, L. (1993) *Empresas de trabajadores y economia de mercado*, Santiago, Programa de Economia del Trabajo, Academia de Humanismo Christiano.

Rival, M., Eynaud, P. and Gautier, A. (2008) "Associations et entrepreneuriat institutionnel," in Hoarau, C. and Laville, J. L. (eds) *La Gouvernance des associations*, Toulouse: Erès, pp. 215–225.

Salamon, M. -D. and Young, D. (2002) *The State of Nonprofit America*, Washington, DC: Brookings Institution.

Sarria Icaza, A. M. and Tiriba, L. (2006) "Économie populaire," in Laville, J. L. and Cattani, A.D. (eds) *Dictionnaire de l'autre économie*, Paris: Gallimard, pp. 258–268.

Servet, J. -M. (2006) *Banquiers aux pieds nus: La microfinance*, Paris: Odile Jacob.

Servet, J. -M. (2013) "Le principe de réciprocité aujourd'hui: Un concept pour comprendre et construire l'économie solidaire," in Hillenkamp, I. and Laville, J. L. (eds) *Socioéconomie et démocratie: L'actualité de Karl Polanyi*, Toulouse: Erès, pp. 187–213.

Singer, P. (2006) "Economie solidaire," in Laville, J. L. and Cattani, A. D. (eds) *Dictionnaire de l'autre économie*, Paris: Gallimard Folio.

Sousa Santos Boaventura, B. de and Rodríguez Garavito, C. (2013) "Alternatives économiques: Les nouveaux chemins de la contestation," in Hillenkamp, I. and Laville, J. L. (eds) *Socioéconomie et démocratie: L'actualité de Karl Polanyi*, Toulouse: Erès, pp. 127–147.

Van Griethuysen, P. (2010) "Pourquoi le développement durable s'est-il imposé là où l'écodéveloppement a échoué? Débats pour la suite du monde," in Abraham, Y. -M., Louis, M. and Hervé, P. (eds) *Développement durable ou décroissance soutenable?* Montréal: Ecosociété, pp. 60–79.

Wanderley, F. (2009) *Crecimiento, empleo y bienestar social ¿Por qué Bolivia es tan desigual?* La Paz: Plural.

Yunus, M. (2008) *Creating a World Without Poverty*, New York: Public Affairs.

Index

Page numbers in *italics* denote tables, those in **bold** denote figures.

For Product Safety Concerns and Information please contact our EU
representative GPSR@taylorandfrancis.com Taylor & Francis Verlag GmbH,
Kaufingerstraße 24, 80331 München, Germany

Printed and bound by CPI Group (UK) Ltd, Croydon, CR0 4YY

08/05/2025

01864495-0001